Spiritual Strategies:

A Manual For Spiritual Warfare

HARVESTIME INTERNATIONAL INSTITUTE

This course is part of the **Harvestime International Institute**, a program designed to equip believers for effective spiritual harvest.

The basic theme of the training is to teach what Jesus taught, that which took men who were fishermen, tax collectors, etc., and changed them into reproductive Christians who reached their world with the Gospel in a demonstration of power.

This manual is a single course in one of several modules of curriculum which moves believers from visualizing through deputizing, multiplying, organizing, and mobilizing to achieve the goal of evangelizing.

© Harvestime International Institute
http://www.harvestime.org

TABLE OF CONTENTS

Suggestions for Group Study	4
Introduction	5
Course Objectives	9

THE CALL TO ARMS

1. The Invisible War	11

INDUCTION

2. Enlisting In God's Army	22

BASIC TRAINING

3. The Commander-In-Chief: The Lord of Hosts	33
4. The Spiritual Forces Of Good: Angels	52
5. The Enemy: Satan	64
6. The spiritual Forces Of Evil: Demons	76
7. Enemy Territory	85
8. Enemy Strategy	97
9. God's Battle Plan	103

MOBILIZATION

10. Offensive And Defensive Warfare	128
11. Defensive Weapons	138
12. Offensive Weapons	149
13. Natural Parallels Of Spiritual Warfare	157

INVASION

14. Entering The Combat Zone: Battling The World And The Flesh.	168
15. The Battle In The Mind	184
16. The Battle With The Tongue	199
17. The Battle Over The Walls	217
18. Battles Over Strategic Territory	227

SPIRITUAL WARFARE ADVANCED TRAINING

19. Transference Of Spirits	242
20. Spiritual Wickedness In High Places	254
21. Dealing With Demonic Powers	268
22. Casualties Of War	293
23. How To Lose A Battle And Win The War	310

FINAL BRIEFING

24. The Final Conflict	321

APPENDIX

Decisive Battles Of The Bible	331
Answers To Inspections	352

SUGGESTIONS FOR GROUP STUDY

FIRST MEETING

Opening: Open with prayer and introductions. Get acquainted and register the students.

Establish Group Procedures: Determine who will lead the meetings, the time, place, and dates for the sessions.

Praise And Worship: Invite the presence of the Holy Spirit into your training session.

Distribute Manuals To Students: Introduce the manual title, format, and course objectives provided in the first few pages of the manual.

Make The First Assignment: Students will read the chapters assigned and take the Self-Tests prior to the next meeting. The number of chapters you cover per meeting will depend on chapter length, content, and the abilities of your group.

SECOND AND FOLLOWING MEETINGS

Opening: Pray. Welcome and register any new students and give them a manual. Take attendance. Have a time of praise and worship.

Review: Present a brief summary of what you studied at the last meeting.

Lesson: Discuss each section of the chapter using the **HEADINGS IN CAPITAL BOLD FACED LETTERS** as a teaching outline. Ask students for questions or comments on what they have studied. Apply the lesson to the lives and ministries of your students.

Inspection: Review the self-tests (Inspection page) students have completed. (Note: If you do not want the students to have access to the answers to the self-tests, you may remove the answer pages from the back of each manual.)

Tactical Maneuvers: You may do these projects on a group or individual basis.

Final Examination: If your group is enrolled in this course for credit, you received a final examination with this course. Reproduce a copy for each student and administer the exam upon conclusion of this course.

MODULE: Deputizing
COURSE: Spiritual Strategies:
A Manual Of Spiritual Warfare

INTRODUCTION

There is a great war being waged in the world today. It is not a conflict between nations, tribes, or government leaders. It is not a rebellion or coup. It is an important invisible battle taking place in the spirit world. The Bible states that God's people are destroyed because of lack of knowledge (Hosea 4:6). One of the main areas in which believers are being defeated due to lack of knowledge is in spiritual warfare.

The early Church viewed their spiritual experience in terms of warfare. Military terminology is used throughout the New Testament. Protection was seen in the armor of God. The Word of God was compared to a sword. Satan's attacks were called fiery darts. Faith was the "good fight" and believers were told to "war a good warfare." The early Church knew they were engaged in an intense spiritual struggle.

The same spiritual battle continues today but instead of fighting the enemy, believers are often building great church buildings, producing musical dramas, holding fellowship meetings, and fighting one another while this great spiritual battle wages around them. Satan has even intensified his attacks against a church that has withdrawn from the front lines of battle.

As the end of time approaches it is even more important for believers to understand spiritual warfare than in the early days of church history. The Apostle Paul warned:

This know also, that in the last days perilous times shall come. (II Timothy 3:1)

In order to be properly prepared for these perilous times, renewed emphasis must be placed on the strategies of spiritual warfare. The Christian life is war. The sooner we recognize and prepare for it, the sooner we will experience victory.

Luke 14:31 says, **"What king, going to make war against another king, sitteth not down first, and consulteth whether he is able with ten thousand to meet him that cometh against him with twenty thousand?"** No king ever entered into a battle without a careful examination of his resources and development of battle strategies. In essence, that is what we are doing in this course. We are making a careful evaluation of the strategy, weapons, and power available to us to win the war against our enemy, Satan.

In the military world, "strategy" is the science of forming and carrying out military operations. It is the method or plan which leads to the goal of victory. In this course you will learn to formulate and carry out spiritual military strategy which will bring victory in the spirit world.

THE MANUAL

Each lesson is presented in military terms consisting of the following sections:

THE CALL TO ARMS:

Chapter 1 explains the invisible war and sounds the "call to arms" for all true believers.

INDUCTION:

All armies in the natural world have induction procedures. These are special things you are required to do in order to join the forces. The same is true of God's army. Chapter 2 explains how to enlist in God's Army.

BASIC TRAINING:

After induction into an army, a soldier always receives basic training. Basic training for God's army is presented in Chapters 3 through 9. The battle lines of the invisible war are defined. The forces of good and evil are discussed, including the Lord of Hosts, angels, Satan, demons, the world, and the flesh. Enemy territory and strategy are identified, and a general overview of God's battle plan presented.

MOBILIZATION:

Training is useless unless an army is mobilized. To "mobilize" means to "put in a state of readiness for active military service." In the "Mobilization" section of this course in chapters 10 through 13, you will learn about offensive and defensive warfare, how to use the weapons of your warfare, and natural parallels of spiritual warfare.

INVASION:

During an invasion in the natural world, an army enters the actual combat zone to conquer its foes and claim territory. Basic training is useless unless what is learned is put into action. Even a mobilized army equipped with weapons is not enough if it stands inactive on the sidelines. To be effective in warfare, you must actually enter the combat zone. In the "invasion" stage, consisting of Chapters 14 through 19, you will enter the combat zone of the world, the flesh, and the Devil. You will study the battle in the mind, with the tongue, over the spiritual walls, in high places, and over strategic territory. In each of these lessons specific strategies of Satan are identified and counter strategies for overcoming the enemy are presented.

SPIRITUAL WARFARE ADVANCED TRAINING:

After gaining some experience in battle, soldiers usually receive advanced training in specific areas of warfare. This portion of the manual is entitled "Spiritual Warfare Advanced Training," the initials of which spell "SWAT." In military action, a "SWAT" team is a specialized group of soldiers used for difficult missions. In the advanced training offered in this manual, you will learn about transference of spirits, how to assist prisoners and casualties of war, and how to deal with demonic powers. You will also learn how to lose a battle and still win the war.

FINAL BRIEFING:

During "final briefing" in Chapter 26 you will study "the final conflict" which will bring this war of the ages to a triumphant conclusion.

APPENDIX:

In the Appendix of this manual, you will examine the historical record of "Decisive Battles Of The Bible" as you continue to develop your spiritual warfare skills.

THE LESSONS

Each lesson in this warfare manual is organized as follows:

OBJECTIVES:

These are the spiritual warfare goals you should achieve by studying the lesson.

KEY VERSE FROM THE ARTICLES OF WAR:

When a nation declares war, they often issue "Articles Of War." This document explains why they are at war, identifies the enemy, and declares the objectives of the war. The Bible is the written Word of the one true God, the Commander of our spiritual army. The Bible contains our "Articles Of War" for spiritual combat. In each lesson, the "Key Verse From The Articles Of War" emphasizes the main concept of the lesson.

INTRODUCTION:

The introduction provides an overview of the content of the chapter.

LESSON:

This presents the "military briefing" for that chapter. A "briefing" is a time of instruction prior to battle which provides information necessary to wage effective warfare.

INSPECTION:

In a natural army, "inspections" occur regularly to check on the preparation and skills of the soldiers. The "Inspection" section of each chapter is an examination to see if you have obtained the objectives of that lesson.

TACTICAL MANEUVERS:

During tactical maneuvers in a natural army, soldiers apply what they have learned to actual combat conditions. This part of each lesson provides opportunity for you to apply what you have learned and to study other materials related to the lesson.

ARE YOU READY?

The exposing of the enemy and his strategies is one of the greatest revelations of God's Word. Even greater is the revelation that as believers we have power over all the powers of the enemy. This manual is by no means an exhaustive study of the subject of spiritual warfare, but it is an in depth Scriptural analysis. As in natural warfare, skill in spiritual warfare is progressive as you enter the combat zone and begin to fight.

OBJECTIVES

Upon completion of this course you will be able to:

- Identify the two spiritual kingdoms.

- Explain what is meant by "spiritual warfare."

- Recognize causes of this great spiritual struggle.

- Identify the spiritual forces of good.

- Identify the spiritual forces of evil.

- Recognize strategies of Satan.

- Effectively use spiritual counter strategies.

- Apply natural parallels of warfare to war in the spirit world.

- Use both offensive and defensive spiritual weapons.

- Detect demon possession.

- Understand how deliverance from demons is obtained.

- Win the war even if you lose a spiritual battle.

- Describe the final conflict which will end the invisible war.

- Identify spiritual warfare principles in decisive battles in the Bible.

THE CALL TO ARMS

A SUMMONS TO THE INVISIBLE WAR

There is a great battle being waged in the spiritual world. It is a personal battle within between the flesh and the spirit. It is a social battle with the evil forces of the world. It is a spiritual battle with evil supernatural powers.

In Old Testament times a trumpet was used to summons God's people to battle. Today, a spiritual summons is sounding throughout the nations of the world. It is a summons to the invisible war. It is a call to arms.

CHAPTER ONE

THE INVISIBLE WAR

OBJECTIVES:

Upon completion of this chapter you will be able to:

- Write the Key Verse from memory.
- Demonstrate understanding of the natural and spiritual realms.
- Define the word "king."
- Define the word "kingdom."
- Identify the two spiritual kingdoms.
- Determine to which kingdom you belong.
- Identify the spiritual forces of good.
- Identify the spiritual forces of evil.
- Explain what is meant by "spiritual warfare."
- Identify the reason for the invisible war.
- Identify the basic principle of understanding spiritual warfare.

KEY VERSE FROM THE ARTICLES OF WAR:

For we wrestle not against flesh and blood, but against principalities, against powers, against the rulers of the darkness of this world, against spiritual wickedness in high places. (Ephesians 6:12)

INTRODUCTION

As you learned in the introduction to this course, there is a great war being waged in the world today. It is not a conflict between nations, tribes, or government leaders. It is not a rebellion or a coup. It is an invisible battle taking place in the spirit world.

This chapter introduces the invisible war in which every believer is engaged. It is a war where no one wears a uniform, but where everyone is a target. The historical and prophetical record of this war is contained in God's Word, the Bible.

THE NATURAL AND SPIRITUAL REALMS

To understand this invisible war, you must first understand the natural and spiritual worlds. Man exists in two worlds: The natural world and the spiritual world. The natural world is that which can be seen, felt, touched, heard, or tasted. It is tangible and visible. The country, nation, city, or village in which you live is part of the natural world. You are a resident in a natural kingdom located on one of the visible continents of the world. You can see the people who are part of your environment. You can communicate with them. You can experience the sights, sounds, and smells around you.

But there is another world in which you live. That world is a spiritual world. You cannot see it with your physical eyes, but it is just as real as the natural world in which you live. Paul speaks of this division of natural and spiritual:

There is a natural body, and there is a spiritual body. (I Corinthians 15:40)

All men have a natural body which lives in the natural world, but man is also a spiritual being with an eternal soul and spirit. Man is body, soul, and spirit. Your spiritual being (soul and spirit) is part of a spiritual world just as your natural body is part of the natural world.

SPIRITUAL DISCERNMENT

Because spiritual warfare is just that--spiritual--it must be understood with a spiritual mind. In our natural, sinful state, we cannot understand spiritual things:

But the natural man receiveth not the things of the Spirit of God: for they are foolishness unto him; neither can he know them, because they are spiritually discerned. (I Corinthians 2:14)

It is necessary to use "spiritual discernment" to understand spiritual things.

Perhaps one of the best examples of natural and spiritual discernment is recorded in II Kings chapter 6. It records the story of a natural battle in which troops of the enemy nation of Syria had surrounded a small town called Dothan where the prophet Elisha was staying. When Elisha's servant, Gehazi, saw the great host of the enemy he became fearful. Elisha prayed that God would open Gehazi's spiritual eyes so he could see the angelic hosts surrounding and protecting them. On this occasion, God actually opened the natural eyes of Gehazi and allowed him to visibly see the superior forces of God aligned for battle.

The story of this battle at Dothan is similar to present spiritual conditions in the Church. There are some, like Elisha, who see clearly into the realm of the spirit. They know there is a conflict occurring, have identified the enemy, and recognize the greater forces of God that assure victory. There are others like Gehazi, who with a little encouragement, will be able to open their spiritual eyes and no longer be fearful of and defeated by the enemy. But sadly, there are many people who, like those in the city of Dothan, are spiritually sleeping. They do not even know that the enemy has surrounded them and is poised for attack.

TWO SPIRITUAL KINGDOMS

Within the natural and spiritual realms of which we are speaking there exists separate kingdoms which are ruled by natural and spiritual leaders.

NATURAL KINGDOMS:

All men live in a natural kingdom of this world. They live in a city or village which is part of a nation. That nation is a kingdom of the world. A natural kingdom is a territory or people over which an actual king or political leader is the sovereign ruler. The Bible speaks of these natural kingdoms as "kingdoms of the world." The kingdoms of the world have come under the power and influence of Satan:

> **Again, the Devil taketh Him (Jesus) up into an exceeding high mountain, and sheweth Him all the kingdoms of the world, and the glory of them;**
>
> **And saith unto Him, All these things will I give thee, if you wilt fall down and worship me. (Matthew 4:8-9)**

John 5:19 sadly reminds us that "the whole world is under the control of the evil one."

SPIRITUAL KINGDOMS:

In addition to the natural kingdoms of this world there are two spiritual kingdoms: The Kingdom of Satan and the Kingdom Of God. Every person alive is a resident of one of these two kingdoms.

The Kingdom of Satan consists of Satan, spiritual beings called demons, and all men who live in sin and rebellion to God's Word. These, plus the world and the flesh, are the spiritual forces of evil at work in the world today.

The Kingdom of God consists of God the Father, Jesus Christ, the Holy Spirit, spiritual beings called angels, and all men who live in righteous obedience to God's Word. These are the spiritual forces of good.

The Kingdom of God is not a denominational church. Denominations are man-made organizations of groups of churches. They have been established for practical purposes of organization and administration. Denominations are major church organizations like Baptist, Assembly of God, Methodist, Lutheran, etc. The Bible speaks of the true Church which is not a denomination or religious organization. The true Church is composed of all those who have become residents of the Kingdom of God.

At the present time in the natural world, the Kingdom of God exists individually within every man, woman, boy or girl who has made Jesus King of their lives. It exists communally in the true church and wherever people make this world the kind of world God wants it to be. In the future, there will be an actual visible manifestation of God's Kingdom.

THE INVISIBLE WAR

The invisible spiritual war is a battle which involves all men and women. Because the Kingdom of Satan is a spiritual kingdom...

> **...we wrestle not against flesh and blood, but against principalities, against powers, against the rulers of the darkness of this world, against spiritual wickedness in high places. (Ephesians 6:12)**

Spiritual warfare is not a natural battle between flesh and blood. It is not a battle of man against man. It is not a visible battle. It is an invisible struggle in the spirit world. It is a battle within and around man. It is not a visible war is because spirits are involved and we learn in Luke 24:39 that a spirit does not have flesh and bones.

Spiritual warfare is "multidimensional," which means it is fought in different dimensions. It is...

1. A social battle between the believer and the world: John 15:18-27
2. A personal battle between the flesh and the spirit: Galatians 5:16-26
3. A supernatural battle between believers and evil spiritual powers: Ephesians 6:10-27

Every person alive is engaged in this battle, whether he realizes it or not. There is no neutral ground. Unbelievers are in bondage to evil and have been taken captive by enemy forces. They are victims of the war.

Believers have been freed from the enemy through Jesus Christ and are victors, but they are still engaged in the war. The key verse for this chapter indicates that we (all believers) wrestle against evil spiritual forces.

"Wrestling" involves close personal contact. No one is exempt from this battle. No one can view it from a distance. You are in the midst of conflict whether you acknowledge it or not. If you believe it will get better, you are wrong. The Christian warfare never ceases.

WHERE THE BATTLE RAGES

This invisible war is being waged on earth:

> **The thief (Satan) cometh (on earth) not but for to steal, and to kill, and to destroy: I am come that they might have life, and that they might have it more abundantly. (John 10:10)**

Satan fights to maintain control of the kingdoms of the world. He does not want them to come under God's authority. The battle also rages within the hearts, minds, and souls of men and women. Satan blinds the minds of unbelievers and attacks believers in the areas of worship, the Word, their daily walk, and their work for God.

HOW THE BATTLE STARTED

The invisible war started in Heaven with an angel named Lucifer who was originally a beautiful angel created by God and was part of the Kingdom of God. Lucifer decided he wanted to take over God's Kingdom. You can read about his rebellion in Isaiah 14:12-17 and Ezekiel 28:12-19. You will study about it in detail later in this course. A group of angels joined Lucifer (now called Satan) in this rebellion. Lucifer and the rebellious angels were cast out of Heaven by God. They formed their own kingdom on earth:

> **And there was war in Heaven: Michael and his angels fought against the dragon (Satan); and the dragon fought and his angels.**
> **(Revelation 12:7)**

> **And the great dragon was cast out, that old serpent, called the Devil, and Satan, which deceiveth the whole world: he was cast out into the earth, and his angels were cast out with him. (Revelation 12:9)**

Lucifer became known as Satan and the angels which followed him in rebellion as demons. Demon spirits can enter, torment, control, and use humans who belong to Satan's Kingdom. They motivate evil acts which are done by men and women. Satan directs his demons in their evil activities. He combines these powerful forces with the world and the flesh to war against all mankind.

REASONS BEHIND THE CONFLICT

Man was originally created in the image of God and for the glory of God (Genesis chapter 2). The invisible war against man started with the first temptation in the garden of Eden (Genesis chapter 3). Satan caused Adam and Eve to sin. This resulted in all men inheriting the basic sin nature and committing individual acts of sin due to this nature:

> **Wherefore, as by one man sin entered into the world, and death by sin; and so death passed upon all men, for that all have sinned. (Romans 5:12)**

It also resulted in the invisible war between man and the forces of evil:

> **And I will put enmity between thee (Satan) and the woman (mankind), and between thy seed (the forces of evil) and her seed (the forces of good represented by the Lord Jesus Christ)... (Genesis 3:15)**

Because of sin, man was separated from God and condemned to death. But God loved man so much that He made a special plan to save him from sin:

> **For God so loved the world, that He gave His only begotten Son, that whosoever believeth in Him should not perish, but have everlasting life.**
>
> **For God sent not His Son into the world to condemn the world; but that the world through Him might be saved. (John 3:16-17)**

Through belief in Jesus, confession of and repentance from sin, men and women can be released from the power of the enemy. The death and resurrection of Jesus not only resulted in salvation from sin. It also defeated the enemy, Satan:

> **...For this purpose the Son of God was manifested, that He might destroy the works of the devil. (I John 3:8)**

But if Satan is defeated, why does the war still rage? Following any war there are always pockets of enemy resistance, rebellious troops that will not give up until forced to do so. Although Jesus defeated Satan, we are living in territory which is still occupied by enemy resistance forces. Understanding spiritual warfare strategies gives us the ability to deal with these evil powers.

Satan is trying to keep men captive in sin. Through deceptive methods he is enticing men and women to temporary lusts of sinful living. He aims for the affections of the soul and spirit which rightfully belong to God:

> **The thief (Satan) cometh not, but for to steal, and to kill, and to destroy; I am come that they might have life, and that they might have it more abundantly. (John 10:10)**

Satan still wants to be the supreme ruler. He is waging an intense battle for the heart, mind, soul, and spirit of man. His strategies are directed at God, His plan, and His people. The battle will continue until the great final conflict which you will study about in the last chapter of this course.

THE MEANING OF SPIRITUAL WARFARE

Spiritual warfare is the analysis of and an active participation in the invisible spiritual war. It includes study of the opposing forces of good and evil, the strategies of Satan, and spiritual strategies for overcoming the enemy. Spiritual warfare is more than a mere analysis of spiritual principles. It includes active participation in warfare by application of these strategies in life and ministry.

One of the most effective strategies of Satan is to keep believers ignorant of his devices. Paul said it is important to know Satan's strategies...

> **...Lest Satan should get an advantage of us: for we are not ignorant of his devices. (II Corinthians 2:11)**

We should learn all we can about Satan's strategies of attack. We must also understand the Scriptural basis of victory over Satan and the forces of evil. We are called to intelligent combat. Basic to the understanding of spiritual warfare is this key principle:

> *You must recognize that all battles of life, whether physical, spiritual, emotional mental, financial or with human personalities are only outward manifestations of a spiritual cause.*

Although in the natural world problems may seem to occur through the circumstances of life, the basis of these natural battles is in the spirit world. Read the story of Job (Job chapters 1-2) which confirms this principle.

We have tried to correct the evils of this world through education, legislation, and improved environment. It has not worked because the visible evils of the world are the results of an underlying spiritual cause. They cannot be corrected by natural means.

TO WHICH KINGDOM DO YOU BELONG?

In the natural world a king is the sovereign ruler of a kingdom. All the territory and people in the kingdom belong to him. He has the power of life and death over his subjects. The same is true in the spiritual world. You are either part of the Kingdom of God or the Kingdom of Satan. Either God or Satan has power over your life.

One of the parables told by Jesus illustrates that all men are either part of the Kingdom of Satan or the Kingdom of God. Jesus compared the world to a field. The good seed in the field were children of the Kingdom of God. The bad seed, which resulted in the growth of tares (weeds), were children of the wicked one:

The field is the world; the good seed are the children of the Kingdom; but the tares are the children of the wicked one. (Matthew 13:38)

People enter the Kingdom of Satan through natural birth. The Bible teaches that all men are born in sin. This means that they have a basic sin nature or the "seed" of sin within. Their natural inclination is to do evil:

Behold, I was shapen in iniquity; and in sin did my mother conceive me. (Psalms 51:5)

Wherefore, as by one man (Adam) sin entered into the world, and death by sin; and so death passed upon all men, for that all have sinned. (Romans 5:12)

For all have sinned and come short of the glory of God. (Romans 3:23)

Because we are born with the basic sin nature, we have all at one time been part of the Kingdom of Satan. All who remain sinners remain part of the Kingdom of Satan.

The whole message of God's written Word, the Holy Bible, is the appeal to man to move from this evil Kingdom of Satan to the Kingdom of God. Men are born into the Kingdom of Satan through natural birth. They must be reborn into the Kingdom of God through spiritual birth. Entrance to the Kingdom of God is by new birth experience explained in John 3.

There are only two divisions in the invisible war. Jesus said, "He that is not with me is against me" (Luke 11:23). You cannot be neutral in this spiritual war. You are on one side or the other. Some believers, because of their fear of confrontation with the enemy, try to ignore the war and form a truce with the enemy. They think if they ignore Satan, he will not bother them. This is one of Satan's main strategies. He tries to render members of God's army immobile by his terror tactics.

But there is no neutrality in this war. You are either a victim or victor. The spiritual "call to arms" is going out...Are you on the side of good or of evil? Are you part of Satan's Kingdom or the Kingdom of God? To which kingdom do you belong? Are you a victim or victor in the invisible war?

INSPECTION

1. Write the Key Verses from the article of war.

   _____

   _____

   _____

2. What are the two divisions made in I Corinthians 15:44-49?

   _____

   _____

3. What are the two invisible kingdoms in the world today?

   _____

   _____

4. List the spiritual forces of evil.

   _____

   _____

   _____

5. List the spiritual forces of good.

   _____

   _____

   _____

   _____

6. Define the word "king."

   _____

   _____

7. Define the word "kingdom."

   _____

   _____

8. What is meant by the term "spiritual warfare"?

   _____

   _____

9. What is the reason behind this great spiritual conflict?

   _____

   _____

   _____

10. What is the basic principle for understanding spiritual warfare?

    _____

    _____

    _____

(Answers to tests are provided at the conclusion of the final chapter in this manual.)

TACTICAL MANEUVERS

1. This course, *"Strategies of Spiritual Warfare,"* focuses on the Kingdom of Satan and the spiritual warfare which rages between his kingdom and the Kingdom of God. The Harvestime International Institute course entitled *"Kingdom Living"* provides a complete study of the Kingdom of God. (If you are enrolled in Harvestime Institute and studying the courses in their suggested order, you have already studied this course.) If you are not enrolled in a Harvestime Institute, you should obtain *"Kingdom Living"* as a companion course to this one. It is important that you gain understanding of both spiritual kingdoms present in the world today.

2. A good spiritual foundation is necessary in order to wage successful spiritual warfare. If you are a new believer, obtain the Harvestime International Institute course entitled *"Foundations Of Faith."* (If you are taking the Harvestime courses in their suggested order, you have already studied this course.)

3. Do you feel you have been a "victim" of spiritual warfare? In what areas of your life or ministry have you been losing the battle? Have you been losing the battle in the... Spiritual realm? Emotional realm? Physical realm? Mental realm? Financial realm? With human personalities? It is important to identify these areas of defeat so you can apply the knowledge you gain in this study to these practical areas of life and ministry.

4. Review the story in II Kings 6 which was discussed in this lesson. Do you know people like Gehazi or those in the city of Dothan? How might you help them?

5. Since spiritual warfare has many dimensions, we must war personally against sin, socially against evil in the world, and supernaturally through the deliverance ministry.

6. Study the Bible as a spiritual warfare manual. It is the historical record of spiritual warfare, revealing the victories and defeats of past battles. It is prophetical, showing the course of our warfare until the time of the final conflict.

INDUCTION

BECOMING PART OF THE ARMY OF GOD

All armies in the natural world have induction procedures--special things you are required to do in order to join the forces.

Are you ready to become part of God's army?

CHAPTER TWO

ENLISTING IN GOD'S ARMY

OBJECTIVES:

Upon completion of this chapter you will be able to:

- Write the Key Verse from memory.
- Define "repentance."
- Explain the importance of repentance.
- Define "conversion."
- Explain the importance of conversion.
- Define "justification."
- Explain what it means to be "saved."
- Use the parable of the prodigal son to describe repentance and conversion.

KEY VERSE FROM THE ARTICLES OF WAR:

I came not to call the righteous, but sinners to repentance. (Luke 5:32)

INTRODUCTION

In the last chapter you learned of the great invisible war in the spiritual world. In this chapter you will learn how to enlist in God's army. In the natural world, armies usually have special induction rituals in which a prospective soldier must participate in order to join the forces. This "induction" makes him part of the army.

God also has a special plan for induction through which you become part of His spiritual army. His plan centers on two important concepts, repentance and conversion, which result in justification.

REPENTANCE

In the natural world, when a soldier joins an army, he must deny any previous allegiance he has had to another army or country. When you join the army of God, you must repent of your allegiance to sin and the Kingdom of Satan. This is done by repentance.

Repentance is "an inward decision or change of mind resulting in the outward action of turning from sin to God and righteousness." Acts 20:21 calls it "repentance toward God." By the act of repenting you turn away from your sin and leave the Kingdom of Satan.

Repentance is a personal decision to change your allegiance from the Kingdom of Satan to the Kingdom of God. This change of mind and turning from sin cannot be done in yourself. It is the power of God which actually brings the change in the mind, heart, and life of a sinner:

> **Then God also to the Gentiles granted repentance unto life. (Acts 11:18)**

Repentance is a gift of God:

> **Him [Jesus] hath God exalted with His right hand to be a Prince and a Savior, for to give repentance...(Acts 5:31)**

Although emotions may be involved in repentance, true repentance is a decision, not just an emotion. Sorrow for sin and the shedding of tears is not enough in itself. This must be accompanied by an inward decision that results in an outward change.

THE IMPORTANCE OF REPENTANCE:

Repentance is important because:

God Commands It:

> **...but [God] now commandeth all men everywhere to repent. (Acts 17:30)**

It Is Necessary To Avoid Spiritual Death:

> **...but, except ye repent, ye shall all likewise perish. (Luke 13:3)**

It Is Necessary For Eternal Life:

Through repentance the penalty of death is removed and eternal life is granted:

> **When they heard these things, they held their peace, and glorified God, saying, Then hath God also to the Gentiles granted repentance unto life. (Acts 11:18)**

It Is Necessary For Forgiveness:

God cannot forgive your sins unless you repent:

> **Then Peter said unto them, Repent, and be baptized every one of you in the name of Jesus Christ for the remission of sins, and ye shall receive the gift of the Holy Ghost. (Acts 2:38)**

It Is God's Desire For All:

God does not want anyone to experience the spiritual death of eternal separation from God in Hell:

> **The Lord...is long suffering to us-ward, not willing that any should perish, but that all should come to repentance. (II Peter 3:9)**

It Is The Reason Jesus Came Into The World:

> **I came not to call the righteous, but sinners to repentance. (Luke 5:32)**

It Is Necessary To Enter God's Kingdom:

> **From that time Jesus began to preach, and to say, Repent: for the Kingdom of Heaven is at hand. (Matthew 4:17)**

When you become part of the Kingdom of God, you are enlisting in God's army.

CONVERSION

When you ask for forgiveness of sins you experience "conversion." Conversion means "to turn." When it is used in connection with Biblical repentance, it means to "turn from the wrong way to the right way." You leave the Kingdom of Satan and join the Kingdom of God.

> **And many of the children of Israel shall He turn to the Lord their God. (Luke 1:16)**

> **And all that dwelt at Lydda and Saron saw Him, and turned to the Lord. (Acts 9:35)**

> **And the hand of the Lord was with them; and a great number believed, and turned unto the Lord. (Acts 11:21)**

Conversion is turning from the darkness of sin to the light of God's righteousness:

> **...to turn them from darkness to light. (Acts 26:18)**

It is turning from the power of Satan to God:

> **...to turn them...from the power of Satan unto God. (Acts 26:18)**

It is turning from worldly things to spiritual things:

> **...Ye should turn from these vanities unto the living God. (Acts 14:15)**

It is turning from false gods to the true and living God:

> **...Ye turned to God from idols to serve the living and true God. (I Thessalonians 1:9)**

THE IMPORTANCE OF CONVERSION:

Conversion must accompany repentance. You must turn from the wrong to the right because...

It Is Necessary To Enter The Kingdom Of God:

Verily I say unto you, except ye be converted, and become as little children, ye shall not enter into the Kingdom of Heaven. (Matthew 18:3)

It Saves From Spiritual Death:

He which converteth the sinner from the error of his way shall save a soul from death and shall hide a multitude of sins. (James 5:20)

It Is Necessary For The Blotting Out Of Sin:

Your sin is written in the records of God until you repent and are converted, then your sins are blotted out:

Repent ye therefore, and be converted, that your sins may be blotted out... (Acts 3:19)

THE PRODIGAL SON

Repentance and conversion are best illustrated by a story Jesus told about the prodigal son. Read the story in Luke 15:11-24. This young man left his father and home, went to a distant land, and through sin wasted all he owned. Eventually this young man realized his condition. He was hungry, lonely, in rags, and tending pigs for a job. Then he made an important decision. He said, "I will arise and go to my father." This inward decision resulted in a change in his outward actions. He went home to his father to seek forgiveness.

REPENTANCE...THE CHANGE OF MIND:

Read Luke 15:17-19. The young man realized his sinful condition. He made a decision to go to his father and repent of his sin. This is an example of repentance, an inward decision which results in outward action.

CONVERSION...ACTING ON THE DECISION:

Luke 15:20 records how the young man arose and left the old life and went to his father to start a new life. This is conversion.

PRODIGAL MAN:

Man is like the prodigal son. In his sinful condition he turned his back on God his Father and Heaven his home. Each step he takes is a step away from God and one step nearer the spiritual death of eternal separation from God. There is a major decision he must make. He must "come to himself" and recognize his spiritual condition. He must make a decision which will result in a change of spiritual direction.

JUSTIFICATION AND SALVATION

There are two other terms used in the Bible which relate to repentance. These terms are "justification" and "salvation." God is the judge of all mankind. When you are living in sin you are condemned before Him:

> **...but he that believeth not is condemned already, because he hath not believed in the name of the only begotten Son of God.**
>
> **And this is the condemnation, that light is come into the world, and men loved darkness rather than light, because their deeds were evil.**
> **(John 3:18-19)**

When you repent from sin and make the decision to turn from your sinful ways, this establishes a right relationship with God. This right relationship or right standing before God is called "justification":

> **Know ye not, that to whom ye yield yourselves servants to obey, his servants ye are to whom ye obey; whether of sin unto death, or of obedience unto righteousness?**
>
> **But God be thanked, that ye were the servants of sin but ye have obeyed from the heart that form of doctrine which was delivered you.**
>
> **Being then made free from sin, ye became the servants of righteousness. (Romans 6:16-18)**

When you are justified by repentance and conversion, you are "saved" from a life of sin as well as from the penalties of sin. This is what it means to be "saved" and what the Bible is speaking of when the term "salvation" is used.

SPIRITUAL WARFARE AND THE BIBLICAL WORLD VIEW

The subject of spiritual warfare must be studied within the context of God's total purpose for the redemption of sinful mankind. Study the parables of the sower and the tares among wheat in Matthew 13. Both parables concern the growth of the Kingdom of God which occurs through the planting of God's Word. Both parables picture the warfare between the two kingdoms with the battle centering on the redemptive purposes of God.

Learning spiritual warfare prepares you to enter the arena of this world and fight for the souls of men and women, boys and girls. This is why authority over Satan was given to the disciples before they were sent out to share the Gospel (Matthew 28:18-20). Satan and his hosts of demons will war against you as you seek to win men to Christ and bring them under the rule of God. Employing Scriptural strategies of spiritual warfare helps you challenge the principalities and powers who rule over individual human lives, societies, and areas of the world.

INDUCTION INTO GOD'S ARMY

Repentance and conversion result in justification and salvation. This is God's plan for induction into His army. If you have not yet been inducted into God's army, the "Tactical Maneuvers" section of this lesson will provide opportunity for you to join. If you are already a member of God's army, the section will assist you in helping others enlist.

Welcome to the army of God!

INSPECTION

1. Write the Key Verse from the Articles Of War.

2. Define "repentance."

3. Explain the importance of repentance.

4. Define "conversion."

5. Explain the importance of conversion.

6. Define "justification."

7. Explain what it means to be "saved."

8. Use the parable of the prodigal son to describe repentance and conversion.

(Answers to tests are provided at the conclusion of the final chapter in this manual.)

TACTICAL MANEUVERS

1. Have you repented and been converted? If not, you need to stop right now in this study and do the following:

    -Repent of your sins.
    -Ask Jesus to forgive you.
    -Accept Him as your Lord and Savior.
    -Turn from your sinful ways (be converted).

2. As a believer, when you sin, you must also repent. Study the following Biblical examples:

THE CORINTHIANS:

The believers at a city called Corinth had to repent:

> **Now I rejoice, not that ye were made sorry, but that ye sorrowed to repentance... (II Corinthians 7:9)**

> **For I fear, lest, when I come...that I shall bewail many which have sinned already and have not repented of the uncleanness and fornication and lasciviousness which they have committed. (II Corinthians 12:20-21)**

THE EPHESIANS:

The believers at Ephesus were told to repent:

> **Remember therefore from whence thou art fallen and repent and do the first works. (Revelation 2:5)**

CHRISTIANS IN PERGAMOS:

God told the Christians in Pergamos:

> **Repent; or else I will come unto thee quickly, and will fight against them with the sword of my mouth. (Revelation 2:16)**

CHRISTIANS IN SARDIS:

> **Remember therefore how thou hast received and heard, and hold fast, and repent. (Revelation 3:3)**

CHRISTIANS IN LAODICEA:

As many as I love, I rebuke and chasten; Be zealous therefore, and repent. (Revelation 3:19)

HOW ABOUT YOU...

Is there unconfessed sin in your life? Wherever there is sin, there must be repentance:

If we say that we have no sin, we deceive ourselves and the truth is not in us. If we confess our sins, He is faithful and just to forgive us our sins, and to cleanse us from all unrighteousness. (I John 1:8-9)

3. Because repentance is necessary for salvation, God made a special plan to enable the message of repentance to reach everyone. The call to repentance began in the New Testament with the ministry of John the Baptist:

The voice of one crying in the wilderness, Prepare ye the way the Lord, make His path straight.

John did baptize in the wilderness, and preach the baptism of repentance for the remission of sins. (Mark 1:3-4)

Repentance was the first message Jesus preached:

Now after that John was put in prison, Jesus came into Galilee, preaching the Gospel of the Kingdom of God,

And saying, the time is fulfilled, and the Kingdom of God is at hand: repent ye, and believe the Gospel. (Mark 1:14-15)

Repentance was preached by believers in the early Church:

And they went out and preached that men should repent. (Mark 6:12)

...Testifying both to the Jews and also to the Greeks, repentance toward God, and faith toward our Lord Jesus Christ. (Acts 20:21)

Today, believers still have the responsibility to spread the message of repentance throughout the world. Jesus gave final instructions to His followers that...

...repentance and remission of sins should be preached in His name among all nations, beginning at Jerusalem. (Luke 24:47)

When you preach the message of repentance, you are actually calling others to enlist in God's army. Will you make a commitment to start drafting others into this great spiritual army?

4. If you are responsible to share the message of repentance and call others to enlist in God's army then you must know how men are persuaded to repent. Men repent because of:

THE GOODNESS OF GOD:

The blessings of God in the life of an ungodly person are not to be mistaken as God's approval of his life style. The goodness of God is one way the Lord appeals to men to turn to Him:

> **Despisest thou the riches of His goodness and forbearance and long suffering; not knowing that the goodness of God leadeth thee to repentance? (Romans 2:4)**

PREACHING:

The preaching of the Word of God causes men to repent. The preaching of Jonah resulted in the whole city of Ninevah repenting:

> **The men of Ninevah shall rise in judgment with this generation and shall condemn it: because they repented at the preaching of Jonas. (Matthew 12:41)**

CHRIST'S CALL:

As the Word of God is preached, people hear and respond to the call of Christ which leads to repentance:

> **I am not come to call the righteous, but sinners to repentance. (Matthew 9:13)**

GOD, THE FATHER:

Jesus said no one could come to Him except the Father draw him. God draws men to repentance:

> **No man can come to me, except the Father which hath sent me draw him... (John 6:44)**

REBUKE:

Rebuke causes men to repent. Rebuke is correction given from the Word of God:

> **...If thy brother trespass against thee, rebuke him; and if he repent, forgive him. (Luke 17:3)**

GODLY SORROW:

As you learned, repentance may be accompanied by emotion. Natural emotion alone is not true repentance, but Godly emotion leads to true repentance:

> **Godly sorrow [for sin] worketh repentance to salvation. (II Corinthians 7:10)**

BASIC TRAINING

PREPARING FOR WAR

In the natural world no soldier is sent to battle without first receiving basic training. This training prepares him to enter the combat zone.

CHAPTER THREE

THE COMMANDER-IN-CHIEF: THE LORD OF HOSTS

OBJECTIVES:

Upon completion of this chapter you will be able to:

- Write the Key Verse from memory.
- Identify the spiritual forces of good.
- Identify personalities of the Trinity of God.
- Describe the nature of the Triune God.
- Explain the function of God the Father in spiritual warfare.
- Summarize the functions of Jesus Christ in spiritual warfare.
- Summarize the functions of the Holy Spirit in spiritual warfare.

KEY VERSE FROM THE ARTICLES OF WAR:

Hear, O Israel: The Lord our God is one Lord. (Deuteronomy 6:4)

INTRODUCTION

In Chapter One you learned of a great spiritual battle being waged between the forces of good and evil. This lesson and the next describe the spiritual forces of good. These include God the Father, Jesus Christ the Son, the Holy Spirit, and angels. They are powerful spiritual forces which assist believers in warfare.

THE TRINITY OF GOD

There are many gods worshiped throughout the world, but there is only one true God. The Holy Bible contains the story of this true God. This one God revealed in three distinct personalities of the Father, the Son Jesus Christ, and the Holy Spirit.

God the Father, Jesus Christ, and the Holy Spirit are described in the Bible in terms of their nature. When we speak of "nature" we mean basic qualities which describe God. These qualities are also known as "attributes" which means "characteristics."

The Bible reveals that God is...

TRIUNE:

God has a triune nature. This means He has three distinct personalities, yet He is one God:

Hear, O Israel: The Lord our God is one Lord. (Deuteronomy 6:4)

The three persons of the Trinity of God are called God the Father, Jesus Christ the Son, and the Holy Spirit. There are several Scriptures which confirm this triune nature of God. When Jesus was being baptized by John the Baptist in the Jordan River, God spoke and the Holy Spirit descended:

> **And Jesus, when He was baptized, went up straightway out of the water: and, lo, the heavens were opened unto Him, and He saw the Spirit of God descending like a dove, and lighting upon Him:**
>
> **And lo, a voice from Heaven saying, This is my beloved Son, in whom I am well pleased. (Matthew 3:16-17)**

Prior to returning to Heaven after His ministry on earth, Jesus spoke of the Holy Spirit coming from God:

> **But when the Comforter is come, whom I will send unto you from the Father, even the Spirit of truth, which proceedeth from the Father, He shall testify of me. (John 15:26)**

The Apostle Peter spoke of the triune nature of God:

> **If ye be reproached for the name of Christ, happy are ye; for the Spirit of glory and of God resteth upon you: on their part He is evil spoken of, but on your part He is glorified. (I Peter 4:14)**

The Apostle Paul spoke of the Trinity in his writings:

> **For the law of the Spirit of life in Christ Jesus hath made me free from the law of sin and death.**
>
> **For what the law could not do, in that it was weak through the flesh, God sending His own Son, in the likeness of sinful flesh, and for sin, condemned sin in the flesh (Romans 8:2-3)**
>
> **The grace of the Lord Jesus Christ, and the love of God, and the communion of the Holy Ghost, be with you all. (II Corinthians 13:14)**
>
> **For through Him (the Son) we both have access by one Spirit unto the Father. (Ephesians 2:18)**

The book of Acts also verifies the triune nature of God:

> **Therefore being by the right hand of God exalted, and having received of the Father the promise of the Holy Ghost, He (Jesus) hath shed forth this, which ye now see and hear. (Acts 2:33)**

ETERNAL:

The Trinity of God is eternal with no beginning and no ending:

> **Lord, Thou hast been our dwelling place in all generations.**
>
> **Before the mountains were brought forth, or ever Thou hadst formed the earth and the world, even from everlasting to everlasting, Thou art God. (Psalms 90:1-2)**
>
> **And Abraham planted a grove in Beersheba, and called there on the name of the Lord, the everlasting God. (Genesis 21:33)**

The eternal nature of God is best illustrated by a circle. The circle has no visible starting point or ending point, yet it exists:

The Eternal Nature Of God

A SPIRIT:

God is a spirit. This means He is without flesh and blood and therefore invisible to the natural eyes of man:

> **God is a Spirit: and they that worship Him must worship Him in spirit and in truth. (John 4:24)**

SOVEREIGN:

God is the sovereign (greatest) power in all the universe. Read Ephesians 1 and Romans 9.

OMNIPRESENT:

This means God is present everywhere:

> **For the eyes of the Lord run to and fro throughout the whole earth... (II Chronicles 16:9)**
>
> **The eyes of the Lord are in every place, beholding the evil and the good. (Proverbs 15:3)**
>
> **Whither shall I go from Thy Spirit? Or whither shall I flee from Thy presence?**
>
> **If I ascend up into Heaven, Thou art there: if I make my bed in Hell, behold, Thou are there. (Psalms 139:7-8)**

OMNISCIENT:

This means God knows all things:

> ...Thou knowest it altogether. (Psalms 139:4)

> ...God is greater than our heart, and knoweth all things. (I John 3:20)

> ...But all things are naked and opened unto the eyes of Him with whom we have to do. (Hebrews 4:13)

OMNIPOTENT:

This means God is all powerful:

> ...I am the Almighty God... (Genesis 17:1)

> ...With God all things are possible. (Matthew 19:26)

> ...For the Lord God omnipotent reigneth. (Revelation 19:6)

> God hath spoken once; twice have I heard this; that power belongeth unto God. (Psalms 62:11)

UNCHANGING:

God does not change His person, nature, purpose, or plans are concerned:

> For I am the Lord, I change not... (Malachi 3:6)

> Jesus Christ the same yesterday, to day, and for ever. (Hebrews 13:8)

HOLY:

God is sinless, absolutely pure:

...Ye shall be holy: for I the Lord your God am holy. (Leviticus 19:2)

JUST:

God is fair and impartial in judgment:

> ...A God of truth and without iniquity, just and right is He. (Deuteronomy 32:4)

FAITHFUL:

God keeps His promises and is absolutely trustworthy.

> **...He abideth faithful: He cannot deny Himself. (II Timothy 2:13)**

BENEVOLENT:

God is good, kind, and desires your welfare:

> **The Lord is good to all: and His tender mercies are over all His works. (Psalms 145:9)**

MERCIFUL:

God shows mercy to sinful mankind:

> **...The Lord God, merciful and gracious, long suffering, and abundant in goodness and truth. Keeping mercy for thousands... (Exodus 34:6-7)**

GRACIOUS:

God shows undeserved kindness to sinful man:

> **...For I am gracious. (Exodus 22:27)**

The Lord is gracious, and full of compassion; slow to anger, and of great mercy. (Psalms 145:8)

LOVING:

God is love:

> **He that loveth not knoweth not God; for God is love. (I John 4:8)**

WISE:

God shows deep understanding and keen discernment.

> **The Lord by wisdom hath founded the earth; by understanding hath He established the heavens. (Proverbs 3:19)**

INFINITE:

God is not subject to natural and human limitations. He is not subject to the limitations of space:

> **But will God indeed dwell on the earth? behold, the heaven and heaven of heavens cannot contain thee: how much less this house that I have built? (I Kings 8:27)**

He is not subject to the limitations of time:

> **The Lord shall reign for ever and ever. (Exodus 15:18)**

GOD THE FATHER

God the Father is the commander of the spiritual forces of good which oppose the spiritual forces of evil. This is His special function in the realm of spiritual warfare.

WHERE IS GOD?

You just learned God is omnipresent, which means He is everywhere in the universe. God's throne is in a place called Heaven but He is also omnipresent.

> **Thus saith the Lord, The heaven is my throne and the earth is my footstool... (Isaiah 66:1)**

NAMES FOR GOD:

The Bible gives other names for God which reveal His ministry to you as you are engaged in this great spiritual conflict. The names for God include:

1. **Jehovah**: Which means Lord. The Bible combines this word with other names for God:

Jehovah-Rapha:	"The Lord that healeth"	Exodus 15:26
Jehovah-Nissi:	"The Lord our banner"	Exodus 17:8-15
Jehovah-Shalom:	"The Lord our peace"	Judges 6:24
Jehovah-Ra'ah:	"The Lord my shepherd"	Psalms 23:1
Jehovah-Tsidkenu:	"The Lord our righteousness"	Jeremiah 23:6
Jehovah-Jireh:	"The Lord who provides"	Genesis 22:14
Jehovah-Shammah:	"The Lord is there"	Ezekiel 48:35

2. **Elohim**: Means God and is used wherever the creative power of God is implied.

3. **Father**: Acts 17:28; John 1:12-13

4. **Adonai**: Means Lord or Master: Exodus 23:17; Isaiah 10:16,33

5. **El:** This is often used in combination with other words for God:

El Shaddai:	"The God who is sufficient for the needs of His People"	Exodus 6:3
Elolam:	"The everlasting God"	Genesis 21:33
El Elyon:	"Most high God who is exalted above other so called gods"	Genesis 14:18,22

6. **Yahweh**: In the Hebrew language in which the Old Testament was written, the word "Yahweh" means God. This word is combined with other words to reveal more about the character of God. God is called:

Yahweh Jireh:	"The Lord provides"	Genesis 22:14
Yahweh Nissi:	"The Lord is my banner"	Exodus 17:15
Yahweh Shalom:	"The Lord is peace"	Judges 6:24
Yahweh Sabbaoth:	"The Lord of Hosts"	I Samuel 1:3
Yahweh Maccaddeshcem:	"The Lord thy Sanctifier"	Exodus 31:13
Yahweh Tsidkenu:	"The Lord our righteousness"	Jeremiah 23:6
Yahweh Shammah:	"The Lord is there"	Ezekiel 48:35
Yahweh Elohim Israel:	"The Lord God of Israel"	Judges 5:3
Quadosh Israel:	"The Holy One Of Israel"	Isaiah 1:4

7. **The Lord Of Hosts:** In the Biblical record, these different names of God were used when requesting God to move in a specific way on behalf of His people. For example, the name Jehovah-Rapham meaning "the Lord that healeth," was used when seeking healing.

The specific name of God which should be used in spiritual warfare is "Yahweh Sabbaoth" which is translated "the Lord of hosts" in the King James version of the Bible. When you call upon that name in warfare, the battle is the Lord's and all the hosts of Heaven come to your aid.

GOD THE SON, JESUS CHRIST

God the Son, Jesus Christ, combines the divine and the human natures in one union. God the Father sent Jesus Christ to earth in human form while yet retaining His divine nature. Jesus was sent by God to earth so man could be pardoned from sin:

For God so loved the world, that He gave His only begotten Son, that whosoever believeth in Him should not perish, but have everlasting life.

For God sent not His Son into the world to condemn the world; but that the world through Him might be saved.

He that believeth on Him is not condemned: but he that believeth not is condemned already, because He hath not believed in the name of the only begotten Son of God. (John 3:16-18)

The story of Jesus is recorded in the Bible in the books of Matthew, Mark, Luke, and John. These books provide a detailed record of the birth, life, death, resurrection, teachings, and ministry of Jesus Christ.

As part of the plan of God, Jesus came to earth in human form, ministered among men, died for the sins of man, was resurrected from the dead, and commissioned His followers to bear the

Gospel to the nations of the world.

WHERE IS JESUS?

Following His resurrection from the dead, Jesus appeared to many people, commissioned His followers, and then returned to Heaven. But remember...even though He is in Heaven He is still omnipresent...His presence is everywhere.

SPECIAL FUNCTIONS:

The special functions of Jesus in relation to spiritual warfare include the following:

1. Redeeming man from sin: It is through the death of Jesus Christ that you are freed from the bondage of sin in which the enemy has ensnared you:

    ...for of whom a man is overcome, of the same is he brought in bondage... (II Peter 2:19)

    Because the creature itself also shall be delivered from the bondage of corruption into the glorious liberty of the children of God. (Romans 8:21)

    Stand fast therefore in the liberty wherewith Christ hath made us free, and be not entangled again with the yoke of bondage. (Galatians 5:1)

2. Authority over the forces of evil: You will study this in detail later in this course. The death of Jesus not only freed mankind from sin, but also resulted in triumph over the forces of evil. Because of this, you have authority over the enemy:

    Then He called His twelve disciples together, and gave them power and authority over all devils and to cure diseases. (Luke 9:1)

3. Destroying the works of the Devil:

    ...For this purpose the Son of God was manifested, that He might destroy the works of the Devil. (I John 3:8)

4. Intercession for believers: In Heaven Jesus is at the right hand of God the Father interceding for believers engaged in spiritual warfare. This means He is talking to the Father on your behalf:

    ...It is Christ that died, yea rather, that is risen again, who is even at the right hand of God, who also maketh intercession for us. (Romans 8:34)

THE NAMES OF JESUS:

The name "Jesus" means "Savior or deliverer" (Matthew 1:21). The name "Christ" means "the anointed one" (John 4:25-26). Additional names given Jesus Christ in the Bible include the following:

Advocate	1 John 2:1
Almighty	Revelation 1:8
Alpha and Omega	Revelation 21:6
Amen	Revelation 3:14
Ancient of Days	Daniel 7:9
Author/Finisher of our Faith	Hebrews 12:2
Author of Eternal Salvation	Hebrews 5:9
Begotten of God	1 John 5:18
Beloved	Ephesians 1:6
Branch	Zechariah 3:8
Bread of Life	John 6:48
Bright and Morning Star	Revelation 22:16
Captain of the Lord's Host	Joshua 5:15
Carpenter's Son	Matthew 13:55
Chief Cornerstone	1 Peter 2:6
Chief Among Ten Thousand	Song of Solomon 5:10
Christ	John 1:41
Counselor	Isaiah 9:6
Deliverer	Romans 11:26
Door	John 10:9
Elect	Isaiah 42:1
Emmanuel	Matthew 1:23
Eternal Life	1 John 5:20
Faithful and True	Revelation 19:11
Faithful Witness	Revelation 1:5
First Begotten	Hebrews 1:6
First and Last	Revelation 22:13
Glorious Lord	Isaiah 33:21
Great High Priest	Hebrews 4:14
Head of the Body	Colossians 1:18
Head over all things	Ephesians 1:22
Headstone	Psalms 118:22
Heir of all things	Hebrews 1:2
Holy One of Israel	Isaiah 41:14
Hope of Glory	Colossians 1:27
I Am	John 8:58
Image of the Invisible God	Colossians 1:15
Jesus Christ Our Lord	Romans 1:3
King of Glory	Psalms 24:7
Lamb of God	John 1:29
Light of the World	John 8:12
Lily of the Valleys	Song of Solomon 2:1
Living Bread	John 6:51
Lord God Almighty	Revelation 4:8
Lord of All	Acts 10:36
Lord Our Righteousness	Jeremiah 23:6

Love	1 John 4:8
Man of Sorrows	Isaiah 53:3
Master	Matthew 23:10
Messiah	Daniel 9:25
Most Holy	Daniel 9:24
Nazarene	Matthew 2:23
Only Wise God	1 Timothy 1:17
Our Passover	1 Corinthians 5:7
Physician	Luke 4:23
Prince of Peace	Isaiah 9:6
Propitiation	Romans 3:25
Redeemer	Isaiah 59:20
Resurrection	John 11:25
Righteous Servant	Isaiah 53:11
Rock	1 Corinthians 10:4
Root of Jesse	Isaiah 11:10
Rose of Sharon	Song of Solomon 2:1
Savior of the World	1 John 4:14
Seed of David	John 7:42
Seed of the Woman	Genesis 3:15
Shepherd	John 10:11
Son of God	Romans 1:4
Son of Man	Acts 7:56
Son of Mary	Mark 6:3
Stone	Matthew 21:42
Sun of Righteousness	Malachi 4:2
Sure Foundation	Isaiah 28:16
Teacher	John 3:2
Truth	John 14:6
Unspeakable Gift	1 Corinthians 9:15
Vine	John 15:1
Way	John 14:6
Wonderful	Isaiah 9:6
Word	John 1:14
Word of God	Revelation 19:13

GOD THE HOLY SPIRIT

The Holy Spirit is part of the triune nature of God, but the Holy Spirit also has an individual personality. The subject of the Holy Spirit is so vast that an entire course entitled *"The Ministry Of The Holy Spirit"* is offered by Harvestime International Institute. This course is recommended for more detailed study of the Holy Spirit.

PERSONALITY OF THE HOLY SPIRIT:

The Bible reveals that the Holy Spirit:

Has a mind:

> And He that searcheth the hearts knoweth what is the mind of the Spirit... (Romans 8:27)

Searches out the human mind:

> But God hath revealed them unto us by His Spirit: for the Spirit searcheth all things, yea, the deep things of God. (I Corinthians 2:10)

Has a will:

> But all these worketh that one and the selfsame Spirit, dividing to every man severally as He will. (I Corinthians 12:11)

The will of the Holy Spirit guides believers by denying permission for certain actions:

> Now when they had gone throughout Phrygia and the region of Galatia, and were forbidden of the Holy Ghost to preach the word in Asia.
>
> After they were come to Mysia, they assayed to go into Bithynia; but the Spirit suffered them not. (Acts 16:6-7)

The will of the Holy Spirit also guides believers by granting permission:

> And after he had seen the vision, immediately we endeavored to go into Macedonia, assuredly gathering that the Lord had called us for to preach the Gospel unto them. (Acts 16:10)

Speaks:

> Then the Spirit said unto Philip, Go near, and join thyself to this chariot. (Acts 8:29)

Loves:

> Now I beseech you, brethren, for the Lord Jesus Christ's sake, and for the love of the Spirit, that ye strive together with me in your prayers to God for me. (Romans 15:30)

Intercedes:

The Holy Spirit intercedes (prays to God) on behalf of believers:

Likewise the Spirit also helpeth our infirmities: for we know not what we should pray for as we ought: but the Spirit itself maketh intercession for us with groanings which cannot be uttered (spoken). (Romans 8:26)

From this list of personality traits you can immediately recognize the important functions of the Holy Spirit in spiritual warfare. The Holy Spirit guides your warfare. He reveals spiritual things that cannot be known naturally. The Holy Spirit speaks the will and words of God to you. He also intercedes for you as you are engaged in spiritual battles.

BAPTISM OF THE HOLY SPIRIT:

There is a spiritual experience called the baptism of the Holy Spirit which involves the sign of speaking in other tongues (Acts 2) and the evidence of power to become an effective witness of the Gospel (Acts 1:8).

To wage successful spiritual warfare, it is important for you to experience the baptism of the Spirit. This is the source of power for spiritual battles. The baptism of the Holy Spirit is discussed in the course *"The Ministry Of The Holy Spirit."*

GIFTS OF THE HOLY SPIRIT:

The Holy Spirit gives special spiritual gifts to believers. These gifts are discussed in detail in the course on the Holy Spirit. The main references listing the gifts of the Holy Spirit are:

-Romans 12:1-8
-I Corinthians 12:1-31
-Ephesians 4:1-16
-I Peter 4:7-11

The gifts of the Holy Spirit are necessary to equip the believer for combat against the forces of evil. The gifts of the Holy Spirit include the following:

Special gifts to equip God's people:

Apostles, prophets, evangelists, pastors, teachers.

Speaking gifts to explain God's truth:

Prophecy, teaching, exhortation, word of wisdom, word of knowledge.

Serving gifts to enable God's work:

Serving, helps, leadership, administration, giving, showing mercy, discerning of spirits, faith, hospitality.

Sign gifts to establish God's authority:

Tongues, interpretation, miracles, healings.

FRUIT OF THE HOLY SPIRIT:

The Holy Spirit also develops spiritual fruit in the life of the believer. The "fruit of the Holy Spirit" refers to the nature of the Spirit revealed in the life of the believer, spiritual qualities which should be evident in the lives of all Christians.

The gifts of the Holy Spirit are for power. The fruit of the Holy Spirit is for character in the life of a believer. If you do not develop Christlike character traits then you will become a victim of the forces of evil. Spiritual fruit is evidence of spiritual maturity. Like fruit in the natural world, it is a product which is the result of the process of life.

There are two types of spiritual fruit. There is the spiritual fruit of reproduction:

> **Ye have not chosen me, but I have chosen you, and ordained you, that ye should go and bring forth fruit, and that your fruit should remain... (John 15:16)**

There is also the inner fruit of Christlike qualities. These qualities are completely opposite of the fleshly nature of man:

> **Now the works of the flesh are manifest, which are these; Adultery, fornication, uncleanness, lasciviousness,**
>
> **Idolatry, witchcraft, hatred, variance, emulations, wrath, strife, seditions, heresies,**
>
> **Envyings, murders, drunkenness, revellings, and such like: of the which I tell you before, as I have also told you in time past, that they which do such things shall not inherit the Kingdom of God.**
>
> **But the fruit of the Spirit is love, joy, peace, long suffering, gentleness, goodness, faith,**
>
> **Meekness, temperance: against such there is no law. (Galatians 5:19-23)**

Although the power of the flesh was defeated at the cross, as a believer you experience this only to the degree that you practice faith in the finished work of Jesus. Therefore, to be effective in denying the power of the sinful nature of the flesh, it is necessary that you develop or "put on" the fruit of the Holy Spirit.

WHERE IS THE HOLY SPIRIT?

Jesus promised His followers that upon His return to Heaven He would send the Holy Spirit to earth to comfort them:

> **And I will pray the Father, and He shall give you another Comforter, that He may abide with you for ever;**
>
> **Even the Spirit of truth: whom the world cannot receive, because it seeth him not, neither knoweth Him; but ye know Him; for He dwelleth with you, and shall be in you. (John 14:16-17)**

One of the main functions of the Holy Spirit is to direct attention to Jesus Christ:

> **But when the Comforter is come, whom I will sent unto you from the Father, even the Spirit of truth, which proceedeth from the Father, He shall testify of me (John 15:26)**

God the Holy Spirit, in spirit form and invisible to the natural eyes of man, is in the world today. He is active in convicting men of sin, drawing men to Jesus Christ, equipping believers with power for spiritual warfare, guiding them, and testifying of Jesus.

The Holy Spirit ministers in many other ways in the world. These are discussed in detail in the Harvestime International Institute course entitled *"Ministry Of The Holy Spirit."*

SENSITIVITY OF THE HOLY SPIRIT:

The Holy Spirit has a sensitive nature. This means He has feelings that can be affected by the actions of man. Because of the sensitive nature of the Holy Spirit the Bible warns that we should not lie to the Holy Spirit (Acts 5:3-4), resist the Spirit (Acts 7:51), quench the Spirit (I Thessalonians 5:19), grieve the Spirit (Psalms 78:40 and Ephesians 4:30), insult the Spirit (Hebrews 6:4-6), blaspheme the Spirit (Matthew 12:31-32), or vex the Spirit (Isaiah 63:10). These actions are discussed in detail in the Harvestime International Institute course on *"The Ministry Of The Holy Spirit."*

It is important that you do not offend the sensitive nature of the Holy Spirit. If the Holy Spirit is offended by your actions He will withdraw His presence. You cannot wage effective spiritual warfare without the power of the Holy Spirit.

TITLES OF THE HOLY SPIRIT:

There are several titles used in the Bible to describe the Holy Spirit. A title is a descriptive phrase which explains a person's position and/or function. It is important that you know the function of the Holy Spirit as you enter spiritual warfare. Look up the following references in your Bible to study the titles given the Holy Spirit.

The Holy Spirit is called:

The Spirit of God:	I Corinthians 3:16
The Spirit of Christ:	Romans 8:9
The Eternal Spirit:	Hebrews 9:14
The Spirit of Truth:	John 16:13
The Spirit of Grace:	Hebrews 10:29
The Spirit of Life:	Romans 8:2
The Spirit of Glory:	I Peter 4:14
The Spirit of Wisdom and Revelation:	Ephesians 1:17
The Comforter:	John 14:26
The Spirit of Promise:	Acts 1:4-5
The Spirit of Holiness:	Romans 1:4
The Spirit of Faith:	II Corinthians 4:13
The Spirit of Adoption:	Romans 8:15

EMBLEMS OF THE HOLY SPIRIT:

The Bible uses several emblems to represent the Holy Spirit. An emblem represents something. It is a symbol which has a special meaning. Look up the following references in your Bible. They each use emblems which represent the Holy Spirit:

The dove:	John 1:32, Song Of Solomon 6:9
Oil:	Luke 4:18, Acts 10:38; Hebrews 1:9
Water:	John 7:37-39; Isaiah 44:3
A seal:	Ephesians 1:13; 4:30; II Corinthians 1:22
Wind:	John 3:8; Acts 2:1-2
Fire:	Exodus 3:2; 13:21; Leviticus 9:24; Acts 2:3

The meaning of each of these emblems of the Holy Spirit is explained in the course on the *"Ministry Of The Holy Spirit."*

SUMMARY

In this chapter you learned of the Triune nature of God and studied about God the Father, the Son Jesus Christ, and the Holy Spirit. With their combined functions in the realm of spiritual warfare they are a powerful force of good in the universe.

But it is not enough just to recognize that the spiritual forces of good exist. The Bible says:

> **Thou believest that there is one God; thou doest well: the devils also believe and tremble. (James 2:19)**

The spiritual forces of evil believe in God and are fearful of Him, but they are still evil. To simply believe in God is not enough. You must acknowledge Him as Lord of your life. You must accept the sacrifice of Jesus Christ for your sin, repent, ask forgiveness, and become a new creature in Christ.

You have not yet completed your study of the spiritual forces of good. The next chapter concerns a mighty host of spirit beings known as angels and describes their function in spiritual warfare.

INSPECTION

1. Write the Key Verse from the Articles Of War.

   _____

   _____

   _____

2. List the spiritual forces of good.

   _____

   _____

   _____

3. Name the three personalities of the Trinity of God:

   God the _____

   God the _____, _____ _____

   God the _____ _____

4. Summarize the special function of God in the realm of spiritual warfare.

   _____

   _____

5. Summarize the functions of Jesus Christ in spiritual warfare.

   _____

   _____

   _____

6. Summarize the functions of the Holy Spirit in spiritual warfare.

_____

_____

7. Column One lists some of the attributes of the Triune god. Column Two lists definitions of these attributes, but they are not in correct order. Look at each attribute in Column One. Then find the correct definition in Column Two. Write the number of the correct definition in the blank provided. The first one is done as an example for you to follow.

1.	_h_	Eternal	a.	Without flesh and blood
2.	____	Sovereign	b.	Present everywhere.
3.	____	Omnipresent	c.	Good, kind
4.	____	Holy	d.	Highest, supreme power
5.	____	Infinite	e.	All powerful
6.	____	Unchanging	f.	Knows all things
7.	____	Benevolent	g.	Sinless
8.	____	A spirit	h.	No beginning or end
9.	____	Omniscient	i.	Does not change.
10.	____	Omnipotent	j.	Fair and impartial in judgment
11.	____	Just	k.	Shows mercy to sinful mankind
12.	____	Merciful	l.	Not subject to natural limitations

8. What is the name of God you should use when entering into spiritual warfare?

_____

(Answers to tests are provided at the conclusion of the final chapter in this manual.)

TACTICAL MANEUVERS

1. If you are studying the Harvestime Institute courses in their suggested order, you will study *"The Ministry Of The Holy Spirit"* after completion of this course. The first chapter of *"The Ministry Of The Holy Spirit"* includes an outline for further study of God the Father and the Son Jesus Christ. If you are not enrolled in the complete Institute program, we suggest you obtain the Harvestime International Institute course entitled *"The Ministry Of The Holy Spirit"* to study upon completion of this course.

2. Additional studies on the life, ministry, and teachings of Jesus Christ are provided in the Harvestime International Institute courses *"Kingdom Living"* and *"Teaching Tactics."*

3. The Harvestime International Institute course entitled *"Foundations Of Faith"* provides detailed instruction on the basic doctrines of the Christian faith. This course is important in gaining understanding of the spiritual forces of good. You have already completed this course if you are studying the subjects in suggested order. If not, we suggest you obtain this course for further study.

4. Are you presently in a spiritual battle? As you pray about your problem, begin to call upon the name of the Lord of Hosts.

5. Think about a battle you are presently facing and study again the functions of God the Father, Jesus Christ, and the Holy Spirit in warfare. How can God assist you in your personal battle? How can Jesus assist you? What is the function of the Holy Spirit in the problem you are facing?

CHAPTER FOUR

THE SPIRITUAL FORCES OF GOOD: ANGELS

OBJECTIVES:

Upon completion of this chapter you will be able to:

- Write the Key Verse from memory.
- Provide a reference which explains what angels are.
- Tell how angels originated.
- Identify two kinds of angels.
- Identify their sphere of activity.
- Summarize the ministry of angels in spiritual warfare.
- Identify attributes of angels.
- Identify various classifications of angels.
- Give a Scripture reference which explains the organization of the angelic host.

KEY VERSE FROM THE ARTICLES OF WAR:

The angel of the Lord encampeth round about them that fear Him, and delivereth them. (Psalms 34:7)

INTRODUCTION

In the last chapter you learned of the Trinity of God which includes God the Father, God the Son Jesus Christ, and God the Holy Spirit. You learned of their origin, attributes, and functions in spiritual warfare.

This chapter continues the study of the spiritual forces of good. It explains the origin, attributes, sphere of activity, classification, and organization of angels. It also explains their ministry in spiritual warfare.

WHAT ARE ANGELS?

Angels are ministering spirits sent by God to do His will:

Are they not all ministering spirits, sent forth to minister for them who shall be heirs of salvation. (Hebrews 1:14)

The title "angel" means messenger.

THE ORIGIN OF ANGELS

Angels were created by God:

> **Praise ye Him, all His angels: praise ye Him, all His hosts.**
>
> **Let them praise the name of the Lord: For He commanded and they were created. (Psalms 148:2 and 5)**
>
> **For by Him were all things created, that are in Heaven, and that are in earth, visible and invisible, whether they be thrones, or dominions, or principalities, or powers: all things were created by Him and for Him. (Colossians 1:16.)**

All the angels were righteous and holy when they were first created. They worshiped and served the one true God. Later, some angels rebelled against God and lost their position as angels. They became part of a force of evil called "demons."

There are now two kinds of angels: Good angels, which are the subject of this chapter, and evil angels (demons) which will be discussed in Chapter Six of this course.

THE ORGANIZATION OF ANGELS

The good Angels have been organized by God in a special order. The Bible does not reveal the details of that order, but it does indicate such organization:

> **For by Him were all things created, that are in Heaven, and that are in earth, visible and invisible, whether they be thrones, or dominions, or principalities, or powers: all things were created by Him and for Him. (Colossians 1:16; See also Ephesians 3:10)**

The organization of the invisible world is described here in terms of thrones, dominions, principalities, and powers. We are not given details of this structure. You will learn later how Satan has imitated this organization in his own structure of evil forces.

THE CLASSIFICATION OF ANGELS

There are literally multitudes of angels (Luke 2:13-15) who are apparently classified according to the duties they perform. These are the main classifications of angels:

MESSENGERS:

This class of angels is most likely the largest in number. These are the angels composing the innumerable group, visualized by Daniel (Daniel 7:10), who carry out the will of God in Heaven and earth. This is the group that usually relates to the believer in terms of spiritual warfare. They interpret God's will, protect, provide guidance, bring answers to prayer, announce, warn, instruct, bring judgment, encourage, sustain, deliver, and intercede on behalf of believers.

ELECT ANGELS:

Only one reference is made to elect angels in I Timothy 5:21. There is no further information given about this group.

CHERUBIM:

This classification of angels is first mentioned in Genesis 3:24. They are also mentioned as part of the ark of the covenant (Exodus 25:18-22). Ezekiel mentions these beings and describes them as having four appearances; the face of a lion, the face of an ox, the face of a man, and the face of an eagle (Ezekiel 1:3-28; 10:22). This symbolism of the cherubim suggests they are the living creatures surrounding the throne of God in Revelation 4:6. They appear to be the highest order of angels, the guardians of God.

SERAPHIM:

This group is mentioned in Isaiah 6:2,6. Their position is above the throne of God in contrast to the position of cherubims who surround His throne. The duty of these angels seems to be to lead Heaven in the worship of God.

LIVING CREATURES:

This group of angels are mentioned in Revelation 4:6,8; 5:6. This title presents these angels as manifesting the fullness of divine life, whose chief ministry appears to be worship of God.

INDIVIDUAL ANGELS

In addition to the different classifications of angels, there are some individual angels mentioned by name in the Bible:

MICHAEL:

Michael the archangel is mentioned by name in Daniel 10:13,21; 12:1; Jude 9; and Revelation 12:7. He is the only angel who is called an archangel. He is represented as having charge over an army of angels in Revelation 12:7 and is said to be the prince of the people of Israel in Daniel 10:13,21; 12:1.

GABRIEL:

The meaning of his name is "mighty one." He is mentioned in Daniel 8:16; 9:21; and in Luke 1:19,26. He is always used to deliver an important message from God. It is Gabriel who interpreted the vision for Daniel in 8:16; 9:21 and who announced the birth of John and Jesus Luke 1:19,26.

SPECIAL GROUPS OF ANGELS:

The Bible also mentions special groups of angels which include:

Angels of the seven churches:	Revelation 1:20
Four angels who control the winds:	Revelation 1:7
Seven angels who stand before God:	Revelation 8:2
Seven angels who administer the seven last plagues:	Revelation 15:1,7
Twenty-four elders (these may be angelic beings):	Revelation 4 and 5

THE ATTRIBUTES OF ANGELS

You will remember from the last chapter that attributes are personality traits or characteristics of an individual. Angels...

- Are spirits: Hebrews 1:14
- Are sexless: Luke 20:34-36
- Are immortal: Matthew 22:28-30
- Have both visible and invisible forms: Numbers 22:22-35
- Appear with the likeness of human form: Genesis 19:1-22; 18:2,4,8
- Have emotions: Luke 15:1-10 (angels rejoicing).
- Have appetites: Genesis 18:8
- Are glorified beings: Luke 9:26
- Are intelligent: II Samuel 14:20
- Are meek: Jude 9
- Are powerful: Psalms 103:20; II Peter 2:11
- Have no need to rest: Revelation 4:8
- Travel at an unrecorded speed: Revelation 8:13; 9:1
- Speak languages: I Corinthians 13:1
- Are innumerable: Luke 2:13; Hebrews 12:22; Psalms 68:17; Mark 1:13; Revelation 5:19
- Are immortal: Luke 20:34-36
- Do not marry or have children: Luke 20:34-36
- Are obedient: Psalms 103:20
- Are holy: Revelation 14:10; Mark 8:38
- Are reverent: Their highest activity is the worship of God. Nehemiah 9:6; Philippians 2:9-11; Hebrews 1:6

THEIR SPHERE OF ACTIVITY

Angels are active in both Heaven and earth. The source of their power is both granted and governed by God. They have access to the presence of God in Heaven:

...In Heaven their angels do always behold the face of my Father which is in Heaven. (Matthew 18:10)

They are also active on earth. This is documented by the varied ministries and many appearances of angels to people recorded in the Bible.

THE MINISTRY OF ANGELS

Angels minister in many ways in both Heaven and earth. Look up each of the following references in your Bible. As you study these verses you will understand the importance of angels in spiritual warfare.

The ministry of angels in Heaven includes:

-Worship: Revelation 4:8; 5:11-12; Isaiah 6:3; Psalms 103:20; 148:1-2
-Standing ready to do God's will: Psalms 103:20-21
-Ministering to the godly who have died in Christ Jesus: Jude 9; Luke 16:22
-Representing children in a special way: Matthew 18:10
-Rejoicing over those who accept the Gospel: Luke 15:10

The ministry of angels on earth includes:

-Ruling nations: Daniel 10
-Ministering to believers in times of testing: Matthew 4:11
-Strengthening believers: Luke 22:43
-Interpreting God's will for men: Zechariah 1:9; Daniel 7:16
-Guiding believers: Acts 8:26.
-Bringing judgment on individuals and nations: Acts 12:23; Genesis 19:3; II Samuel 24:16; Revelation 16:1
-Bringing answers to prayer: Daniel 9:21-22
-Announcing: Luke 1:11-20; Matthew 1:20, 21
-Warning: Matthew 2:13;
-Instructing: Matthew 28:2-6; Acts 10:3-6; Daniel 4:13-17
-Encouraging: Acts 27:23; Genesis 28:12
-Revealing: Acts 7:53; Galatians 3:19; Hebrews 2:2; Daniel 9:21-27; Revelation 1:1
-Sustaining: Matthew 4:11; Luke 22:43
-Preserving: Genesis 16:7; 24:7; Exodus 23:20; Revelation 7:1
-Protecting: Psalms 91:11
-Delivering: Numbers 20:16; Psalms 34:7; Isaiah 63:9; Daniel 3:28; 6:22; Genesis 48:16; Matthew 26:53; Acts 12:1-19
-Destroying: Acts 12:20-23
-Interceding: Zechariah 1:12; Revelation 8:3,4

The future activities of angels will include:

-Participating in the return of Jesus: I Thessalonians 4:16
-Gathering the elect: Matthew 24:31
-Warning and preaching during the tribulation: Revelation 14:6-9
-Separating the wicked from the righteous: Matthew 13:39 and 49
-Binding Satan: Revelation 20

ANGELS AND SPIRITUAL WARFARE

The Messenger angels are the group that usually relates to the believer in terms of spiritual warfare. They interpret God's will, protect, provide guidance, bring answers to prayer, announce, warn, instruct, bring judgment, encourage, sustain, deliver, and intercede on behalf of believers in battle.

Many believers have not availed themselves of the aid available from angels because they have not been taught regarding their function in spiritual warfare. They are "ministering spirits" and can minister for you as well as to you. You can ask God to dispatch angels to assist you in battle. King David did this. He prayed...

> **Let the angel of the Lord persecute them...Let the angel of the Lord chase them... (Psalms 35:5-6)**

Read the following Biblical accounts of angels participating in warring against the enemy: II Kings 19:35; II Chronicles 32:21; Isaiah 37:36; Revelation 12:7.

IMPORTANT WARNINGS

Angels are holy beings with important ministries on behalf of believers. They are part of the spiritual forces of good as is the Trinity of God. But the Bible gives some warnings concerning angels:

DO NOT WORSHIP THEM:

You are not to worship angels:

> **Let no man beguile you of your reward in a voluntary humility and worshiping of angels, intruding into those things which he hath not seen, vainly puffed up by his fleshly mind. (Colossians 2:18)**

> **And I John saw these things, and heard them. And when I had heard and seen, I fell down to worship before the feet of the angel which shewed me these things.**

> **Then saith he unto me, See thou do it not: for I am thy fellow servant and of thy brethren the prophets, and of them which keep the sayings of this book: Worship God. (Revelation 22:8-9)**

REJECT ANGELS PREACHING "ANOTHER GOSPEL":

Some people have claimed to see angels who gave them a "new revelation" contrary to God's written Word. Entire religious movements have been founded on such false revelations. The Bible warns:

But though we, or an angel from Heaven, preach any other gospel unto you than that which we have preached unto you, let him be accursed. (Galatians 1:8)

You are not to listen to a man, an angel, or any other being that would guide you contrary to God's Word. As you will learn later in this course, one of the main strategies of Satan is deception. The Bible warns:

And no marvel; for Satan himself is transformed into an angel of light. (II Corinthians 11:14)

DO NOT PROVOKE THE ANGELS:

Read the story of Balaam in Numbers 22, a prophet who was acting in disobedience to God. You will note that he was opposed by an angel of the Lord. When you are disobedient to God, the angels may actually hinder you. You will be fighting a battle, but it will not be warfare against the enemy. Be careful that you do not provoke the angels of God (Ecclesiastes 5:1-6).

INSPECTION

1. Write the Key Verse from the Articles Of War.

   _____

2. Angels minister in both_____and_____.

3. How did angels originate?

   _____

   _____

4. Summarize the ministry of angels as related to spiritual warfare.

   _____

5. List as many of the attributes of angels as you can recall from this chapter.

   _____

   _____

6. Give a Bible reference which explains what angels are.

   _____

7. Is this statement True or False? You are not to worship angels. The statement is_.

8. Is this statement True or False? If an angel appears and reveals something that does not agree with God's written Word, you should listen to him because he is a direct messenger from the Lord.

   The statement is_____.

9. Use the words below to complete the paragraphs. Use each word only once.

Messengers

Elect angels

Cherubim

Seraphim

Living Creatures

_____ Only one reference is made to this group of angels (I Timothy 5:21). No further information is given in the Bible about this group.

_____ This group of angels is most active in terms of spiritual warfare and probably includes the largest number of angels.

_____ This group of angels appear to be the highest order of angels; guardians of God. They surround the throne of God. Their chief ministry is to worship God.

_____ Their position is above the throne of God. They lead Heaven in worship of God.

10. There are two kinds of angels: These are_____ angels and_____ angels which are also called demons.

11. What verse reveals that God has an organization of the various classes of angels?

_____

(Answers to tests are provided at the conclusion of the final chapter in this manual.)

TACTICAL MANEUVERS

1. Use the following outline to study further about angels:

ANGELS IN THE OLD TESTAMENT:

Rescued Hagar: Genesis 16:7-12
Announced the birth of Isaac: Genesis 18:1-15
Announced the destruction of Sodom: Genesis 18:16-33
Destroyed Sodom and rescued Lot: Genesis 19:1-29
Prevented the slaying of Isaac: Genesis 22:11-2
Guarded Jacob: Genesis 28:12; 31:11; 32:1; 48:16
Commissioned Moses: Exodus 3:2
Led Israel: Exodus 14:19; 23:20-23; 32:34
Arranged the marriage of Isaac and Rebecca: Genesis 24:7
Gave the law: Acts 7:38; Galatians 3:19; Hebrews 2:2
Rebuked Balaam: Numbers 22:31-35
Appeared to Joshua: Joshua 5:13-15
Rebuked Israel for idolatry: Judges 2:1-5
Commissioned Gideon: Judges 6:11-40
Announced the birth of Samson: Judges 13
Punished Israel: II Samuel 24:16-17
Rescued Elijah: I Kings 19:5-8
Surrounded Elisha: II Kings 6:14-17
Saved Daniel from lions: Daniel 6:22
Conquered the Assyrian army: II Kings 19:35 and Isaiah 37:36
Camp round about God's people: Psalms 34:7; 91:11
Mentioned frequently as messengers to the prophets from God.

ANGELS IN THE LIFE OF JESUS:

Announced the birth of John: Luke 1:11-17
Named him: Luke 1:13
Announced the birth of Jesus to Mary: Luke 1:26-37
Announced the birth of Jesus to Joseph: Matthew 1:20-21
Named Jesus: Matthew 1:21
Announced the birth of Jesus to the shepherds: Luke 2:8-15
Sang: Luke 2:13-14
Directed the flight to Egypt: Matthew 2:13,20
Ministered to Jesus at His temptation: Matthew 4:11
Came to Jesus in Gethsemane: Luke 22:43
Rolled away the stone at His tomb: Matthew 28:2
Announced His resurrection: Matthew 28:5-7

Presented Him to Mary Magdalene: John 20:11-14
Angels ascended on Him: John 1:51
He could have twelve legions of angels: Matthew 26:53
Angels will come with Him when He returns to earth: Matthew 25:31; 16:27; Mark 8:38; Luke 9:26
Angels will be the reapers: Matthew 13:39
They will gather the elect: Matthew 24:31

They will divide the wicked from the righteous: Matthew 13:41,49
They carried the beggar to Abraham: Luke 16:22
They rejoice over sinners who repent: Luke 15:10
They represent little children: Matthew 18:10
He will confess His people before angels: Luke 12:8
They have no sex and cannot die: Luke 20:35-36
The Devil has evil angels: Matthew 25:41

ANGELS IN THE BOOK OF ACTS:

Opened prison doors: 5:19
Directed Philip to the Ethiopian: 8:26
Directed Cornelius to send for Peter: Chapter 10
Delivered Peter from prison: 12:7-19
Struck Herod dead: 12:23
Stood by Paul during the storm: 27:23
Also mentioned in: 6:15; 7:30,35,38,53; 11:13; 23:8-9

ANGELS IN THE EPISTLES:

Elect angels: I Timothy 5:21
Angels are innumerable: Hebrews 12:22
Angels minister to heirs of salvation: Hebrews 1:13-14
Angels will return with Jesus: II Thessalonians 1:7
We are not to worship angels: Colossians 2:18

ANGELS IN THE BOOK OF REVELATION:

Dictated the book to John: 1:1-2; 22:16
Presided over the seven churches: Chapters 1-2
Were interested in the sealed book: 5:2
Sang praise to the Lamb: 5:11-12
Were given special power on earth: 7:1-4
Sealed the elect: 7:1-4
Fell down before God: 7:11
Were used to answer prayers of the saints: 8:3-5
Sounded the seven trumpets: 8:6
Ruled the locust army: 9:11
Loosed 200,000,000 horsemen: 9:15-16
Announced the end of time: 10:1,2,6

Fought with the dragon and his angels: 12:7
Proclaimed the Gospel to the nations: 14:6
Proclaimed the fall of Babylon: 14:8; 18:2
Pronounced doom of the beast's followers: 14:9-10
Announced the harvest of the earth: 14:15-18
Had the last seven plagues: 15:1
Announced judgment on Babylon: 17:1,5
Participated in destruction of Babylon: 18:21
Showed John the New Jerusalem: 21:9
Forbid John to worship them: 22:8-9

2. Study the appearance of the angel in Judges 13. Note that the angel returns to Heaven through worship which apparently opens the way through the "Satanic atmosphere" around us to permit angels to operate on our behalf. Review the story of Daniel and note that the hindrance by the prince of Persia (a Satanic power) was broken by prayer and fasting.

3. There is no Biblical support that a believer can command his angel to do whatever he desires, but you can ask God to dispatch them in your behalf. Think about a battle you are facing and then ask God to send His "ministering spirits" to work in that situation.

4. Read Psalms 78:36,40 and Ecclesiastes 5:6. Israel had a special angel caring for them until they provoked him in the wilderness. If God sends an angel to your aid and you provoke him by sin and unbelief, he may depart from you. It is well to take heed to the warning in Exodus 23:20-22. You may also entertain an angel and not be aware of it...See Hebrews 13:2.

CHAPTER FIVE

THE ENEMY: SATAN

OBJECTIVES:

Upon completion of this chapter you will be able to:

- Write the Key Verse from memory.
- Identify Satan as your spiritual enemy.
- Explain how Satan originated.
- Describe his former position.
- Explain how Satan fell from his original position.
- Identify the results of Satan's sin.
- List attributes of his nature.
- Identify his sphere of activity.
- Summarize the activities of Satan.

KEY VERSE FROM THE ARTICLES OF WAR:

Be sober, be vigilant, because your adversary the devil, as a roaring lion, walketh about, seeking whom he may devour. (I Peter 5:8)

INTRODUCTION

In previous chapters you learned of a great invisible war that is in progress in the spirit world. You studied the spiritual forces of good engaged in this warfare. These include God the Father, the Son, the Holy Spirit, and the angels.

This chapter introduces your spiritual enemy, a powerful force of evil known as Satan. You will learn of his origin, his former position, how he fell from his former position, and of those he took with him when he fell. You will learn the attributes of his nature, his sphere of activity, and receive an introduction to his strategies. In the following two chapters you will continue this study of the spiritual forces of evil as you learn about demons, the world, and the flesh.

In warfare in the natural world, a soldier must first identify the enemy before entering the battlefield. He must study all available information on the enemy, his nature, and strategies. This is why military forces spend much time gathering intelligence information on the enemy.

The same is true in the spirit world. You can only war effectively if you identify your enemy, understand his nature, and recognize his strategies. As you have learned, the evil forces you face are not clothed in flesh. They are spiritual hosts of wickedness.

THE ORIGIN OF SATAN

Satan was originally created by God:

> **All things were made by Him; and without Him was not any thing made that was made. (John 1:3)**

> **For by Him were all things created, that are in Heaven, and that are in earth, visible and invisible, whether they be thrones, or dominions, or principalities, or powers; all things were created by Him and for Him. (Colossians 1:16)**

God does not create evil. Satan was perfect when he was originally created by God, but was given a free will to choose good or evil:

> **Thou was perfect in thy ways from the day that thou wast created till iniquity was found in thee. (Ezekiel 28:15)**

THE FORMER POSITION OF SATAN

The Bible describes the original position of Satan in Ezekiel 28:12-17. Read this passage in your Bible before proceeding with this lesson. When Satan was originally created, he was an angel of God. He was one of the Cherubim class of angels, holy, wise, beautiful, and perfect. He was the leader among the cherubs and is called a "guardian" or "covering" cherub. His name was originally Lucifer which means "light bearer" (Isaiah 14:12). He was decked with precious stones set in gold (Ezekiel 28:13; Exodus 28:15-11). He was given a position on God's holy mountain and apparently led in worship (Ezekiel 28:13).

What a brilliant, beautiful picture of Satan in his original position is given in the Word of God. He is described as a gem of precious stones. But a gem has no light of its own. It is not beautiful in a dark room. Its beauty is in its ability to reflect light from without.

When God created Lucifer, He made him with a capacity to reflect the glory of God to a greater degree than any other created being. God was the light that made Lucifer radiate beauty.

THE FALL OF SATAN

But Satan did not retain this glorious position. The Bible describes his rebellion and fall:

> **How art thou fallen from Heaven, O Lucifer, son of the morning. How art thou cut down to the ground which didst waken the nations.**

> **For thou hast said in thine heart, I will ascend into Heaven, I will exalt my throne above the stars of God: I will sit also upon the mount of the congregation in the sides of the north;**
>
> **I will ascend above the heights of the clouds; I will be like the Most High.**
>
> **Yet thou shalt be brought down to Hell, to the sides of the pit. (Isaiah 14:12-15)**
>
> **Thine heart was lifted up because of thy beauty, thou hadst corrupted thy wisdom by reason of thy brightness. (Ezekiel 28:17)**

Satan's fall from his angelic position occurred because of pride and rebellion demonstrated in five wrong attitudes. Satan said:

I WILL ascend unto Heaven: He desired to occupy the abode of God--Heaven--desiring equal recognition.

I WILL exalt my throne above the angels (stars) of God: He not only desired to occupy God's abode, but he also coveted His rule over the angelic hosts.

I WILL sit also upon the mountain of the congregation: According to Isaiah 2:2 and Psalms 48:2, this is the center of God's earthly rule. Satan desired to rule the earth as well as the angels.

I WILL ascend above the heights of the clouds: The clouds speak of the glory of God. Satan wanted God's glory for himself. (The following verses document clouds in relation to the glory of God: Exodus 13:21; 40-28-34; Job 37-15-16; Matthew 26:64; Revelation 14:14- 16).

I WILL be like the Most High: As we learned in Chapter Three of this course, God has many names by which He is called. Why did Satan choose this particular name? He selected this title because it reflects God as "possessor of Heaven and earth."

RESULTS OF SATAN'S SIN

Here are the terrible results of Satan's sin:

1. BANISHMENT FROM HEAVEN:

Because of his rebellion, Satan was cast out of Heaven by God:

> **...I will cast thee as profane out of the mountain of God...I will cast thee to the ground... (Ezekiel 28:16-17)**

2. CORRUPTION OF CHARACTER:

Lucifer, once created for God's glory, became Satan with a character that opposed all God is and does.

3. PERVERSION OF POWER:

Satan's power was once used for God's glory. Now it is turned to disruptive and destructive purposes. According to Isaiah 14 he weakens the nations (verse 12), causes the earth and governments to tremble (verse 16), and those taken as his prisoner have no relief (verse 17).

4. DESTINED TO THE LAKE OF FIRE:

Satan was destined to the lake of fire (Isaiah 14:15).

5. AFFECTED OTHER ANGELS OF GOD:

When Satan fell from Heaven he did not fall alone. He took with him a portion of the angelic host of Heaven who participated in his rebellion against God. This group of angels are now part of an evil force of demons which you will study about in the next chapter.

6. ENTRANCE OF SIN IN THE UNIVERSE:

When Satan rebelled, sin entered the universe. As a result, there were two actions God could have taken:

> 1. He could have struck down Satan and killed him. But if God had brought down the first enemy in this way, there would always have been the possibility of another rebellion. The history of Heaven would have been clouded with similar disasters.

> 2. The other action open to God was the one which the Bible indicates He took. The claims of Satan to superior power should have their complete trial on earth in the span of eternity we call time. When God created the first man and woman, the trial on earth began. You can read the story of the temptation of Adam and Eve by Satan and their fall into sin in Genesis chapter

> 3. You will study more about this when you analyze the strategies of Satan later in this course.

The battle is still in progress on earth. That is what spiritual warfare is all about. Satan is still seeking power, position, and worship. But as you will learn later in this course, he is already a defeated foe. Jesus overcame the power of Satan through His death and resurrection. The final destiny of Satan is already revealed in the Bible.

WHERE IS SATAN?

Satan, in spirit form, is present in the world:

> **And the Lord said unto Satan, Whence comest thou? Then Satan answered the Lord, and said, From going to and fro in the earth, and from walking up and down in it. (Job 1:7)**

> **Be sober, be vigilant, because your adversary the devil, as a roaring lion, walketh about, seeking whom he may devour. (I Peter 5:8)**

Although Satan is present in the world, he is not omnipresent, which means he cannot be every place in the world at one time as God can. This is why he employs a host of demons to accomplish his plans.

SATAN'S ACTIVITIES

Satan has access to the presence of God and operates on the earth, including the "air" or region above the earth:

> **Now there was a day when the sons of God came to present themselves before the Lord, and Satan came also among them.**

> **And the Lord said unto Satan, Whence comest thou? Then Satan answered the Lord, and said, From going to and fro in the earth, and from walking up and down in it. (Job 1:6-7)**

> **Wherein in time past ye walked according to the course of this world, according to the prince of the power of the air, the spirit that now worketh in the children of disobedience. (Ephesians 2:2)**

We may summarize the activities of Satan by noting that they are always directed against God, His plan, and His people. He will attack you in the areas of worship of God, the Word of God, your Christian walk, and your work for God. More specific activities of Satan will be dealt with in detail in later lessons.

THE ATTRIBUTES OF SATAN

As you have already learned, Satan is a spirit, but he also has attributes of a real personality. The Bible teaches that he is:

INTELLIGENT AND SUBTLE:

> **But I fear, lest by any means, as the serpent beguiled Eve through his subtility, so your minds should be corrupted from the simplicity that is**

in Christ. (II Corinthians 11:3)

EMOTIONAL:

And the dragon was wroth with the woman... (Revelation 12:17) **SELF-WILLED:**

And that they may recover themselves out of the snare of the devil, who are taken captive by him at his will. (II Timothy 2:26)

POWERFUL:

...Prince of the power of the air... (Ephesians 2:2)

DECEITFUL:

Put on the whole armour of God, that ye may be able to stand against the wiles of the devil. (Ephesians 6:11)

FIERCE AND CRUEL:

Be sober, be vigilant; because your adversary the devil, as a roaring lion, walketh about, seeking whom he may devour. (I Peter 5:8)

DECEPTIVE:

And no marvel: For Satan himself is transformed into an angel of light. (II Corinthians 11:14)

THE NAMES OF SATAN

The Bible gives many names for Satan which reveal more about his nature and activities. As you previously learned, Satan was originally called the "anointed cherub" and "Lucifer" before his rebellion. Other names for Satan are:

Abaddon: (Hebrew word for a destroying angel)	Revelation 9:11
Accuser of the Brethren:	Revelation 12:10
Adversary:	I Peter 5:8
Angel of bottomless pit:	Revelation 9:11
Angel of light:	II Corinthians 11:4
Apollyon (Greek word for destroyer):	Revelation 9;11
Beelzebub:	Matthew 12:24; Luke 11:15; Mark 3:22
Belial:	II Corinthians 6:15
Deceiver:	Revelation 12:9; 20:3
Destroyer:	Revelation 9:11; I Corinthians 10:10

Devil: (Means slanderer)	I Peter 5:8; Matthew 4:1
Dragon:	Revelation 12:3
Enemy:	Matthew 13:39
Evil One:	I John 5:19
God of this world:	II Corinthians 4:4
King of Tyrus:	Ezekiel 28:12-15
Liar, father of lies:	John 8:44
Murderer:	John 8:44
Prince of the devils:	Matthew 12:24
Prince of this world:	John 12:31; 14:30; 16:11
Prince of the power of the air:	Ephesians 2:2
Satan: (means adversary, opposer)	John 13:27
Serpent:	Revelation 12:9; II Corinthians 1:3
Tempter:	Matthew 4:3; I Thessalonians 3:5
Roaring Lion:	I Peter 5:8
Ruler of darkness:	Ephesians 6:12
Spirit that works in the children of disobedience:	Ephesians 2:2

You can recognize the power of Satan from his attributes and names. Because he is a deceptive, powerful enemy the Bible warns:

Be sober, be vigilant, because your adversary the devil, as a roaring lion, walketh about, seeking whom he may devour. (I Peter 5:8)

Neither give place to the devil. (Ephesians 4:27)

SATAN IS NOT...

Unlike God, Satan is not omniscient (knowing all things). If Satan could foresee the future he never would have allowed Jesus to die on the cross. He would have known that the death of Jesus would overthrow his power and provide a way of escape from the bondage of sin for all mankind.

Satan is not omnipotent (all powerful). Jesus said the power of God within you is greater than the power of Satan. For those who believe in Jesus, Satan is already a defeated foe (John 12:31). He is strong only to those who yield to him. His power is limited by the power of God (Job 1:10-12) and he is only able to overcome a believer as they yield control to him.

Because Satan is not omnipresent (present everywhere) he dispatches a host of demons throughout the earth to do his will and accomplish his purposes. You will learn more about them in the following chapter.

INSPECTION

1. Write the Key Verse from the Articles Of War.

2. How did Satan originate?

3. What was his former position?

4. What caused the fall of Satan?

5. What were the results of Satan's sin?

6. Where is Satan's sphere of activity?

7. What are the general activities of Satan?

8. List as many attributes of Satan as you can recall from this chapter.

(Answers to tests are provided at the conclusion of the final chapter in this manual.)

TACTICAL MANEUVERS

1. Study the Biblical record of the words of Satan. His words serve as a further introduction to his strategies: Genesis 3:1,4,5; Job 1:7-12; Job 2:1-6; Matthew 4:1-11; Luke 4:1-13.

2. Satan is an exact opposite of the Holy Spirit. The Spirit was sent by God to draw men to Himself. Satan is committed to draw men away from God.

Holy Spirit	**Satan**	**References**
Spirit of truth	Spirit of Error	I John 4:6
True	A liar	John 14:17; 8:44
Life giving	A murderer	I Corinthians 15:45; John 8:44
Holy	Evil	Romans 1:4; Matthew 6:13
Like a dove	Like a serpent	Matthew 3:16; Revelation 12:9
Our helper	Our adversary	Romans 8:26; I Peter 5:8
Gives utterance	Makes men dumb	Acts 2:4; Mark 9:17
Advocate	Slanderer	John 14:16; Job 1:9-11
Stronger than Satan	Strong armed man	Luke 11:21-22

3. Jesus said Satan...

-Is an enemy:	Matthew 13:39
-Is the wicked one:	Matthew 13:38
-Is the prince of this world:	John 12:31; 14:30
-Is a liar and the father of lies:	John 8:44
-Is a murderer:	John 8:44
-Fell from Heaven:	Luke 10:18
-Has a kingdom:	Matthew 12:26
-Sows tares among the wheat:	Matthew 13:38-39
-Snatches the Word from hearers:	Matthew 13:19; Mark 4:15; Luke 13:16
-Bound a woman for eighteen years:	Luke 13:16
-Desired to have Peter:	Luke 22:31
-Has angels:	Matthew 25:41
-Is prepared for eternal fire:	Matthew 25:41

4. In studying this lesson on Satan, have you identified areas in which the enemy is active in your life? Has he deceived you and lied to you? Has he subtly crept into your life to destroy and rob you of joy, peace, or your Christian testimony? It is important to determine this, because areas in which Satan is operative in your life are battlefields in which you will apply the strategies you will learn in this course.

5. Satan is compared to a snake or serpent in the natural world. Consider the spiritual application of the following natural principles:

> The venom of poisonous snakes falls into three categories:
> Neurotorins: Which affect the nerves.
> Hemotorins: Which affect the blood.
> Cardiotorins: Which affect the heart.

Satan also affects your nerve (courage), your heart (to attack your worship and service of God), and tries to prevent the work of the blood of Jesus (salvation, healing, deliverance) in your life. Snakes protect themselves by:

> -Disguise: Some snakes are very hard to see because they look like the dirt or trees in which they are found.
>
> -Imitation: Some snakes protect themselves by imitation. One example is the African tree viper which "freezes" itself and sticks its neck out like a twig on a tree.
>
> -Increased size: The puff adder protects itself by blowing itself up as big as possible.

Frightening sounds: Some snakes hiss or rattle, making frightening sounds to scare you away. Your spiritual enemy comes disguised as an "angel of light" and imitates the things of God. He also tries to frighten you by appearing large and threatening.

Snakes capture their food in four different ways:

> -Strike: A swift attack.
>
> -Constriction: Where the snake wraps itself around the target and slowly squeezes out its life.
>
> -Throwing weight around over the prey to overcome it.
>
> -Biting and holding the target in its fangs while slow poison paralyzes the target.

Sometimes the snake's teeth are broken off in the struggle, but snakes are constantly developing new teeth. The most dangerous part of a snake is its mouth. It shoots enough venom to paralyze, then devours its prey.

Do you see how these methods parallel those used in attacks of Satan? Sometimes he attacks with swift and deadly strikes. Other times he constricts your spiritual life with the cares of the world and sinful weights and entanglements. He is always trying to "throw his weight around" to terrorize you, and he loves to hold you in bondage while paralyzing you with his deadly venom.

Snakes locate their prey by picking up dust on their tongue which relays information to their brain. If you stand still, a snake cannot locate you. Satan spots you best when the dust is stirred up and you are running in confusion and fear. When the dust is settled and you stand against him fearlessly, just like snake, he cannot strike you. This is why the Bible says "stand still."..and "keep on standing."

In a panic situation, a snake will shoot all of its venom at once and is then rendered defenseless for awhile until it can produce more venom. It is possible that this is what occurred in the wilderness temptation when Jesus used the Word of God against Satan's attacks and caused Satan to "depart from him for a season."

Here are some ways to avoid snake bite in the natural world. Note that they are also applicable in the spiritual realm:

1. Recognize poisonous snakes (know your enemy).

2. Wear protective clothing (your spiritual armor).

3. Avoid known snake territory (do not go into areas of known temptation or Satanic activity).

4. Have a friend with you (this illustrates the importance of being part of the Body of Christ).

5. Avoid walking after dark or in darkened areas. Snakes avoid direct sunlight. (as believers, we no longer walk as children of the dark but as children of light!)

6. Do not put your hands or feet into places you cannot look (guard your fleshly senses).

7. Do not sit down without looking around carefully (stationary targets are easier to hit than moving targets).

8. Do not go out of your way to kill a snake. Thousands of people are bitten each year because they try to kill them without knowing anything of their habits or habitats. (We are to resist the Devil when we encounter him, not go looking for him).

9. Know what to do in case of snakebite (defensive warfare).

In case of snakebite, the first thing that is done in the natural world is to make a cut in the shape of a **cross** (+) over each fang mark and then suck the poison out. What an illustration of the work of the cross of Jesus Christ in freeing us from the "poison" of sin.

We have authority over serpents. In Genesis 3, God pronounced a curse upon the serpent (Satan). He said that his head would be bruised by the seed of the woman (Jesus) and that the heel of the seed (Jesus) would be bruised by the serpent.

The "bruise" on the "heel" of Jesus speaks of the pressure resulting from bruising Satan's head on the cross of Calvary. When Jesus bruised the head of Satan, it was much like severing the head of a poisonous snake in the natural world. A snake's head can be severed from its body, but it still can bite for hours afterwards. The heart has been known to keep beating for two days and the snake's body can continue to move.

Jesus severed the head of the "serpent" at Calvary, but the serpent still has life. He is still active in the world today and he still has power. But Satan has no authority. The only authority he has in your life is what you give him and the power and authority within you (Jesus) is greater than his power.

CHAPTER SIX

THE SPIRITUAL FORCES OF EVIL: DEMONS

OBJECTIVES:

Upon completion of this chapter you will be able to:

- Write the Key Verse from memory.
- Recall the origin of demons.
- Explain their original position.
- Identify their sphere of activity.
- Identify the attributes of demons.
- Explain how demon forces are organized.
- Summarize the activities of demons.

KEY VERSE FROM THE ARTICLES OF WAR:

> **Now the Spirit speaketh expressly, that in the latter times some shall depart from the faith, giving heed to seducing spirits and doctrines of devils. (I Timothy 4:1)**

INTRODUCTION

In the previous chapter you learned about Satan. In this chapter you will study about the "troops," known as demons, which are under Satan's command. Some people ignore the subject of demons completely. Others have a compulsive interest in them. You should not minimize the power of demon spirits in the world today, yet you must not become so preoccupied with them that you see a demon in everything that happens and in everyone around you. You should take a simple, literal, Biblical approach to the subject of demons. Do not study secular books about such powers of evil. Your only sources of study in these areas should be the Word of God or good Christian literature.

THE ORIGIN OF DEMONS

God originally created all of the angels, some of which later became demons:

> **All things were made by Him; and without Him was not any thing made that was made. (John 1:3)**

> **For by Him were all things created, that are in Heaven, and that are in earth, visible and invisible, whether they be thrones, or dominions, or principalities, or powers; all things were created by Him and for Him. (Colossians 1:16)**

THEIR ORIGINAL POSITION AND FALL

Demons were originally like the other angels of God with the same attributes and positions as the good angels described in Chapter Four of this course. When Satan rebelled against God, a portion of the angels participated in his rebellion. God cast them out of Heaven, along with Satan. They were no longer good spiritual beings (angels). They became evil spiritual beings (demons):

> **And there was war in Heaven: Michael and his angels fought against the dragon (Satan); and the dragon fought and his angels.**
>
> **And prevailed not; neither was their place found any more in Heaven. And the**
>
> **great dragon was cast out, that old serpent, called the Devil, and Satan, which deceiveth the whole world: he was cast out into the earth, and his angels were cast out with him. (Revelation 12:7-9)**

If demons are not "fallen" angels, then we have no other Biblical explanation for their existence. Satan cannot create his own forces, because all things were created by God. There are two groups of these fallen angels. One group is actively opposing God and His people on earth. Another is confined in chains:

> **For if God spared not the angels that sinned, but cast them down to Hell, and delivered them into chains of darkness to be reserved unto judgment...**
> **(II Peter 2:4)**
>
> **And the angels which kept not their first estate, but left their own habitation, he hath reserved in everlasting chains under darkness unto the judgment of the great day. (Jude 6)**

There are confined demons and active demons. The leader of both groups is Satan, who is called the "prince" of devils (Matthew 12:24). Hell is prepared for the Devil and his angels. It will be their final destiny:

> **Then shall He (Jesus) say also unto them on the left hand, Depart from me, ye cursed, into everlasting fire, prepared for the devil and his angels.**
> **(Matthew 25:41)**

When Jesus confronted two men possessed by demons, their response was:

> **...What have we to do with thee, Jesus, thou Son of God? art thou come hither to torment us before the time? (Matthew 8:29)**

The demons in the possessed men knew their final destiny was a place of eternal torment. Since Hell is a place of torment and was prepared for Satan and his angels, then demons must be the fallen angels.

THEIR SPHERE OF ACTIVITY

Throughout the Bible, demons are shown as active on earth. Since Satan is not omnipresent (present everywhere), he uses demons to do his will and accomplish his purposes throughout the world. They constitute the "powers of the air" (Ephesians 2:2) and the "powers of darkness" (Colossians 1:13) and are all under the control of Satan.

THE ATTRIBUTES OF DEMONS

In their original sinless condition, demons, demons had the same attributes as the good angels previously studied. In their present evil state these demons:

Are spirits:	Matthew 8:16; Luke 10:17, 20
Can appear visibly:	Genesis 3:1; Zechariah 3:1; Matthew 4:9-10
Can speak:	Mark 5:9, 12; Luke 8:28; Matthew 8:31
Believe:	James 2:19
Exercise their wills:	Luke 11:24; 8:32
Demonstrate intelligence:	Mark 1:24
Have emotions:	Luke 8:28; James 2:19
Have recognition:	Acts 19:15
Have supernatural strength:	Acts 19:16; Mark 5:3
Have supernatural presence:	Daniel 9:21-23
Are eternal:	Matthew 25:41
Have their own doctrine:	I Timothy 4:1-3
Are evil:	Matthew 10:1; Mark 1:27; 3:11

THE NAMES OF DEMONS

Demons are called evil spirits six times and unclean spirits 23 times in the New Testament. They are also called devils (Mark 1:32) and the devil's angels (Matthew 25:41)

THE ORGANIZATION OF DEMON FORCES

Let us review how God organized His angelic host...

> **For by Him were all things created, that are in Heaven, and that are in earth, visible and invisible, whether they be thrones, or dominions, or principalities, or powers: All things were created by Him, and for Him. (Colossians 1:16)**

Satan is an imitator, not an originator. He has organized his demons in a structure similar to that of God's forces:

> **For we wrestle not against flesh and blood, but against principalities, against powers, against the rulers of the darkness of this world, against spiritual wickedness in high places. (Ephesians 6:12)**

Satan has organized his forces into:

Principalities: Satan has apparently divided the world into principalities. A principality is the territory or jurisdiction of a prince. Satan has placed a prince over each principality. The prince of the power of Persia is mentioned in Daniel 10. This is how Satan works on a national level influencing governments and nations.

Powers and rulers of darkness of this world: These two categories of demons are at work in the social, political, and cultural systems of the world. You will learn about how to deal with these and the spirits over principalities as you study spiritual strategies for overcoming the world in Chapter Fourteen.

Spiritual wickedness in high places: High places in the Old Testament were where worship was carried on. This is how Satan works in the religious structures of the world. You will learn more about this in Chapter Twenty as you study about spiritual wickedness in high places.

These organized groups vary in size. For example, Mary Magdalene had seven demons in her prior to her deliverance. Luke 8:30 mentions a "legion" of demons. A legion in the Roman army which ruled at the time of Jesus referred to 6,100 foot soldiers and 726 horsemen!

These organized forces of demons...

Are United:

In the case of the demon possessed man recorded in Luke 8:30 the demons were united in their purpose, which in this example was possession of the man. The same is true in Matthew 12:45 and in the case of Mary Magdalene who had seven demons (Luke 16:9). Jesus spoke of the unity of demon powers when He said:

> **And if Satan cast out Satan, he is divided against himself; how shall then his kingdom stand? (Matthew 12:26)**

Have Different Degrees Of Wickedness:

This is illustrated by the demon who said he would return with other evil spirits:

> **When the unclean spirit is gone out of a man, he walketh through dry places, seeking rest, and findeth none.**
>
> **Then he saith, I will return into my house from whence I came out; and when he is come, he findeth it empty, swept, and garnished.**
>
> **Then goeth he and taketh with himself seven other spirits more wicked than himself and they enter in and dwell there: And the last state of that man is worse than the first... (Matthew 12:43-45)**

Can Change Their Functions:

The demon in I Kings 22:21-23 declared he would be a lying spirit. This indicates he was not one previously for he said "I will be...".

Are Of Different Kinds:

The Bible teaches that man has a body, soul, and spirit. There are three major kinds of demons that attack the body, soul, and spirit of man:

1. Evil or unclean spirits: They are responsible for immoral acts, unclean thoughts, oppression, possession, depression, and other strategies of Satan which we will study later. They afflict the mind and the soulish nature of man. (Matthew 10:1; 12:43; Mark 1:23-26)

2. Spirits of infirmity: These spirits afflict the physical body. (Luke 13:11)

3. Seducing spirits: Seducing spirits afflict the mind, soul, and spirit of man, influencing him to believe false doctrines as indicated in I Timothy 4:1. These spirits seduce people to believe a lie and be damned to eternal punishment. They are spirits of false doctrine, cults, false Christs, and false teachers.

THE ACTIVITIES OF DEMONS

Demons follow orders given by their prince, Satan. We can summarize the activities of demons by noting that they are always directed against God, His plan, and His people. Demons are used by Satan to attack the Word of God, your worship of God, your walk with God, and your work for God.

In Chapter Eight you will learn details of the enemy's strategy in spiritual warfare. Satan uses his demons to accomplish this strategy throughout the world. Demons extend Satan's power by promoting deception and wickedness. They affect individuals, governments, nations, and the world system. They promote rebellion and slander both God and men. They promote idolatry, false doctrines, and blind men and women to the truth of the Gospel.

These demons attack unbelievers driving them to commit terrible evil acts, to murder, injure, commit suicide, etc. They affect the mind with emotional problems and the body with physical infirmities. Demons attack believers by temptation, deception, depression, and oppression. They try to keep you in bondage to habits and fear. They accuse and slander you and create division among the people of God. They target your spiritual walk with God and fight against the Word of God, the worship of God, and your work for God. They also attack your physical body.

Unbelievers are defenseless against the attacks of demonic powers, but believers have powerful spiritual weapons and strategies for dealing with this mighty spiritual force of evil. You will learn about these weapons and strategies as you continue this study of spiritual warfare.

INSPECTION

1. Write the Key Verse from the Articles Of War.

   _____

   _____

2. How did demons originate?

   _____

   _____

3. What is their sphere of activity?

   _____

4. Summarize their activities.

   _____

5. List as many attributes of demons as you can recall from the discussion in this chapter.

   _____

   _____

6. How are demon forces organized?

   _____

   _____

7. What was the original position of demons?

   _____

   _____

   _____

   _____

8.   Why did they become demons?

_____

_____

_____

9.   Give a brief definition of each of the following ranking of demons:

Principalities:

_____

_____

Powers And Rulers Of Darkness:

_____

_____

Spiritual Wickedness In High Places:

_____

_____

(Answers to tests are provided at the conclusion of the final chapter in this manual.)

TACTICAL MANEUVERS

1. To learn more about the spiritual forces of evil, study the following Biblical references on the subject of demons:

   Genesis: 3:1-15; 6:1-4; 41:8; 44:5
   Exodus: 7:8-13; 20-24; 8:6-7, 18-19; 9:11; 22:18
   Leviticus: 17:7; 19:26,31; 20:6,27
   Numbers: 22:7; 23:23
   Deuteronomy: 18:9-14, 20-22; 32:17
   Judges: 8:21,26
   I Samuel: 15:23; 16:14; 18:10; 28:1-15
   I Kings: 5:4; 18:28; 22:19-38
   II Kings: 9:22; 17:17; 21:1-9; 23:5,24
   I Chronicles: 21:1
   II Chronicles: 33:1-10
   Job: 1:1-12; 2:1
   Psalms: 78:49; 91:6; 106:36-38
   Isaiah: 3:18-19; 8:19; 14:12-17; 47:11-15
   Jeremiah: 27:9
   Ezekiel: 21:21; 28:11-19
   Daniel: 1:20; 2:2,27; 4:6-9; 5:7, 11, 15
   Hosea: 4:12
   Micah: 5:12
   Zechariah: 3:1,2; 10:2
   Malachi: 3:5
   Matthew: 4:1-11, 24; 8:16, 28-34; 9:32-34; 10:1, 25: 11:18; 12:22-30, 11:43-45; 13:19,
   39: 15:21-28; 17:14-21; 24:24; 25:41
   Mark: 1:12-13, 21-28, 32, 34, 39; 3:11-12, 15, 22-30; 5:1-20; 6:7, 13; 7:24-30; 8:33; 9:17-29, 38-40; 13:22; 16:9, 17
   Luke: 4:1-13, 33-37; 6:18; 7:21,33; 8:2, 26-39; 9:1, 37-42, 49-50; 10:17-20; 11:14-26; 13:10-17, 32; 22:3, 31; 24:39
   John: 6:70; 7:20; 8:44, 48-49; 10:20-21; 12:31; 13:27; 14:30; 16:11; 17:15
   Acts: 5:3, 16; 8:7, 9-11, 18:24; 10:38; 13:6-12; 16:16-19; 19:12-20; 26:18
   Romans: 8:38-39; 16:20
   I Corinthians: 5:5; 7:5; 10:20-21
   II Corinthians: 2:11; 4:4, 6:14, 15, 17; 11:13-14; 12:7
   Galatians: 1:4; 3:1; 4:8-9; 5:19-21
   Ephesians: 1:21; 2:2; 4:26-27; 6:11, 12, 16
   Colossians: 1:13; 2:15
   I Thessalonians: 2:18; 3:5
   II Thessalonians: 2:1-10; 3:3
   I Timothy: 1:20; 3:6; 4:1-3
   II Timothy: 1:7; 2:26; 4:18
   Hebrews: 2:14

James: 2:19; 3:15; 4:7
I Peter: 5:8
II Peter: 2:4, 19
I John: 2:13, 18; 3:8, 12; 4:1-4, 6; 5:18
Jude: 1:6, 9
Revelation: 2:9, 13, 24; 3:9; 9:1-11, 20-21; 12:1-13; 13:1-18; 16:13-16; 18:2; 19:20; 20:1-14: 21:8

2. Study the Old Testament record of demonic powers:

Satan in the form of a serpent is mentioned seven times in Genesis 3:1-24 and Isaiah 27:1.

Satan is also mentioned in I Chronicles 21:1; II Samuel 24:1; Psalm 109:6; Zechariah 3:1-2; and 14 times in the book of Job.

Evil spirits are mentioned eight times in the record of King Saul: I Samuel 16:14-23; 18:10; 19:9.

Lying spirits are mentioned six times in I Kings 22:21-23.

Familiar spirits are mentioned six times in Leviticus 20:27 and I Samuel 28.

Religious spirits and spirits of physical harlotry are identified in the book of

Hosea.

Demons are identified with the gods of pagan nations four times: Leviticus 17:7; Deuteronomy 32:17; II Chronicles 11:15; Psalms 106:19-39.

Evil princes who rule nations are identified in the Psalms, the prophets, and specifically in Daniel 10:10-21.

Unclean perverse spirits are mentioned twice: Isaiah 19:14

3. Think about this: While demonic forces are God's enemies, at the same time they are subject to His will and used by Him to defeat themselves: See I Samuel 16:14; 18:10; 19:9; I Kings 22:20-22; and Isaiah 19:14.

CHAPTER SEVEN

ENEMY TERRITORY

OBJECTIVES:

Upon completion of this chapter you will be able to:

- Write the Key Verses from memory.
- Define what is meant by the word "world" as it is used in this lesson.
- Identify the prince of the world.
- Explain the reason for the current world system.
- Describe the attitude of the world toward believers.
- Define what is meant by the word "flesh" as it is used in this lesson.
- Explain what is meant by the "lust of the flesh."
- Explain how lust develops.
- Explain the results of unconquered lust.
- Identify a Scripture reference which lists the works of the flesh.

KEY VERSES FROM THE ARTICLES OF WAR:

> **Love not the world, neither the things that are in the world. If any man love the world, the love of the Father is not in him.**
>
> **For all that is in the world, the lust of the flesh, and the lust of the eyes, and the pride of life, is not of the Father, but is of the world.**
> **(I John 2:15-16)**

INTRODUCTION

There is only one enemy, but as you have learned in previous lessons he works through a mighty force of demons. As the Key Verse of this chapter reveals, Satan not only uses demons but he also works through the evil forces of the flesh and the world:

> **Love not the world, neither the things that are in the world. If any man love the world, the love of the Father is not in him.**
>
> **For all that is in the world, the lust of the flesh, and the lust of the eyes, and the pride of life, is not of the Father, but is of the world.**
> **(I John 2:15-16)**

The purpose of this chapter is to identify and discuss the enemy forces of evil known as the world and the flesh. Beware! You are entering a hostile grounds. The world and the flesh are enemy territory.

PART ONE: THE WORLD

The word "world" has different meanings in Scripture. It can mean the earth or universe in its physical order. It is used to refer to Gentiles which are all nations other than the Jewish nation.

But the word "world" also is used to refer to the present condition of human affairs in opposition to God. It is the system that runs the inhabited earth, a system that is opposed to God and the Lord Jesus Christ. It is this meaning that is used in this lesson. The "world" is the corporate group of flesh-centered individuals who make up the human race. Flesh, in this context, is not referring to the actual flesh of your body. It is a term which describes the basic evil human nature of man which is in willful rebellion against God.

As your enemy, the world is the whole organized system of social, economic, materialistic, and religious philosophies which have their expression through organizations, personalities, and governments. It is not a specific government, organization, or person, but the worldly system upon which these are based. The world system is an extension of man's fleshiness. It provides an atmosphere, environment, and system which promotes fleshly sins. It surrounds man with that which appeals to his fleshly desires.

THE PRINCE OF THE WORLD:

Satan is the "prince" or ruler of the world system:

> **Now is the judgment of this world: now shall the prince of this world be cast out. (John 12:31)**

> **Hereafter I will not talk much with you: for the prince of this world cometh, and hath nothing in me. (John 14:30)**

Satan is also called the god of this world:

> **In whom the god of this world hath blinded the minds of them which believed not... (II Corinthians 4:4)**

The kingdoms of the world are presently influenced by Satan. They are guided by Satanic philosophy and principles. They are flesh-centered and flesh-governed:

> **Again, the Devil taketh him up into an exceeding high mountain, and sheweth Him all the kingdoms of the world, and the glory of them;**

> **And saith unto Him, All these things will I give thee, if thou wilt fall down and worship me. (Matthew 4:8-9)**

Some day they will become the kingdoms of our Lord:

> **And the seventh angel sounded: and there were great voices in heaven saying, The kingdoms of this world are become the kingdoms of our Lord and of His Christ; and He shall reign for ever and ever. (Revelation 11:15)**

THE REASON FOR THE CONDITION OF THE WORLD:

Sin is the reason for the present condition of the world. When Adam and Eve were originally created by God, they were given dominion over the world. This meant they had control over the world, to guide its systems and inhabitants according to the plan of God. When they sinned against God, they lost that dominion. (Genesis 1-3)

When Jesus was crucified for the sins of all mankind and resurrected from the dead, He reclaimed the world. He pronounced judgment on the spiritual forces of evil:

> **And having spoiled principalities and powers, He made a shew of them openly, triumphing over them in it. (Colossians 2:15)**

Although Jesus reclaimed the world from the power of the enemy, Satan does not yet acknowledge that claim. Satan still is at work in the world with his evil powers. Satan will not acknowledge the claims of Jesus over the kingdoms of the world until the final conflict which you will study about in the last chapter of this course.

The present situation is similar to military conditions that often occur in the natural world. A political or military power will take control of a nation but their claims will not be acknowledged by rebel troops within that nation. The rebel troops continue to war throughout the country. They try to take possession of territory not rightfully theirs and overpower the citizens. They often use tactics of terror to accomplish these purposes.

The situation in the spirit world is similar. Jesus reclaimed dominion over the world, the enemy, and his evil forces. But the rebel troops of Satan still war throughout the world. They try to take possession of territory not rightfully theirs and influence men and women for evil. This battle, which is our "spiritual warfare," will continue until the final conflict.

THE STRUCTURE OF THE WORLD:

The world structure is in direct opposition to God, His plan, purposes, and people:

The Evil World System:

The present world system is evil:

> **Who gave Himself for our sins, that He might deliver us from this present evil world, according to the will of God and our Father. (Galatians 1:4)**

The world system is without God:

> **...having no hope, and without God in the world. (Ephesians 2:12)**

There is much deception in the world to ensnare believers to become part of the world system:

> **For many deceivers are entered into the world...(II John 7)**

The world is already judged and under condemnation by God:

> **But when we are judged, we are chastened of the Lord, that we should not be condemned with the world. (I Corinthians 11:32)**

The Elements Of The World:

The "elements of the world" refer to the elementary principles that govern the world. They lead to spiritual bondage:

> **Even so we, when we were children, were in bondage under the elements of the world. (Galatians 4:3)**

The Rudiments Of The World:

These are the regulations on which the world structure rests. They are different from the principles upon which God structures His Kingdom:

> **Wherefore if ye be dead with Christ from the rudiments of the world, why, as though living in the world, are ye subject to ordinances. (Colossians 2:8,20)**

The Spirit Of The World:

The spirit of the world is in direct opposition to the Holy Spirit:

> **Now we have received, not the spirit of the world, but the spirit which is of God; that we might know the things that are freely given to us of God. (I Corinthians 2:12)**

The Philosophy Of The World:

Philosophies are principles of knowledge. Worldly philosophies are not based on Christ:

> **Beware lest any man spoil you through philosophy and vain deceit, after the tradition of men, after the rudiments of the world, and not after Christ. (Colossians 2:8)**

The Wisdom Of The World

Worldly wisdom is not God's wisdom:

> **For the wisdom of this world is foolishness with God. (I Corinthians 3:19)**

The Course Of The World:

The "course" of the world is the cycle of the present world, its routine, the way in which it operates:

> **Wherefore in times past ye walked according to the course of this world, according to the prince of the power of the air, the spirit that now worketh in the children of disobedience. (Ephesians 2:2)**

The Voices Of The World:

The many "voices" in the world are contrary to the voice of God:

> **There are, it may be, so many kinds of voices in the world, and none of them is without signification. (I Corinthians 14:10)**

The Peace Of The World:

The peace of the world is temporary, fragile, and sometimes deceptive:

> **Peace I leave with you, my peace I give unto you: not as the world giveth give I unto you. Let not your heart be troubled, neither let it be afraid. (John 14:27)**

The Sorrow Of The World:

Godly sorrow differs from that of the world:

> **For godly sorrow worketh repentance to salvation not to be repented of: but the sorrow of the world worketh death. (II Corinthians 7:10)**

The Attitude Of The World:

The world hates God:

> **...Know ye not that the friendship of the world is enmity with God? Whosoever therefore will be a friend of the world is the enemy of God. (James 4:4)**

The world hates believers:

> **If the world hate you, ye know that it hated me before it hated you. If ye were of the world, the world would love his own; but because ye are not of the world, but I have chosen you out of the world, therefore the world hateth you. (John 15:18-19)**

Since the world is made up of flesh centered individuals who hate believers, we need to learn more about this powerful force called "the flesh."

PART TWO: THE FLESH

The world is an evil social force of Satan that works from the outside to attack believers. It is the corporate organization of fleshly individuals. The flesh is an evil force working from within the believer. The same "fleshly spirit" that operates in the world will operate in your life if you

allow it to do so. The word "flesh" as used in Scripture can refer to the actual body of man and beast. But this is not what we are talking about when we use the word "flesh" in this lesson.

The Bible also uses the word "flesh" to describe the basic sin nature of man. The flesh is the center of willful defiance and rebellion against God:

> **For I know that in me (that is, in my flesh) dwelleth no good thing; for to will (to do good) is present with me; but how to perform that which is good I find not.**
>
> **For the good that I would I do not; but the evil which I would not, that I do.**
>
> **Now if I do that I would not, it is no more I that do it, but sin that dwelleth in me. (Romans 8:18-20)**

The flesh is a compulsive inner force which expresses itself in rebellion through sin. It is this meaning of flesh which is used in this lesson. The words "carnal" and "old man" are also used to describe the fleshly nature of man. All men have this basic, sinful, fleshly nature:

> **Wherefore, as by one man sin entered into the world, and death by sin, and so death passed upon all men, for that all have sinned. (Romans 5:12)**
>
> **For all have sinned and come short of the glory of God. (Romans 3:23)**

THE LUST OF THE FLESH:

> **This I say then, Walk in the Spirit, and ye shall not fulfill the lust of the flesh. (Galatians 5:16)**

What is the lust of the flesh? First let us define the word "lust." Lust is "strong desire, soulish emotions, the natural tendency of man towards evil." The Bible warns that we should not lust after evil things:

> **Now these things were our examples, to the intent we should not lust after evil things, as they also lusted. (I Corinthians 10:6)**

Lusting after evil things which will please your fleshly nature is "lust of the flesh." It is how Satan attacks from within. It is like a civil war within a nation, with your spirit and flesh warring against each other.

HOW LUST DEVELOPS:

Lust, or sinful desire, first enters through the natural senses. The eye sees something evil or the ear hears something wicked. A touch, a taste, or even a smell can even foster lust. This is how Satan uses the environment of the world to tempt the flesh. These natural senses trigger an evil thought or desire in the mind. This is lust. The lustful thought is what tempts you to do evil:

> **Let no man say when he is tempted, I am tempted of God; for God cannot be tempted with evil, neither tempteth He any man.**
>
> **But every man is tempted, when he is drawn away of his own lust, and enticed. (James 1:13-14)**

Remember, God never tempts you. You are tempted when you are drawn by your own sinful, fleshly lusts. But you do not have to yield to this temptation. God always provides a way of escape:

> **There hath no temptation taken you but such as is common to man: But God is faithful, who will not suffer you to be tempted above that ye are able; but will with the temptation also make a way of escape that ye may be able to bear it. (I Corinthians 10:13)**

Since the mind is used to tempt the flesh, Paul warns:

> **For to be carnally (fleshly) minded is death; but to be spiritually minded is life and peace.**
>
> **Because the carnal mind is enmity against God: for it is not subject to the law of God, neither indeed can be. (Romans 8:7-8)**

You will learn later how the mind is one of the main battlefields of spiritual warfare.

THE RESULTS OF LUST:

If you yield to lust, temptation results and if you yield to temptation, it results in sin which leads to death:

> **Then when lust hath conceived, it bringeth forth sin, and sin, when it is finished, bringeth forth death. (James 1:15)**

The world is corrupt because of lust:

> **...having escaped the corruption that is in the world through lust. (II Peter 1:4)**

Your flesh is corrupt because of lust:

> **That ye put off concerning the former conversation the old man, which is corrupt according to the deceitful lusts... (Ephesians 4:22)**

THE RELATIONSHIP OF THE SPIRIT TO THE FLESH:

> **For the flesh lusteth against the Spirit, and the Spirit against the flesh; and these are contrary the one to the other; so that ye cannot do the things that ye would. (Galatians 5:17)**

When you are saved and filled with the Holy Spirit, that Spirit indwells your spirit. The Holy Spirit in your spirit opposes the lusts of the flesh. Your flesh wars against your spirit and the Spirit of God within you. The flesh entices you to sinful lusts. This is why you often cannot live the way you desire to live.

Paul described this battle between the spirit and the flesh in Romans chapter 7:

> **I find then a law, that when I would do good, evil is present with me. For I delight in the law of God after the inward man (the spirit);**
>
> **But I see another law in my members (the flesh), warring against the law of my mind and bringing me into captivity to the law of sin which is in my members. (Romans 7:21-23)**

THE WORKS OF THE FLESH:

The lusts of the flesh, if not conquered, lead to sinful works of the flesh which result in spiritual death:

> **Now the works of the flesh are manifest, which are these: Adultery, fornication, uncleanness, lasciviousness,**

Idolatry, witchcraft, hatred, variance, emulations, wrath, strife, seditions, heresies,

Envyings, murders, drunkenness, revellings, and such like; of the which I tell you before, as I have also told you in time past, that they which do such thing shall not inherit the Kingdom of God. (Galatians 5:19-21)

This list can be divided into four categories of sins:

- Worship Sins: Idolatry and witchcraft.

- Sexual Sins: Adultery, fornication, uncleanness, and lasciviousness.

- Personal Sins: Drunkenness and revellings.

- Relationship Sins: Hatred, variance, emulations, wrath, strife, seditions, envyings, and murders.

Each of these sinful works are defined in detail in the Harvestime International Institute course *"Ministry Of The Holy Spirit."* They are contrasted to the fruit of the Holy Spirit which should be developed in the lives of believers.

POWERFUL EVIL FORCES

The world and the flesh combine with Satan and his demons to war against believers. These are the spiritual forces of evil. In the following lessons you will learn strategies of spiritual warfare to combat these powerful spiritual forces of evil.

INSPECTION

1. Write the Key Verses from the Articles Of War.

2. What is meant by the word "flesh" as it is used in this lesson?

3. What is meant by the word "world" as it is used in this lesson?

4. Who is the prince of this world?

5. Summarize characteristics of the present world system.

6. What is the reason for the sinful condition of the current world system?

_____

_____

7. What is the attitude of the world toward believers?

_____

_____

_____

_____

8. What is meant by the "lust of the flesh"?

_____

_____

_____

9. How does lust develop?

_____

_____

10. What happens if you do not control lust?

_____

11. Give a Scripture reference which identifies the works of the flesh.

_____

(Answers to tests are provided at the conclusion of the final chapter in this manual.)

TACTICAL MANEUVERS

1. Study further on the works of the flesh in Galatians 5:19-21.

2. Contrast to these evil works the fruit of the Spirit in Galatians 6:22-23.

3. Read John 1:1-15 and chapter 3. Observe God's great love for the world despite its sinful, fleshly condition. What did God do to show His love? What was the response of the world?

4. Study further about temptation.

    -Satan is called the tempter: Matthew 4:3; I Thessalonians 3:15
    -God does not tempt men to do evil: James 1:13-14
    -You are tempted by:
    -Men: Matthew 16:1; 19:3; 22:35; Mark 8:11; 10:2; Luke 11:16; John 8:6
    -Satan: Matthew 4:1; Mark 1:13; Luke 4:2; I Corinthians 7:5
    -Your lusts: James 1:13-14
    -Riches: I Timothy 6:9
    -You are to pray not to be led into temptation: Matthew 26:41; Luke 11:4; Mark 14:38; 22:46
    -Jesus was tempted, but did not sin: Hebrews 2:18; 4:15
    -You are blessed if you endure temptation: James 1:12
    -God can deliver you from temptation: Hebrews 4:15; II Peter 2:9; I Corinthians 10:13
    -Temptation brings heaviness but you should count every temptation a joy James 1:2; I Peter 1:6

5. Are you experiencing lust which has led to temptation and then to sin? Follow the strategy in I John 1:8-9.

6. It is within the context of describing the warfare between the Holy Spirit and the flesh that Paul identifies the works of the flesh which war within believers. See Galatians 5:16-26.

CHAPTER EIGHT
ENEMY STRATEGY

OBJECTIVES:

Upon completion of this chapter you will be able to:

- Write the Key Verses from memory.
- Summarize the strategy of the enemy in relation to God.
- Summarize the strategy of the enemy in relation to the nations.
- Summarize the strategy of the enemy in relation to unbelievers.
- Summarize the strategy of the enemy in relation to believers.

KEY VERSES FROM THE ARTICLES OF WAR:

> **Be sober, be vigilant; because your adversary the Devil, as a roaring lion, walketh about, seeking whom he may devour;**
>
> **Whom resist steadfast in the faith, knowing that the same afflictions are accomplished in your brethren that are in the world. (I Peter 5:8-9)**

INTRODUCTION

This lesson presents an overview of the general strategies of our enemy, Satan. In the next lesson, you will be given an overview of "The Battle Plan" of God. In later lessons, after you have been armed with your spiritual weapons, you will be given more specific counterstrategies to overcome all the evil plans of the enemy. But first, you need to understand the general strategy of the enemy in relation to God, the nations, unbelievers, and believers.

THE ENEMY AND GOD

Satan's original sin was that he wanted to be like God, so his present power and activities are directed primarily against God. All of his other activities and his very nature are viewed as stemming from his original rebellious ambition.

For example, Satan's attack on the first man and woman, Adam and Eve, was really an attack on the character and control of God (Genesis 3:1-5). Satan also induced Cain to murder Abel in opposition to God (I John 3:10-12). You can study every attack of Satan recorded in Scripture and you will discover that it is actually an attack on God and His activities and nature.

Satan is in direct opposition to God in every activity and quality of nature. For example, God is love whereas Satan is hateful and promotes hatred (I John 3:7-15). God is life and creates life while Satan promotes death and destruction (Hebrews 2:14).

Satan not only opposes God and His nature, but he also opposes God's program. He denies the existence of God (Psalms 14:1-3), promotes lies (Ephesians 2:2; II Thessalonians 2:8-11); and is behind false religions, the occult, and cults with their false doctrines and practices. Satan's religious system results in false teachers, prophets, and "christs." You will study more about this later as you study "Spiritual Wickedness In High Places."

Satan will reach the climax of his rebellion against God and His plans during the time of "The Final Battle" discussed in the last chapter of this course. Despite these evil strategies, Satan and his hosts of demonic powers are no threat to our Almighty God.

THE ENEMY AND THE NATIONS

Satan is called the "god of this world" which includes men who are not believers and demonic angels. (II Corinthians 4:4) He offered the nations to Jesus during the temptation of Christ, and our Lord did not dispute the legitimacy of the offer. He simply refused to rebel against God in submitting to Satan's way of obtaining the rule (Matthew 4:8-10).

Satan uses his demons to influence and deceive the nations, leading the leaders and people astray from God. This is why there are cruel dictators and ungodly political systems in many nations. It also accounts for the wars and divisions between the nations. Satan especially influences leaders against the Church and God's chosen people, Israel. He also works through governments to hinder the spread of the Gospel.

During the tribulation period Satan will actually direct the affairs of a group of ten nations through the Antichrist. After the second coming of Christ, Satan will be bound for a thousand years (Revelation 20:3). Upon his release, he will deceive the nations one last time to assemble them against Jerusalem and God (Revelation 20:7-10). In the end, every kingdom of earth and the Kingdom of Satan will become the Kingdoms of our Lord and Savior, Jesus Christ.

THE ENEMY AND UNBELIEVERS

The enemy has a very powerful strategy operating against unbelievers. He blinds their minds to the Gospel (II Corinthians 4:3-4) and snatches away the truth of the Gospel when they do hear it so that no response will occur (Luke 8:12). As a result, the Gospel sounds foolish and irrelevant to those who are lost in sin (I Corinthians 1:18).

Satan also snares many unbelievers in false religions (I Timothy 4:1-3) and leads them to walk according to the "course of the world" which is the philosophy of the age. That philosophy may vary from generation to generation and culture to culture, but it is always creature-centered and creature-promoting rather than God-centered. Satan is constantly sowing the seeds of rebellion (sin) in the hearts and minds of unbelievers.

One of the purposes of the Holy Spirit is to war against Satan for the souls of unbelievers. The Holy Spirit works to convict men and women of their sinful rebellion against God (John 16:7-11).

THE ENEMY AND BELIEVERS

When you accept Jesus Christ as Savior, it certainly does not mean the battle is over! You have won one major confrontation when you are saved, but in reality, your intense struggle has only begun.

You will learn many specific strategies of Satan as you continue to study this course and are armed with spiritual weapons and mobilized to enter enemy territory. But all of these attacks can be summarized in four major areas. In the life of a believer Satan attacks:

THE WORD OF GOD:

Satan will cause you to question the Word of God and will add to, take from, or distort the Scriptures. Remember that this happened in the very first temptation of Eve. This is why it is important for you to study and understand God's Word so you will not be deceived by these attacks.

YOUR WORSHIP OF GOD:

Satan's original rebellion involved his desire to be worshiped, so he especially targets the worship of believers. He will try to prevent you from worshiping or lead you into false or fleshly worship.

YOUR WALK WITH GOD:

Satan attacks your personal walk with God. He accuses and slanders you, tempts you to engage in the works of the flesh, to be occupied with the world, and to rely upon your own human wisdom and strength. If Satan can win territory in your personal walk with God, it will make it easier for him to defeat you in the next area which is...

YOUR WORK FOR GOD:

Satan also attacks your work for God. He will try to deter you from accomplishing God's will by persecution, disaster, discouragement, prayerlessness, and busy involvement with the cares of the world. Satan also tries to affect your work for God by infiltrating the Church with false teachers and disciples (II Corinthians 11:13-15; II Peter 2:1-19; Matthew 13:38-39).

While God sows good seed through your ministry, the enemy sows tares which are the "sons of the wicked one." He promotes division within the Body of Christ trying to affect the work of God and His purposes in your life and ministry.

SO---WHAT CAN YOU DO?

Satan's strategies are certainly varied and powerful as he works against God, the nations, unbelievers, and believers.

Having spent the last four lessons studying the enemy, the spiritual forces of evil, enemy territory, and strategy, you may be a bit overwhelmed at this point. But as you will learn in the next chapter, God has a "battle plan" far greater and more powerful than any scheme of the enemy.

You are now ready to study that plan and then be armed with your spiritual weapons and mobilized for battle.

INSPECTION

1. Write the Key Verses from the Articles Of War.

___

2. Summarize the strategy of the enemy in relation to God.

___

3. Summarize the strategy of the enemy in relation to the nations.

___

4. Summarize the strategy of the enemy in relation to the unbelievers.

___

5. Summarize the strategy of the enemy in relation to believers.

___

(Answers to tests are provided at the conclusion of the final chapter in this manual.)

TACTICAL MANEUVERS

1. Analyze the nation in which you live. What strategies of the enemy do you see operative in your nation?

2. Analyze unbelievers around you for whom you are praying. Has the enemy blinded their eyes to the Gospel? Is he snatching away the Gospel message being presented to them? Are they being indoctrinated in false religion? Are they living in the "course of the world" and its lifestyle? Make these items a matter of prayer.

3. Note the fourfold accusations of Satan:

    -He accuses God before the believer: Genesis 3:1-5
    -He accuses the believer before God: Job 1-2; Revelation 12:9-10
    -He accuses the believer before his own conscience: Jeremiah 31:34; Romans 8:33-39
    -He accuses the believer through other believers: Matthew 16:13-23; Romans 8:33-39.

4. Think about your own life. In the space provided below, analyze how Satan has attacked you in regards to the Word of God, your worship, walk with God, or work for God:

The Word of God:

_____

Worship of God:

_____

Walk with God:

_____

Work for God:

_____

In following lessons you will learn specific counter strategies for winning battles in each of these areas.

CHAPTER NINE

GOD'S BATTLE PLAN

OBJECTIVES:

Upon completion of this chapter you will be able to:

- Write the Key Verse from memory.
- Identify the purpose of God.
- Identify the purpose for which Jesus came into the world.
- Explain the six point battle plan for spiritual warfare.

KEY VERSE FROM THE ARTICLES OF WAR:

> **He that committeth sin is of the Devil; for the Devil sinneth from the beginning. For this purpose the Son of God was manifested, that He might destroy the works of the Devil. (I John 3:8)**

INTRODUCTION

This chapter introduces the basic battle for spiritual warfare. It is a strategy resting upon understanding the purposes of our warfare and based upon communication with our Commander-in-Chief by prayer, fasting, and the written Word of God.

When you do not understand God's purpose and plan, you may be tempted to become discouraged in the conflicts of life. This is why many Christian soldiers fail in warfare: They do not understand the divine purpose behind the battle.

> **...For if their purpose or activity is of human origin, it will fail. But if it is from God, you will not be able to stop these men. You will only find yourselves fighting against God. (Acts 5:38-39 New International Version)**

THE PURPOSE OF WARFARE

From the beginning of time, every natural battle that has been fought always had a purpose for which it was waged. Before we examine God's battle plan, it is important to understand the purpose of spiritual warfare. This involves understanding the purposes of God the Father and Jesus Christ the Son.

THE PURPOSE OF GOD:

It is God's purpose that...

> **...in the dispensation of the fullness of times He might gather together in one all things in Christ, both which are in Heaven, and which are on earth... (Ephesians 1:10)**

From the beginning of time, Satan has battled against the fulfillment of this purpose. Your own warfare in the spirit world is related to this purpose of God. Satan battles to bring your heart, mind, spirit, and soul into allegiance to him instead of the Lord Jesus Christ.

God works in you to accomplish His purpose:

> **For it is God which worketh in you both to will and to do His good pleasure. (Philippians 2:13)**

God also works through your life to accomplish His purposes:

> **Neither yield ye your members as instruments of unrighteousness unto sin: but yield yourselves unto God, as those that are alive from the dead, and your members as instruments of righteousness unto God. (Romans 6:13)**

When you yield yourself to become "an instrument of righteousness unto God," it means you bring your life and ministry in harmony with His purpose and plans. By doing this, you become a target for God's enemy, Satan.

THE PURPOSE OF JESUS:

Jesus said:

> **He that committeth sin is of the Devil; for the Devil sinneth from the beginning. For this purpose the Son of God was manifested, that He might destroy the works of the Devil. (I John 3:8)**

The reason Jesus came into the world was to destroy the works of Satan. This immediately set Him in opposition to the enemy:

> **The thief cometh not, but for to steal, and to kill, and to destroy: I am come that they might have life and that they might have it more abundantly. (John 10:10)**

From the beginning of His earthly ministry, Jesus set about destroying the works of Satan:

- He revealed the bondage of sin (John 8:34).
- He forgave sins (Matthew 9:1-8; Mark 2:1-12,17; Luke 4:17-32).
- He stressed the heart condition rather than the deception of outward appearance (Matthew 15:16-20; Mark 7:20-23; Luke 6:45; 11:39).
- He healed the sick (Matthew 11:5).
- He raised people from the dead (Mark 5:35-43; Luke 8:49-56; John 11).
- He released people from demonic powers (Matthew 8:16).

In summary, He destroyed the works of Satan in the hearts, souls, minds, and bodies of men and women:

> **The blind receive their sight, and the lame walk, the lepers are cleansed, and the deaf hear, the dead are raised up, and the poor have the Gospel preached to them. (Matthew 11:5)**

Jesus not only destroyed the works of Satan, He also exposed the devious strategies of the enemy:

- He taught on the deception of Satan which would increase during the last days on earth Matthew 24-25; Mark 13; Luke 17:22-37; 21:8-36; Matthew 24-25).
- He warned of Satan who was able to destroy the soul (Matthew 10:28).
- He spoke of the necessity of binding the strong man (Satan) before spoiling his goods (Matthew 12:26-30; Mark 3:23-27; Luke 11:17-24).
- He revealed how Satan tries to prevent the Word of God from being effective in the hearts of men and women (Matthew 13:38; Mark 4:15; Luke 8:12).
- He exposed those who were not right with God as being of their "father, the devil" (John 8:44-47).
- He revealed Satan as the "prince of the world" (John 14:30).

THE GREAT DIVISION

Although Jesus came to bring the peace of God (John 14:27; Philippians 4:7), and peace with God (Romans 5:1), His coming also brought division:

> **Think not that I am come to send peace on earth: I came not to send peace, but a sword.**
>
> **For I am come to set a man at variance against his father, and the daughter against her mother, and the daughter in law against her mother in law.**
>
> **And a man's foes shall be they of his own household. (Matthew 10:34-36)**

Jesus divided all men into two battle camps. It is not possible to be neutral:

No man can serve two masters: for either he will hate the one, and love the

other; or else he will hold to the one, and despise the other. Ye cannot serve God and mammon. (Matthew 6:24)

He that is not with me is against me... (Luke 11:23)

Jesus spoke of this great division in a story about two paths, one which was straight and narrow and one which was broad. He warned of the deception of Satan's broad path which many took (Matthew 7:13-14). Through the account of the rich man and Lazarus (Luke 16:19-31), Jesus removed the veil between life and death. He let men see the end result of choosing the wrong way.

Because He destroyed and exposed the works of Satan, Jesus was under assault throughout His earthly life. The enemy constantly tried to destroy Him or prevent Him from fulfilling the mission for which He had come. The moment He was born, an attempt was made on His life. During His public ministry there were several plots on His life and at least one attempt which was aborted. He met the opposition of demonic powers, religious leaders, His own followers, and Satan.

When you align yourself with the plan and purposes of Jesus by accepting Him as your Savior, you become part of the army that wars against Satan. The purposes of Jesus become your purposes and this sets you in a tactical position of direct opposition to the enemy.

THE BATTLE PLAN

There are many different Scriptural strategies that can be used in spiritual warfare, but the basic battle plan for believers is revealed by observing how Jesus dealt with the enemy. The basic battle plan for spiritual warfare is based on six major points. These are:

-The Word Of God
-Delegated Power And Authority
-Prayer
-Fasting
-Keys Of The Kingdom
-The Name Of Jesus

THE WORD OF GOD

One direct confrontation between Jesus and Satan came during a special period of temptation by the enemy. In this encounter, one of the major portions of our spiritual battle plan was revealed. Before proceeding with this lesson, read the accounts of this temptation recorded in Matthew 4:1-11, Mark 1:12-13, and Luke 4:1-13.

First Satan tried to get Jesus to turn stones into bread. The power of Jesus which soon was to turn water into wine surely could have turned stones into bread. But to do so in this situation would have been acting independently of God and using His power for personal benefit.

Next Satan tried to get Jesus to cast Himself down from the top of the temple. Note that Satan said "Cast thyself down." Satan could not cast Him down, because the power of Satan is a limited power. Satan can persuade you to sin, but he cannot cast you down. As you have learned, every man is tempted when he is drawn away by his own lust. He is not forced, but enticed. In this temptation, Satan used God's Word to back up his appeal, but he misapplied it (Matthew 4:6). Misapplication of God's Word is a major strategy of Satan.

In both of the first two temptations Satan said "IF you are the Son of God," do these things. For Jesus to have complied would have been admission that the verification of His sonship by God was inadequate. God had already spoken from Heaven confirming this relationship (Matthew 3:17). Satan always centers his attacks on your relationship with God. The final temptation was an appeal by Satan for worship. In return, Satan would deliver to Jesus all the kingdoms of the world.

In these three situations of temptation you can see the evil forces of the world, the flesh, and the Devil warring against Jesus. Jesus met the temptations of Satan with the Word of God. The Bible is a very important spiritual weapon and part of the armor of God which you will study about later. It is called "the sword of the Spirit." The Word of God is the only divinely inspired manual of spiritual warfare. Other books are useful only as they are in harmony with God's Word.

In meeting the temptations of Satan, Jesus used the Word of God. Jesus quoted specific Scriptures applicable to the immediate battle. He did not quote passages of chronology or history from the Old Testament. Jesus said, "It is written again..." When you use specific Scriptures, be sure they are in balance with the remainder of the Word of God. They must be viewed in their context and applied in harmony with the total revealed Word of God.

In order to use the Word of God effectively in spiritual warfare, you must know the Word of God. You must study, meditate on, and memorize it. Many defeats in life come because we do not know God's Word:

> **Jesus answered and said unto them, Ye do err, not knowing the scriptures, nor the power of God. (Matthew 22:29)**

The Word of God is our manual for warfare and reveals God's spiritual battle plan.

DELEGATED POWER AND AUTHORITY

The second part of the battle plan is based upon the power and authority over Satan which Jesus delegated to His followers:

> **Then He called His twelve disciples together and gave them power and authority over all devils, and to cure diseases. (Luke 9:1)**

Authority and power are two different things. Consider the example of a policeman. He has a badge and a uniform which are symbols of his authority. His authority comes because of the position he holds with the government. But because all people do not respect that authority, the policeman also carries a weapon. The weapon is his power.

Your authority over the enemy comes through Jesus Christ and your position in Him as believers. Your power over the enemy comes through the Holy Spirit:

> **And behold, I send the promise of My Father upon you; but tarry ye in the city of Jerusalem, until ye be endued with power from on high. (Luke 24:49)**

Like the policeman, you must have both authority and power to be effective. Believers receive authority through the new birth experience and their position in Christ, but some never go on to receive the power of the Holy Spirit, which is to be combined with the authority for effective warfare.

The power Jesus gave is directed power for specific purposes. These include:

POWER OVER THE ENEMY:

> **Then He called His twelve disciples together and gave them power and authority over all devils, and to cure diseases. (Luke 9:1)**

POWER OVER SIN:

> **And when He had said this, He breathed on them, and saith unto them, Receive ye the Holy Ghost:**
>
> **Whosoever sins ye remit, they are remitted unto them; and whosoever sins ye retain, they are retained. (John 20:22-23)**

POWER TO EXTEND THE GOSPEL:

> **But ye shall receive power, after that the Holy Ghost is come upon you: and ye shall be witnesses unto me both in Jerusalem, and in all Judaea, and in Samaria, and unto the uttermost part of the earth. (Acts 1:8)**

PRAYER

Prayer is the third part of the basic battle plan. Here is a detailed outline to assist you in studying about prayer:

THE DEFINITION OF PRAYER:

Prayer is communion with God. It takes different forms, but basically it occurs when man talks with God and God talks with man. Prayer is described as:

Calling upon the name of the Lord:	Genesis 12:8
Crying unto God:	Psalms 27:7; 34:6
Drawing near to God:	Psalms 73:28; Hebrews 10:22
Looking up:	Psalms 5:3
Lifting up the soul:	Psalms 25:1
Lifting up the heart:	Lamentations 3:41
Pouring out the heart:	Psalms 62:8
Pouring out the soul:	I Samuel 1:15
Crying to Heaven:	II Chronicles 32:20
Beseeching the Lord:	Exodus 32:11
Seeking God:	Job 8:5
Seeking the face of the Lord:	Psalms 27:8
Making supplication:	Job 8:5; Jeremiah 36:7

THE PRAYER LIFE OF JESUS:

Prayer was an important strategy of the Lord Jesus:

Jesus made prayer a priority:

-He prayed any time of the day or night: Luke 6:12-13
-Prayer took priority over eating: John 4:31-32
-Prayer took priority over business: John 4:31-32

Prayer accompanied any event of importance:

-At His baptism: Luke 3:21-22
-During the first ministry tour: Mark 1:35; Luke 5:16
-Before the choice of the disciples: Luke 6:12-13
-Before and after the feeding of the 5,000: Matthew 14:19,23; Mark 6:41,46; John 6:11,14-15
-At the feeding of the 4,000: Matthew 15:36; Mark 8:6,7

-Before the confession of Peter: Luke 9:18
-Before the transfiguration: Luke 9:28,29
-At the return of the seventy: Matthew 11:25; Luke 10:21
-At the grave of Lazarus: John 11:41-42
-At the blessing of the children: Matthew 19:13
-At the coming of certain Greeks: John 12:27-28
-Before the hour of His greatest anguish: Matthew 26:26-27; Mark 14:22-23; Luke 22:17-19
-For Peter: Luke 22:32
-For the giving of the Holy Spirit: John 14:1-6
-On the road to Emmaus: Luke 24:30-31
-Prior to His ascension: Luke 24:50-53
-For His followers: John 17
-The prayer Jesus taught is recorded in Matthew 6:9-13.

KINDS OF PRAYER:

Paul calls for believers to pray always with "all prayer" (Ephesians 6:18). Another translation of the Bible reads "praying with every kind of prayer" (Goodpseed Translation). This refers to the various levels and types of prayer.

LEVELS OF PRAYER:

There are three levels of intensity in prayer: Asking, seeking, and knocking:

> **Ask, and it shall be given you; seek, and ye shall find; knock, and it shall be opened unto you:**
>
> **For every one that asketh receiveth; and he that seeketh findeth, and to him that knocketh it shall be opened. (Matthew 7:7-8)**

Asking is the first level of prayer. It is simply presenting a request to God and receiving an immediate answer. In order to receive, the condition is to ask:

> **...ye have not, because ye ask not. (James 4:2)**

We have the powerful spiritual weapon of prayer, and yet many do not use it. They do not ask, and because of this, they do not receive.

Seeking is a deeper level of prayer. This is the level of prayer where answers are not as immediate as at the asking level. The 120 gathered in the upper room where they "continued" in prayer is an example of seeking. These men and women sought fulfillment of the promise of the Holy Spirit and continued "seeking" until the answer came. (Acts 1-2)

Knocking is a deeper level yet. It is prayer that is persistent when answers are longer in coming. It is illustrated by the parable Jesus told in Luke 11:5-10. The knocking level is the most intense level of spiritual warfare in prayer. It is illustrated by the persistence of Daniel who continued to knock despite the fact he saw no visible results as Satan hindered the answer from God. (Daniel 10)

TYPES OF PRAYER:

There are various types of prayer illustrated in the model prayer given by the Lord (Matthew 6:9-13). Types of prayer include:

1. Worship and praise:

You enter into God's presence with worship and praise:

> **Enter into His gates with thanksgiving, and into His courts with praise; be thankful unto Him, and bless His Name. (Psalms 100:4)**

Worship is the giving of honor and devotion. Praise is thanksgiving and an expression of gratitude not only for what God has done but for what He is. You are to worship God in spirit and in truth:

> **But the hour cometh, and now is, when the true worshippers shall worship the Father in Spirit and in truth: for the Father seeketh such to worship Him.**
>
> **God is a Spirit, and they that worship Him must worship Him in spirit and in truth. (John 4:23-24)**

Praise and worship can be with:

Singing:	Psalms 9:2,11; 40:3; Mark 14:26
Audible praise:	Psalms 103:1
Shouting:	Psalms 47:1
Lifting up of the hands:	Psalms 63:4; 134:2; I Timothy 2:8
Clapping:	Psalms 47:1
Musical instruments:	Psalms 150:3-5
Standing:	II Chronicles 20:19
Bowing:	Psalms 95:6
Dancing:	Psalms 149:3
Kneeling:	Psalms 95:6
Lying down:	Psalms 149:5

The warrior of God in the spirit world is shown with...

> **...the high praises of God...in their mouth, and a two edged sword in their hand. (Psalms 149:6)**

2. Commitment:

This is prayer committing your life and will to God. It includes prayers of consecration and dedication.

3. Petition:

Prayers of petition are requests. Requests must be made according to the will of God as revealed in His written Word. Petitions may be at the levels of asking, seeking, or knocking. Supplication is another word for this type of prayer. The word supplication means "beseeching God or strongly appealing to Him in behalf of a need."

4. Confession and repentance:

A prayer of confession is repenting and asking forgiveness for sin:

> **If we confess our sins, He is faithful and just to forgive us our sins and to cleanse us from all unrighteousness. (I John 1:9)**

5. Intercession:

Intercession is prayer for others. An intercessor is one who takes the place of another or pleads another's case. The Bible records that at one time God looked on the earth and saw there was no intercessor:

> **And He saw that there was no man, and wondered that there was no intercessor: therefore His arm brought salvation unto Him, and His righteousness, it sustained Him. (Isaiah 59:16)**

When God saw there was no intercessor He supplied the need. He sent Jesus:

> **For there is one God, and one mediator between God and men, the man Christ Jesus. (I Timothy 2:5)**

> **...It is Christ that died, yea rather, that is risen again, who is even at the right hand of God, who also maketh intercession for us. (Romans 8:34)**

> **Wherefore He is able also to save them to the uttermost that come unto God by Him, seeing He ever liveth to make intercession for them. (Hebrews 7:25)**

> **My little children, these things write I unto you, that ye sin not. And if any man sin, we have an advocate with the Father, Jesus Christ, the righteous. (I John 2:1)**

An advocate in a court of justice is a legal assistant or counselor who pleads another's cause. Intercession in spiritual warfare is prayer to God on behalf of another person.

Sometimes this intercession is made with understanding. You intercede in your own native language:

> **I exhort therefore, that first of all, supplications, prayers, intercessions, and giving of thanks, be made for all men. For kings, and for all that are in authority... (I Timothy 2:1-2)**

At other times, intercession is made by the Holy Spirit. It may be with groanings resulting from a heavy spiritual burden. It may be in an unknown tongue. It may be intercession for another or the Holy Spirit making intercession for you. When this happens, the Holy Spirit speaks through you praying directly to God and according to the will of God. You do not understand this type of intercession:

> **Likewise the Spirit also helpeth our infirmities; for we know not what we should pray for as we ought; but the Spirit itself maketh intercession for us with groanings which cannot be uttered. (Romans 8:26)**

This is the deepest level of intercessory prayer and the most effective in spiritual warfare.

THE MODEL PRAYER:

During the earthly ministry of Jesus His disciples once came to Him with an interesting request:

> **... one of His disciples said unto Him, Lord, teach us to pray... (Luke 11:1)**

The disciples did not ask how to preach or perform miracles. They did not seek lessons on how to build lasting relationships. They did not inquire regarding the wonders of physical healing. They asked to be taught how to pray.

What created this desire? It was the visible effects of prayer in the life and ministry of Jesus. The disciples had witnessed the powerful results of this spiritual strategy in action.

Read the model prayer and observe the various types of prayer we have discussed:

Our Father, which art in Heaven, Hallowed be thy name.	Praise and worship
Thy kingdom come. Thy will be done in earth, as it is in Heaven.	Commitment
Give us this day our daily bread.	Petition

And forgive us our debts, as we forgive our debtors.   Confession and Intercession

And lead us not into temptation, but deliver us from evil   Petition

For thine is the Kingdom, and the power   Praise and worship
and the glory, forever. Amen.

(Matthew 6:9-13)

HOW TO PRAY:

Look up each of the following references in your Bible to learn how you should pray:

-Prayer is to be made to God: Psalms 5:2
-Empty repetition is forbidden, but earnest repetition is not: Matthew 6:7; Daniel 6:10; Luke 11:5-13; 18:1-8
-You sin by neglecting to pray for others: I Samuel 12:23
-Pray with understanding (in a known tongue): Ephesians 6:18
-Pray in the Spirit: Romans 8:26; Jude 20
-Pray according to the will of God: I John 5:14-15
-Pray in secret: Matthew 6:6
-Quality rather than quantity is stressed. Prayer is not successful because of "much speaking": Matthew 6:7
-Pray always: Luke 21:36; Ephesians 6:18
-Pray continually: Romans 12:12
-Pray without ceasing: I Thessalonians 5:17
-Pray to the Father in the name of Jesus: John 15:16
-With a watchful attitude: I Peter 4:7
-Pray according to the example of the model prayer: Matthew 6:9-13
-Pray with a forgiving spirit: Mark 11:25
-Pray with humility: Matthew 6:7
-Sometimes accompany prayer with fasting: Matthew 17:21
-Pray fervently: James 5:16; Colossians 4:12
-Pray with submission to God: Luke 22:42
-Use the strategies of binding and loosing in prayer: Matthew 16:19

WHAT YOU SHOULD PRAY FOR:

-The peace of Jerusalem: Psalms 122:6
-Laborers in the harvest: Matthew 9:38
-That you enter not into temptation: Luke 22:40-46
-Them that despitefully use you (your enemies): Luke 6:28
-All the saints: Ephesians 6:18
-The sick: James 5:14
-One for another (bearing each other's burdens): James 5:16
-For all men, kings, and those in authority: I Timothy 2:1-4

-For daily needs: Matthew 6:11
-For wisdom: James 1:5
-For healing: James 5:14-15
-For forgiveness: Matthew 6:12
-For God's will and Kingdom to be established: Matthew 6:10
-For relief from affliction: James 5:13

PRAY THE PROMISES:

> **Ye ask, and receive not, because ye ask amiss, that ye may consume it upon your lusts. (James 4:3)**

God answers prayer according to His promises. When you do not ask on the basis of these promises, your prayer is not answered. It is similar to how a father relates to his children. No parent commits to give his youngsters anything they want or ask for. He makes it clear that he will do certain things and not do other things. Within these limits the father answers his child's requests.

It is the same way with God. He has given promises and they form the proper basis for prayer. Learn what God has promised and pray according to the promises of God. One way to do this is to go through the Bible and mark all the promises God has made. Use your Bible as you pray and base your prayers upon these promises.

HINDRANCES TO PRAYER:

-Sin of any kind: Isaiah 59:1-2; Psalm 66:18; Isaiah 1:15; Proverbs 28:9
-Idols in the heart: Ezekiel 14:1-3
-An unforgiving spirit: Mark 11:25; Matthew 5:23
-Selfishness, wrong motives: Proverbs 21:13; James 4:3
-Power hungry, manipulative prayers: James 4:2-3
-Wrong treatment of marriage partner: I Peter 3:7
-Self-righteousness: Luke 18:10-14
-Unbelief: James 1:6-7
-Not abiding in Christ and His Word: John 15:7
-Lack of compassion: Proverbs 21:13\
-Hypocrisy, pride, meaningless repetition: Matthew 6:5; Job 35:12-13
-Not asking according to the will of God: James 4:2-3
-Not asking in Jesus' name: John 16:24
-Satanic demonic hindrances: Daniel 10:10-13; Ephesians 6:12
-Not seeking first the Kingdom: It is only when you seek first the Kingdom of God that you are promised the "other things": Matthew 6:33
-God has a higher purpose in denying your request: II Corinthians 12:8-9
-When you do not know how to pray as you should, prayer is hindered. This is why it is important to let the Holy Spirit pray through you: Romans 8:26

WHEN NOT TO PRAY:

It is important to learn how to wait before the Lord in prayer for His guidance and direction before acting. But it is equally important to know when not to pray. When God calls you to action, you must act, not continue to pray.

For example, at the bitter waters of Marah when Moses cried unto the Lord, God showed him exactly what to do to sweeten the waters. There was no need to wait further on the Lord in prayer. Moses was to act upon what God had revealed. The same was true of Joshua when he prayed about the terrible defeat of Israel at Ai. God revealed there was sin among the people of Israel. He actually told Joshua...

> **Get thee up; wherefore liest thou thus upon thy face? Israel hath sinned...Up, sanctify the people... (Joshua 7: portions of 10, 12, and 13)**

It was not the time to pray. It was the time to act upon the direction given in prayer. Some people use prayer as an excuse to avoid involvement and acting upon what God has told them to do.

Others continue to pray when God has already answered but they did not like the answer. Review the story of Balaam in Numbers 22. Note especially verses 18-19. Balaam had no right to go to God with the same matter for God had clearly forbidden him to have anything to do with it (see verse 12).

FASTING

Fasting is the fourth part of our battle plan. It is combined with prayer to wage effective warfare in the spirit world.

THE DEFINITION OF FASTING:

Fasting, in the most simple definition, is going without food.

TYPES OF FASTS:

According to the Bible there are two types of fasts. The total fast is when you do not eat or drink at all. An example of this is found in Acts 9:9. The partial fast is when the diet is restricted. An example of this is in Daniel 10:3.

PUBLIC AND PRIVATE FASTING:

Fasting is a personal matter between an individual and God. It is to be done in private and not boasted about:

> **Moreover when ye fast, be not as the hypocrites, of a sad countenance; for they disfigure their faces, that they may appear unto men to fast. Verily I say unto you, they have their reward.**

> **But thou, when thou fastest, anoint thine head, and wash thy face;**
>
> **That thou appear not unto men to fast, but unto thy Father which is in secret and thy Father which seeth in secret shall reward thee openly. (Matthew 6:16-18)**

Leaders may call a public fast and request the whole church fellowship to fast:

> **Blow the trumpet in Zion, sanctify a fast, call a solemn assembly. (Joel 2:15)**

THE PURPOSES OF FASTING:

There are definite spiritual purposes for fasting. It is important that you understand these, for if you fast for the wrong reasons it will be ineffective.

Study each of the following references regarding the purposes of fasting. They reveal the great power of fasting in spiritual warfare. You fast:

- To humble yourself: Psalms 35:13; 69:10
- To repent of sin: Joel 2:12
- For revelation: Daniel 9:2; 3:21-22
- To loose bands of wickedness, lift heavy burdens, set the oppressed free, and break every bondage: Isaiah 58:6
- To feed the poor, both physically and spiritually: Isaiah 58:7
- To be heard of God: II Samuel 12:16,22; Jonah 3:5,10

Fasting does not change God. It changes you. God relates to you on the basis of your relationship to Him. When you change, then the way God deals with you is affected. You do not fast to change God, because God does not change. Read the book of Jonah for an example of how this occurred in the city of Ninevah.

LENGTH OF THE FAST:

How long you fast depends upon what God speaks into your spirit. He may lead you to fast a short or lengthy time. Remember the story of Esau and Jacob? Jacob was originally making a meal for himself but denied himself in order to obtain the birthright. How much better if Esau had fasted that one meal!

KEYS OF THE KINGDOM

Jesus gave to believers the keys of the Kingdom. Those keys include the power to bind and loose and they are the fifth part of our basic battle plan:

> **And I will give unto thee the keys of the Kingdom of Heaven; and whatsoever thou shalt bind on earth shall be bound in Heaven; and whatsoever thou shalt loose on earth shall be loosed in Heaven. (Matthew 16:19)**

Jesus taught the importance of binding evil spirits before casting them out, but the principle of binding and loosing is more than casting out demons. You can bind the power of the enemy to work in your life, home, community, and church fellowship. You can loose men and women from the bondage of sin, depression, and discouragement of the enemy.

The principle of binding and loosing is an important strategy to overcome the power of the enemy. It is a key to the Kingdom of God. In every situation with which you are confronted...every problem, every challenge...there is a spiritual key. That key is in exercising the principle of binding and loosing. When you recognize what to bind and what to loose and act upon this discovery, the enemy will be defeated.

THE NAME OF JESUS

The final part of the basic battle plan is found in the name of Jesus. The Word of God is to be applied in His name, we pray, fast, and use our delegated power and authority and the keys of the Kingdom in His name:

> **If ye shall ask any thing in my name, I will do it. (John 14:14)**
>
> **...Verily, verily, I say unto you, Whatsoever ye shall ask the Father in my name, He will give it you. (John 16:23)**
>
> **And these signs shall follow them that believe, in my name shall they cast out devils; they shall speak with new tongues;**
>
> **They shall take up serpents; and if they drink any deadly thing, it shall not hurt them: they shall lay hands on the sick, and they shall recover. (Mark 16:17-18)**
>
> **And Jesus came and spake unto them, saying, All power is given unto me in Heaven and in earth.**
> **Go ye therefore, and teach all nations, baptizing them in the name of the Father, and of the Son, and of the Holy Ghost;**
>
> **Teaching them to observe all things, whatsoever I have commanded you; and, lo, I am with you alway, even unto the end of the world. (Matthew 28:18-20)**

You are to teach, baptize, cast out demons, heal the sick, and overcome every power of the enemy through the name of Jesus. It is more powerful than any other name:

> **Far above all principality, and power, and might, and dominion, and every name that is named, not only in this world, but also in that which is to come. (Ephesians 1:21)**
>
> **Wherefore God also hath highly exalted Him, and given Him a name which is above every name;**

> **That at the name of Jesus every knee should bow, of things in Heaven, and things in earth, and things under the earth;**
>
> **And that every tongue should confess that Jesus Christ is Lord, to the glory of God the Father. (Philippians 2:9-11)**

A WINNING STRATEGY

Jesus faced every temptation of the enemy which we face, but He overcame these temptations without sin. Because He entered the arena of spiritual warfare, He understands your battles and strengthens you:

> **For we have not an high priest which cannot be touched with the feeling of our infirmities; but was in all points tempted like as we are, yet without sin. (Hebrews 4:15)**

Because He emerged victorious, you can also be a victor:

> **For in that He Himself hath suffered being tempted, He is able to succor them that are tempted. (Hebrews 2:18)**

Read the story of the death and resurrection of Jesus in Matthew 26-28; Mark 14-16; Luke 22-24; and John 18-21. The death and resurrection of Jesus Christ was the greatest confrontation that ever occurred between the power of Satan and the power of God.

Through the death of Jesus, Satan thought he had destroyed God's plan. He had killed God's only Son. He had destroyed the King who was to reign over God's Kingdom. But Jesus said:

> **Thinkest thou that I cannot now pray to my Father, and He shall presently give me more than twelve legions of angels?**
>
> **But how then shall the Scriptures be fulfilled, that thus it must be? (Matthew 26:53-54)**
>
> **...My Kingdom is not of this world: if my Kingdom were of this world, then would my servants fight, that I should not be delivered to the Jews: but now is my Kingdom not from hence. (John 18:36)**
>
> **...Thou couldest have no power at all against me, except it were given thee from above...(John 19:11)**

Jesus did not die because His power was less than that of the enemy. His death did not end the plan for God's Kingdom. It was not time for His Kingdom to be visibly established in the world.

The death of Jesus actually fulfilled the plan of God. Men could now be saved from the bondage of sin and the penalty of the "second death" (eternal separation from God because of sin).

Great though it was, salvation from sin was not the only victory gained by Jesus through His death on the cross. Through His death and resurrection, Jesus defeated all the power of the enemy:

> **...When He ascended up on high (was resurrected) He led captivity captive, and gave gifts unto men.**
>
> **(Now that He ascended, what is it but that He also descended first into the lower parts of the earth?**
>
> **He that descended is the same also that ascended up far above all Heavens, that He might fill all things.) (Ephesians 4:8-10)**
>
> **And having spoiled principalities and powers. He made a shew of them openly, triumphing over them in it. (Colossians 2:15)**

Jesus defeated every power of the enemy, including death. He also passed judgment upon Satan:

> **Now is the judgment of this world: now shall the prince of this world (Satan) be cast out. (John 12:31)**

Jesus made a way of salvation. He defeated death and the principalities and powers of the enemy. He restored to man dominion over all things. He pronounced judgment on Satan which will be fulfilled in the future.

As you have learned, the present situation is similar to conditions which have existed in certain countries in the natural world. The powers of rebel forces will be overthrown by the government. The rebel leader will be under judgment, but still at large. Resistance forces under his direction still war in the land.

Jesus has conquered Satan and set his judgment, but he is still at large and his forces of demonic powers, the flesh, and the world are still at war in the land. They attempt to control territory that is rightfully that of the Conqueror. They try to blind men to the fact Satan has been defeated and is under judgment. They try to control homes, churches, and nations.

That is where the warfare of the believer comes into focus. Jesus has defeated the enemy but Satan remains at large in the world. It is our task to open the eyes of men and women to his deception and regain control of territory that is rightfully ours. Your personal battle will continue until judgment on Satan is executed or until you go to be with Jesus through death, whichever comes first:

> **To the intent that now unto the principalities and powers in heavenly places might be known by the church the manifold wisdom of God. (Ephesians 3:10)**

VICTORS, NOT VICTIMS

Through Jesus, you are a victor over the enemy rather than a victim of the enemy:

> **And hath put all things under His feet, and gave Him to be the head over all things to the Church.**
>
> **Which is His body, the fullness of Him that filleth all in all. (Ephesians 1:22-23)**

All things are "under the feet" of Jesus. This means He has conquered them. He is the head of the Church, and we are the body. It is stated that all things are under His feet, which means under His body, the Church. This means we are victors, not victims. You can be kept from the power of Satan. Jesus Himself prayed for us to be kept from the power of the enemy:

> **I pray not that thou shouldest take them out of the world, but that thou shouldest keep them from the evil.**
>
> **Neither pray I for these alone, but for them also which shall believe on me through their word. (John 17:15,20)**

You are a conqueror, not through your own power, but through the powers of a greater One:

> **...In all these things we are more than conquerors through Him that loved us. (Romans 8:37)**

When the spiritual battle gets rough, just remember that the Bible assures that God's purposes will be accomplished:

> **The Lord of hosts hath sworn, saying, Surely as I have thought, so shall it come to pass; and as I have purposed so shall it stand. (Isaiah 15:24)**
>
> **This is the purpose that is purposed upon the whole earth; and this is the hand that is stretched out upon all the nations.**
>
> **For the Lord of hosts hath purposed and who shall disannul it? and his hand is stretched out, and who shall turn it back? (Isaiah 15:26-27)**

The Lord of Hosts has a purpose, and no force of the world, flesh, demons, Hell, or Satan himself will disannul it.

INSPECTION

1. Write the Key Verse from the Articles Of War.

___

___

2. What is the purpose of God?

___

___

3. For what purposes did Jesus come into the world?

___

___

___

4. What is God's six point battle plan for spiritual warfare?

___

___

___

___

___

___

(Answers to tests are provided at the conclusion of the final chapter in this manual.)

TACTICAL MANEUVERS

1. In this lesson you learned of the importance of the Word of God in spiritual warfare. Harvestime International Institute offers two courses that will increase your ability to know and use the Word of God. Write for information on *"Creative Bible Study Methods"* and *"Basic Bible Survey."*

2. In this lesson you learned that Jesus came to destroy the works of Satan. Read more about the purposes of Jesus in the following verses: Luke 4:18-19; 4:43; 19:10; 24:46-49; John 6:38; 9:4; 12:46; 18:37. Read the statement of God's purpose as it relates to Jesus: John 3:16-18; Ephesians 1:9-10.

3. Jesus had many encounters with evil spirits. But evil spirits and temptation by Satan were not the only battles Jesus fought. Satan also used men who were close to Jesus to war against Him:

Peter:

Simon Peter was one of the twelve disciples chosen by Jesus, yet at times Peter was used
by Satan to war against Jesus. When Jesus had revealed His forthcoming death, Peter began to rebuke Him for saying such things (Mark 8:32). Jesus said to Peter...

...Get thee behind me, Satan; for thou savourest not the things that be of God, but the things that be of men. (Mark 8:33)

Jesus did not mean Peter was actually Satan, rather that Peter was being used by Satan at that particular moment.

One of the chief strategies of Satan is to use those close to you to try to keep you from doing God's will. As Jesus, you must put their persuasions behind you. Is Satan using someone close to you to try to keep you from doing God's will?

At a later time, when Peter pledged loyalty to the Lord, Jesus said to him:

...Simon, Simon, behold, Satan hath desired to have you, that he may sift you as wheat;

But I have prayed for thee, that thy faith fail not: and when thou art converted, strengthen thy brethren. (Luke 22:31-32)

Jesus knew that when the time of crucifixion drew near Peter would deny Him. He saw how the enemy desired to sift everything good out of Peter's life. But Jesus also could see the great potential in Peter. He realized that someday he would emerge as a great leader of the early church.

Judas:

Judas was one of the original twelve disciples chosen by Jesus. Jesus knew from the beginning how the enemy would use this man:

Jesus answered them, Have not I chosen you twelve, and one of you is a devil?

He spake of Judas Iscariot, the son of Simon; for he it was that should betray Him, being one of the twelve. (John 6:70-71)

Read of Jesus' betrayal by Judas in Matthew 26:20-25 and John 13:21-30. Has Satan used close associates to betray and wound you? As Jesus, you cannot let that deter you from the purpose God has set for you.

4. Read Malachi 1:13. The prophet reports that in his time some were so bored with their religious observances that they said, "Behold, what a weariness." Perhaps these people never had learned how to worship?

    Study more about worship: Psalms 5:7; 22:27; 29:2; 45:11; 66:4; 86:9; 95:6; 96:9 97:7; 99:5,9; Exodus 34:14; I Chronicles 16:29; Matthew 15:9; Mark 7:7; John 4:23-24; Philippians 3:3.

    The Harvestime International Institute Course entitled *"Mobilization Methodologies"* contains further instruction on the subject of worship.

5. Study more about praise in the book of Psalms. Mark the word "praise" every time it occurs in Psalms then go back and study all the verses you have marked.

6. Here are some more facts about prayer:

    Answers to prayer are granted:
Immediately at times:	Isaiah 65:24; Daniel 9:21-23
Delayed at times:	Luke 18:7
At times, different from our desires:	II Corinthians 12:8-9
Beyond our expectations:	Jeremiah 33:3; Ephesians 3:20

    Different postures may be used in prayer:
Standing:	I Kings 8:22; Mark 11:25
Bowing down:	Psalms 95:6
Kneeling:	II Chronicles 6:13; Psalms 95:6; Luke 22:41; Acts 20:36
Falling on the face:	Numbers 16:22; Joshua 5:14; I Chronicles 21:16; Matthew 26:39
Spreading forth the hands:	Isaiah 1:15; II Chronicles 6:13
Lifting up the hands:	Psalms 28:2; Lamentations 2:19; I Timothy 2:8

Common problems you will need to overcome in order to pray:
Lack of time
Distractions
Tiredness
Lack of desire

Organizing The Prayer Forces:

Prayer is one of the most powerful weapons of spiritual warfare. The New Testament reveals the following structure for organizing prayer forces to wage warfare more effectively:

Personal prayer: Prayer is to be made on an individual basis in private: Matthew 6:6

Two praying together: Praying of two together is the smallest unit of corporate prayer: Matthew 18:19

Small groups: Small group cells consist of more than two individuals joining together in prayer. There is great power when two or three people join together for this purpose: Matthew 18:20

Total congregational prayer: The entire church should join together in times of corporate prayer: Acts 1:14-15

Prayer Promises:

Study the following promises regarding prayer. They reveal the great power of this weapon in spiritual warfare:

-The Father knows what you need even before you ask: Matthew 6:8
-If any two agree in prayer, it will be answered: Matthew 18:19
-All things are possible with God: Matthew 19:26; Luke 18:27
-Prayer combined with faith is effective: Matthew 21:22; Mark 11:24
-The effectual fervent prayer of the righteous availeth much: James 5:16
-If you ask in the name of Jesus, it will be done: John 14:14

7. Study further on fasting:

   -Fasting is one of the things that approves us as ministers of God: II Corinthians 6:3-10
   -Prayer with fasting was used in organizing the Church: Acts 14:23
   -We are to "give ourselves" to fasting: I Corinthians 7:5

8. Jesus said you would have power to tread on "serpents and scorpions." In Chapter Five you studied the natural and spiritual parallels of a serpent. Here are some facts about scorpions that can be applied spiritually:

Scorpions avoid others. A scorpion will fight to the death. It will seize its prey, crush it, and then inject deadly poison from its stinger. If you are stung by a scorpion, you may experience pain, speech difficulties, restlessness, weakness, and numbness.

Scorpions live in dark places and die when exposed to the heat (light). First the scorpion will try to escape, then it begins to strike frantically with its tail. In the natural world, army ants are the main enemy of the scorpion.

Can you apply these truths spiritually as we did with the facts about snakes in Chapter Five?

MOBILIZATION

ACTIVE MILITARY SERVICE IN GOD'S ARMY

To "mobilize" means to put in a state of readiness for active military service. "Mobilization" is the process of being deployed as part of the spiritual forces of God's army.

CHAPTER TEN

OFFENSIVE AND DEFENSIVE WARFARE

OBJECTIVES:

Upon completion of this chapter you will be able to:

- Write the Key Verse from memory.
- Define "offensive warfare."
- Define "defensive warfare."
- Identify the common factor in both offensive and defensive warfare.
- Summarize the role of the Holy Spirit in offensive and defensive warfare.
- Use the natural example of wrestling to explain offensive and defensive warfare strategies.

KEY VERSE FROM THE ARTICLES OF WAR:

Neither give place to the Devil. (Ephesians 4:27)

INTRODUCTION

There are two types of warfare in the natural world: Offensive and defensive. The Bible also teaches both defensive and offensive spiritual strategies. You must learn to fight both defensively and offensively. The only other option is desertion, which is unacceptable.

This lesson provides an introduction to both offensive and defensive warfare. The following two chapters examine in detail your defensive and offensive spiritual weapons.

DEFENSIVE WARFARE

Defensive warfare is battle waged to defend territory. It is warfare that waits for the enemy to strike, then pulls its forces together in defensive response. The defender must respond to his opponent and his decisions are forced on him by the attacker. This type of warfare does not advance into enemy territory. It defends territory already claimed. It is important, however, because the spiritual forces of evil are constantly attacking you as a believer. If you do not know how to defend yourself, you will become a victim of these attacks.

OFFENSIVE WARFARE

Offensive warfare is aggressive warfare. It is not a warfare of waiting and responding in defense. It is warfare which takes the initiative of attack. The enemy is identified, his strategy recognized, and offensive advances against him are made in the spirit world. In offensive warfare the attacker has the advantage of making decisions first. Offensive warfare gains territory rather than defends it.

Offensive advances are the only type of spiritual warfare which will reach the world with the Gospel of Jesus Christ. We cannot remain in our comfortable homes and churches and practice defensive strategies only. The army of God must advance into enemy territory. It must go to the strongholds of Satan with the power of the Gospel message. We must wage aggressive offensive spiritual battle.

THE COMMON FACTOR

There is one thing in common about offensive and defensive warfare. Both involve personal action by the believer. In natural warfare, unused weapons do not inflict causalities on the enemy nor win wars. The same is true in the spirit world. Your spiritual weapons are affected by your will to use them. It is true that God empowers for battle, but you have a personal responsibility in both defensive and offensive spiritual strategies.

In Old Testament battles, the Lord fought for and with His people, Israel. But first, they had to position themselves on the battlefield. When God sees a spiritual weapon being used in His name and a man or woman on the battlefield daring to attempt the impossible, the Lord of Hosts is moved to action.

Read the story of Elisha in II Kings 13:14-19. In this object lesson using the bow and arrows, there are some spiritual parallels that will help you understand your part in the battle:

1. DEMONSTRATE YOUR INTENTION TO FIGHT:

Elisha told King Joash, "Take up the bow and arrows." Paul said, "Take the sword of the Spirit" and declare war. By taking up your offensive and defensive weapons, you are demonstrating your intention to fight.

2. PUT YOUR HANDS ON THE WEAPON:

Elisha told the king to put his hands upon the bow, then Elisha laid his hands upon the king's hands. The strategy for victory is your hand upon the weapon and His hand over yours.

3. OPEN THE WINDOW:

Open up the window of the place where the enemy is victorious. Israel's foe was to the east, so Elisha told the king to open the window eastward. God wants you to open up the "windows" of every area of your life to expose the failure, defeat, and bondage of the enemy.

4. SHOOT:

Elisha told the king, "Shoot," and the king shot. Then Elisha said, "The Lord's arrow of victory over Syria." The open window is not enough. The weapon in your hand is not sufficient. Even God's hand upon your hand will not win the battle. You must follow the command of the Lord of Host to "SHOOT!" This is your part in the warfare...to actually use the weapon that is in your hand which is guided by the hand of the Lord.

5. KNOW THE OBJECTIVE:

Elisha told the King to take the arrows and hit them upon the ground as a symbol of his victory over Syria. The king did so, but he "smote thrice and stayed (stopped)." Elisha told him that because he limited God by hitting the ground only three times, his military victory would be limited. This happened because the King did not understand the objective of warfare. Elisha had said the Lord wanted to totally consume the enemy (verse 17). By striking the ground only three times, the King settled for only partial victory.

The Lord's objective for you is total victory in every area of your life and ministry. If you fail to understand this objective then your victory will be limited.

6. WIN FIRST IN THE SECRET CHAMBER:

What happened between Elisha and King Joash in the secret chamber that day determined the outcome of the battle with Syria. It is what happens in the secret chamber with the Lord that determines your victories in the actual battles of life.

DEVICES OF SATAN

Basic to both offensive and defensive warfare is knowledge of the strategies of Satan:

> **Lest Satan should get an advantage of us: for we are not ignorant of his devices. (II Corinthians 2:11)**

The word "devices" means a scheme, project, plot or underhanded plan of evil character. Satan can gain advantage over you when you are ignorant of his devices and fail to respond in offensive and defensive battle.

THE MINISTRY OF THE HOLY SPIRIT

Earlier in this course you learned of the spiritual force of good known as the Holy Spirit. The Holy Spirit is important in both offensive and defensive warfare. The Holy Spirit knows the strategies of Satan and intercedes for believers engaged in battle:

> **Likewise the Spirit also helpeth our infirmities; for we know not what we should pray for as we ought: but the Spirit itself maketh intercession for us with groanings which cannot be uttered....because He maketh intercession for the saints according to the will of God. (Romans 8:26-27)**

The Holy Spirit gives power to claim enemy territory:

> **But ye shall receive power after that the Holy Ghost is come upon you: and ye shall be witnesses unto me both in Jerusalem, and in all Judaea, and in Samaria, and unto the uttermost part of the earth. (Acts 1:8)**

Gifts of the Holy Spirit are valuable weapons of offensive and defensive battle. The gifts of the word of knowledge and the word of wisdom provide supernatural revelation for spiritual warfare. The gift of discerning of spirits reveals the deception of the enemy.

The **special** gifts of pastor, prophet, apostle, evangelist and teacher assist in equipping us for battle. The **speaking** gifts of the Holy Spirit provide special instructions from God and the serving gifts of the Spirit enable the army of God to move forward in spiritual advance.

WRESTLING: A NATURAL PARALLEL OF SPIRITUAL TRUTH

One of the most powerful verses on offensive spiritual combat is...

> **For we wrestle not against flesh and blood, but against principalities, against powers, against the rulers of the darkness of this world, against spiritual wickedness in high places. (Ephesians 6:12)**

God's choice of the word "wrestle" is significant. Wrestling is a natural parallel of a great spiritual truth. Wrestling in the natural world is a sport of mastery in strength. To wrestle means "to contend in struggle for power over an opponent."

Consider these facts about wrestling in the natural world as applied to your spiritual warfare:

1. PREPARATION AND TRAINING:

A wrestler in the natural world must train to be successful at his sport. He must practice wrestling. He must have a proper diet. He must learn the rules of wrestling and they must be carefully followed to win the match.

A believer must learn the rules of spiritual warfare in order to be victorious. A proper "diet" of God's Word and prayer is necessary for successful spiritual wrestling. As in wrestling in the natural world, skill is gained through practice.

The primary purpose of training in the natural world is to prepare the wrestler to perform at peak efficiency while experiencing the least amount of fatigue. This is true also in the spirit world. Some people are easily fatigued and defeated spiritually because they are not properly trained for spiritual warfare.

2. THE NATURE OF THE STRUGGLE:

Individual championship wrestling is not a team sport. When a wrestler tires there is no substitute team member to send in. Wrestling involves intimate, face to face, personal contact with the opponent.

The same is true in the spirit world. Believers are involved in intimate, face to face combat with the enemy. No other believer can take your place in this spiritual combat. There are no "time outs" in wrestling as in other sports. There are no "time outs" in the spiritual world either. Satan never rests from this war. The believer must never be off guard.

3. THE STRATEGIES:

There are both offensive and defensive strategies in natural wrestling which are applicable in the spiritual world. Stalling is one technique used in wrestling. Stalling is avoiding confrontation with an opponent. Points are lost in the judging system for stalling. You also "lose points" when you "stall" spiritually and do not aggressively wrestle your enemy. Some believers spend their entire lives stalled in confrontation with the enemy. They never aggressively wrestle and gain the victory.

4. UPSET BALANCE:

Another important strategy in natural wrestling is to upset the balance of the opponent. Once an opponent's balance has been destroyed, he is kept struggling to regain it.

The Bible speaks much of the importance of balance or "temperance." One of the strategies of Satan in the spiritual realm is to try to upset balance. Many cults have resulted because of improper balance on doctrinal issues. Homes, church fellowships, and even nations have been defeated because of improper balance by wrong emphasis or lack of emphasis in certain areas.

There are two types of balance involved in wrestling: Physical and mental balance. Before physical balance can be destroyed, mental balance must first be attacked. To accomplish this, a strategy of surprise is used. A move is initiated that is distracting and a surprising. While the wrestler focuses on this, the intended technique is applied. By leading an opponent to believe some move is about to be attempted, he will try to avoid the imagined danger and leave himself open to the actual attack.

How true this is in the spiritual world! Satan upsets balance through the strategy of surprise. He upsets your mental balance by distracting attacks and while you are fearfully focused on these, he launches his intended assault in another area of your life.

5. ANTICIPATION:

Anticipation is important in natural wrestling. A wrestler who can discern when a particular move is going to be made is usually able to block or counter attack. When the intended move is made it is not as likely to be successful since it is anticipated and the wrestler is prepared.

The same is true in the spirit world. If you are not ignorant of Satan's devices and anticipate his strategies, then you are prepared. You are not thrown off balance when attacks occur.

6. BAITING:

There are moves in wrestling which are made to "bait" an opponent, to tempt and entice him into making a move which will weaken his position. In the spirit world Satan is constantly tempting you to moves which will weaken your spiritual position.

In natural wrestling, moves are planned to place an opponent in a position that leaves him open to attack. Situations are purposely created to do this and advantage is taken of an opponent's weakened position at the instant it occurs.

Spiritually, Satan creates situations which leave you open to attack Then he immediately takes advantage of your weakened position. But you must remember as you wrestle that it is Satan who holds the weakened position. The power within you is greater than his power. He has already been dealt the final weakening blow by the Lord Jesus Christ. But you must exercise the advantage given you by the Lord in order to win the match.

7. ATTACK AND COUNTERATTACK:

In natural wrestling, every move you make sets you up for a response from the opponent. The same is true in the spirit world. When you make a move for God, Satan will always counterattack with a move of his own.

8. MOBILITY:

In wrestling, a mobile opponent is considered dangerous. This is why you want to pin your opponent down. In the spiritual world, Satan is a mobile opponent. He goes "to and fro" as a lion seeking to devour. You must be on guard for his constant mobility. Satan also recognizes the effectiveness of your mobility. He wants to prevent you from being on the move for God. This is why he strives to throw you and pin you down spiritually.

9. RECOVERY:

Any error made in wrestling results in an action that can be taken advantage of by the opponent. How true spiritually! Any error you make in spiritual wrestling is quickly taken advantage of by the enemy. It is important in wrestling to learn how to recover from a fall. It is necessary to be able to convert the bottom position into an advantage. There are moves of escape and reversal which will enable this.

In spiritual wrestling you may at times experience a fall and be temporarily pinned by the enemy. But you do not have to remain in this position. God has given strategies in His Word which, if followed, will convert your disadvantage into an advantage. He has provided strategies for escape and reversal spiritually just as are used in natural wrestling.

The life of Joseph is an excellent example of this. He had the disadvantages of being sold into slavery and put in prison. But he converted disadvantages to advantages. In the end, he triumphed over the enemy.

There are other moves in wrestling which result in taking an opponent down from behind, dragging, pinning, throwing, and pulling him. Can you recognize similar moves by the enemy spiritually?

10. THE OBJECTIVE:

The objective of wrestling in the natural world is to defeat the opponent by causing him to fall or pinning him to the ground. This results from a series of strategic moves and/or by wearing the opponent down.

Satan constantly wars against believers trying to wear them down. His objective is to cause believers to fall, throw them, and trap in the bondage of sin. His goal is to destroy your supportive points, just as a wrestler does to his opponent in the natural world. The goal is to make you prostrate spiritually.

11. SCORING:

Victory in natural wrestling also comes through a process of scoring by the judges. The wrestler with the highest points for the most effective strategic moves wins the match.

Your spiritual opponent has already been judged. Satan was overcome by the most effective move in all history, the death and resurrection of Jesus Christ. You wrestle with an enemy who is already judged as a loser in the match. Because of this you do not need to be afraid of his power or strategies in the wrestling match in which you engage. You do not have to fall or be pinned by the bondage of sin. You can stand confidently in the wrestling match of spiritual warfare and resist him steadfastly in the faith.

12. MENTAL ATTITUDE:

Mental attitude is very important in wrestling. In a study on the subject, the following attitudes were said to be necessary for championship wrestling in the natural world. These attitudes also are true in the spiritual realm:

> **Desire:** To wish and want to win is not enough. The champion wrestler must have a will to win. Desire is an emotion which transcends all else in life.
>
> **Persistence:** Sustained effort is required for championship wrestling. A champion wrestler will not accept defeat.
>
> **Purpose:** Winning is the goal and purpose of wrestling. To achieve this goal he must not only know he is master of the situation, but he must also let his opponent know.

INSPECTION

1. Write the Key Verse from the Articles Of War.

   _____

   _____

2. What is defensive warfare?

   _____

   _____

3. What is offensive warfare?

   _____

   _____

4. What common factor exists in both offensive and defensive spiritual warfare?

   _____

   _____

5. Summarize the role of the Holy Spirit in offensive and defensive warfare.

   _____

   _____

6. Summarize what you learned about offensive and defensive warfare from the natural example of wrestling.

   _____

   _____

(Answers to tests are provided at the conclusion of the final chapter in this manual.)

TACTICAL MANEUVERS

1. You are not to trust in "chariots" (natural weapons) of men: Psalms 20:7. God has "spiritual" chariots. Read about them in Psalms 68:17; 104:3; Isaiah 19:1; and II Kings 2:11.

2. You need to wage both offensive and defensive warfare because Satan is a destroyer: John 10:10; I Corinthians 10:10; Matthew 10:28.

    -If you obey God, He will not let the destroyer come in: Exodus 12:23
    -God keeps you from the destruction of Satan: Psalms 17:4
    -Satan is your adversary, the one you fight against: I Peter 5:8.
    -You are not to give him room to operate against you: I Timothy 5:14.
    -If you obey God, He will be an enemy to your adversaries: Exodus 23:22.

3. You do not have to be defeated by Satan. Study the following references:

    -You can chase the enemy: Leviticus 26:7-8; Deuteronomy 32:30; Joshua 23:10

    -You can have victory: Deuteronomy 7:21; I Chronicles 29:11; Psalms 5:11; 18:29; 24:8; 91:1; Isaiah 49:19; I Corinthians 15:57; I John 5:4

    -The Lord is your fortress: II Samuel 22:2; Psalms 18:2; 31:3; 71:3; 91:2; 144:2; Jeremiah 16:19

    -You have dominion over the enemy: Psalms 8:6; 49:14; 72:8; 119:133; Daniel 7:27; Ephesians 1:21

    -Safety comes from the Lord: Proverbs 18:10; 21:31; 29:25. Psalms 91 is the Psalm of safety.

    -God delivers you from distress: Psalms 25:17; 107:6,13; 19:28

    -You can capture enemy thoughts: II Corinthians 10:5

    -God looses bonds of the enemy: Psalms 116:16; Romans 8:15-21; Galatians 5:1

4. When Paul speaks of wrestling, he is talking about wrestling with the enemy, not with God as did Jacob. Be sure when you are wrestling it is not God grappling with you to break the spirit of self-sufficiency in order to transform you from a "Jacob" to an "Israel."

5. Review Chapter Three of this manual and list the functions of the Holy Spirit in both offensive and defensive warfare:

Ministry Of The Holy Spirit

In Offensive Warfare   **In Defensive Warfare**

CHAPTER ELEVEN

DEFENSIVE WEAPONS

OBJECTIVES:

Upon completion of this chapter you will be able to:

- Write the Key Verse from memory.
- Describe your defensive spiritual weapons.
- Give a Scripture reference that lists the armor of God.
- Identify each piece of the armor of God.
- Explain the function of each piece of armor.

KEY VERSE FROM THE ARTICLES OF WAR:

Put on the whole Armor of God, that ye may be able to stand against the wiles of the Devil. (Ephesians 6:11)

INTRODUCTION

You have learned that the great spiritual battle in which you are engaged cannot be fought with natural weapons. It must be fought both offensively and defensively with spiritual weapons. You already studied "God's Battle Plan" in Chapter Nine. You learned the basic battle strategy includes:

- The Word of God
- Delegated power and authority
- Prayer
- Fasting
- Keys of the kingdom
- The name of Jesus

In addition to these basic warfare strategies, the Bible reveals that you have a whole arsenal of spiritual weapons. In this chapter you will learn about your defensive spiritual weapons. In the next lesson you will study offensive weapons.

DEFENSIVE STRATEGIES

The Bible teaches the following defensive actions which must be taken by the believer:

SUBMIT AND RESIST:

Submit yourselves therefore to God. Resist the Devil, and he will flee from you. (James 4:7)

Note the order in this verse: First submit, then resist. Many people skip over the first step of submission and try resisting the Devil, only to discover it does not work. Defeat results when you act independently of God. It is the humble, not the arrogant and self-confident, who overcome the enemy. You will be able to resist Satan only as you submit to God. To "resist" means to "stand firm against and oppose the enemy at every point." The Scripture does not teach us to go looking for demons, but to resist them when they approach us.

RESIST SATAN STEADFASTLY IN FAITH:

Be sober, be vigilant; because your adversary the Devil, as a roaring lion, walketh about, seeking whom he may devour.

Whom resist steadfast in the faith, knowing that the same afflictions are accomplished in you brethren that are in the world. (I Peter 5:8-9)

To resist "in the faith" means to resist on the authority of God's Word.

DON'T GIVE PLACE TO SATAN:

Do not leave room for Satan to operate in your life:

Neither give place to the Devil. (Ephesians 4:27

RECOVER YOURSELF FROM SATAN'S SNARE:

You must recover yourself from Satan's snare by applying Biblical strategies:

And that they may recover themselves out of the snare of the devil, who are taken captive by him at his will. (II Timothy 2:26)

ABSTAIN FROM FLESHLY LUSTS:

To "abstain" means to keep yourself from something and refuse to do it:

Dearly beloved, I beseech you as strangers and pilgrims, abstain from fleshly lusts which war against the soul. (I Peter 2:11)

For this is the will of God, even your sanctification, that ye should abstain from fornication. (I Thessalonians 4:3)

Abstain from all appearance of evil. (I Thessalonians 5:22)

STAND YOUR GROUND:

> **Wherefore take unto you the whole Armor of God, that ye may be able to withstand in the evil day, and having done all, to stand...Stand therefore..(Ephesians 6:13-14a)**

When you "stand your ground" you are defending that which is rightfully yours.

BEWARE OF EVIL, SHUN IT, AND PUT IT OFF:

Study Ephesians 4:17-32. The "putting off" of all the evil behavior listed there is defensive warfare.

Don't be led aware by the error of the wicked:

> **Ye therefore, beloved, seeing ye know these things before, beware lest ye also being led away with the error of the wicked, fall from your own steadfastness. (II Peter 3:17)**

> **But shun profane and vain babblings; for they will increase unto more ungodliness. (II Timothy 2:16)**

To "shun" means to avoid or turn away from. You should avoid every evil thing related to the enemy.

TRY THE SPIRITS:

Trying the spirits prevents deception.

> **Beloved, believe not every spirit whether they are of God: because many false prophets are gone out into the world. (I John 4:1)**

To "try" means to "test." You are not operating in unbelief when you try the "spirits" of those with whom you come in contact or in operation in and around you. If they are true, they will pass the test.

SHUN FALSE TEACHERS:

When you receive false teachers into your home you become partakers of their evil. Defend your home from enemy attack:

> **If there come any unto you, and bring not this doctrine, receive him not into your house, neither bid him God speed;**

> **For he that biddeth him God speed is partaker of his evil deeds. (II John 10-11)**

LAY ASIDE WORLDLY AFFAIRS:

You are to lay aside worldly affairs which prevent you from being a good soldier. To "lay aside" is defensive action you must take.

> **Thou therefore endure hardness, as a good soldier of Jesus Christ. No man that warreth entangleth himself with the affairs of this life; that he may please him who hath chosen him to be a soldier. (II Timothy 2:3-4)**

> **Wherefore seeing we also are compassed about with so great a cloud of witnesses, let us lay aside every weight, and the sin which doth so easily beset us, and let us run with patience the race that is set before us. (Hebrews 12:1)**

> **Wherefore lay apart all filthiness and superfluity of naughtiness, and receive with meekness the engrafted word, which is able to save your souls. (James 1:21)**

PUT ON THE ARMOR OF GOD:

> **Put on the whole Armor of God, that ye may be able to stand against the wiles of the Devil. (Ephesians 6:11)**

"Put on" indicates action you must take. The basic description of the armor of God is given in Ephesians 6:10-17. Read this passage in your Bible.

Paul introduces the subject of warfare by emphasizing that the battle is not a natural one and natural weapons are ineffective. Spiritual battles must be fought with spiritual weapons. Paul describes the armor to be used in spiritual warfare:

> **Wherefore take unto you the whole Armor of God, that ye may be able to withstand in the evil day, and having done all, to stand. Stand therefore, having your loins girt about with truth, and having on the breastplate of righteousness;**

> **And your feet shod with the preparation of the Gospel of peace.**

> **Above all, taking the shield of faith, wherewith ye shall be able to quench all the fiery darts of the wicked.**

> **And take the helmet of salvation and the sword of the Spirit, which is the Word of God. (Ephesians 6:13-17)**

The purpose of the armor is to be able to stand against the wiles (deceit, cunning, craftiness) of the enemy, Satan. It is your responsibility to put on the armor:

> **Put on the whole Armor of God, that ye may be able to stand against the wiles of the devil. (Ephesians 6:11)**

But put ye on the Lord Jesus Christ, and make not provision for the flesh, to fulfill the lusts thereof. (Romans 13:14)

The night is far spent, the day is at hand: let us therefore cast off the works of darkness, and let us put on the Armor of light. (Romans 13:12)

The phrase "put on" means to "put on once and for all." Your spiritual armor is not like a athletic uniform you put on at game time. You put on the armor once and for all and leave it on the rest of your life. Just as a soldier on the battlefield does not take his armor off and on, you will not lay down your armor until you go to be with the Lord. If you do not have your armor on at all times, you are vulnerable to the enemy. It is wise to check often that each piece of your spiritual armor is still in place.

The first division of armor covers three things you have done in the past. "Having put" indicates something you have already done if you are a believer.

- Having your loins girt about with truth (verse 14)
- Having on the breastplate of righteousness (verse 14)
- Having your feet shod with the preparation of the Gospel of peace (verse 15)

The second division includes things which are to be put on in the present:

- Taking the shield of faith (verse 16)
- Taking the helmet of salvation (verse 17)
- Taking the sword of the Spirit (verse 17)

In Ephesians 6:11 Paul emphasizes putting on the whole armor of God. Some of us are preoccupied with but one piece of God's armor to the extent that others are neglected. You must have on the whole armor or you may find yourself being an expert in the use of the "sword of the Spirit" and still defeated because you have forgotten the shield of faith.

The Belt:

The first piece of armor to be buckled on is the girdle or belt of truth. In the natural world, a suit of armor was attached to the belt which held the other pieces of armor in place. The truth of God's Word is the spiritual belt to which all other pieces of armor are attached. Satan's first attack on man was on truth:

And the woman said unto the serpent...God hath said, Ye shall not eat of it, neither shall ye touch it, lest ye die.

And the serpent said unto the woman, Ye shall not surely die. (Genesis 3:2-4)

The truth will protect you from lies and doctrinal errors of the enemy. Truth is the undergirding of your spiritual armor. You are to have your loins (your spiritual vital organs) girt (covered) with truth:

Stand therefore, having your loins girt about with truth... (Ephesians 6:14)

What is the truth?

-Jesus said, "I am the truth."John 14:6
-The Holy Spirit is the "Spirit of truth."John 14:17
-God is truth. Romans 3:4
-God's Word is truth. Psalms 119:151
-The Gospel is truth. Colossians 1:5

The Breastplate:

In the natural world, the breastplate covered the upper body of the warrior to protect vital organs such as his heart, lungs, etc. The spiritual breastplate of righteousness does not refer to your righteousness, but to the covering of the righteousness of Christ:

And be found in Him, not having mine own righteousness, which is of the law, but that which is through the faith of Christ, the righteousness which is of God by faith. (Philippians 3:9)

You do not stand on your own merits. You stand in Christ. You cannot face the enemy without the protection of the righteousness of Christ:

By the word of truth, by the power of God, by the Armor of righteousness on the right hand and on the left. (II Corinthians 6:7)

The righteousness of Christ protects your spiritual "vital organs" from attacks of Satan and from unrighteousness. The breastplate of righteousness must be buckled on to the belt of truth.

The Shoes:

There are many types of shoes for different purposes. Some are for walking, others for specific sports activities. A soldier's shoes are another kind...They are shoes designed for warfare. A soldier who cannot advance on the battlefield is disabled in warfare.

"Feet shod with the preparation of the Gospel of peace" indicate a readiness to advance in the spiritual realm. These spiritual shoes protect your will from the temptation of the enemy who would lead you in wrong paths. They indicate your willingness to do every good work and to spread the Gospel to all nations. These spiritual shoes will also enable you to stand against the enemy as Paul encourages you to do (Ephesians 6:14).

The Shield:

In the natural world, the shield was used to provide protection to the warrior's entire body. Your spiritual shield is called the "shield of faith."

There are several types of faith mentioned in the Bible. There is saving faith, the gift of faith, and the spiritual fruit of faith. But the word "faith" when used in relation to the "shield of faith" speaks of defensive faith. This faith is a firm trust and confidence in God which protects your whole being. It protects you from flaming missiles of doubt and unbelief sent by the enemy. This shield of faith is a calm and confident trust in God which deflects all the fiery arrows of the enemy from their target.

The shield of faith is the constant application of God's Word to the issues of life. It is a faith that enables you to overcome the evil forces of the world:

> **For whatsoever is born of God overcometh the world; and this is the victory that overcometh the world, even our faith. (I John 5:4)**

Combined with love of God, faith is most effective:

> **...putting on the breastplate of faith and love...(I Thessalonians 5:8)**

It is faith based on truth:

> **He shall cover thee with His feathers, and under His wings shalt thou trust: His truth shall be thy shield and buckler. (Psalms 91:4)**

It is faith based on salvation:

> **Thou hast also given me the shield of thy salvation: and thy right hand hath holden me up, and thy gentleness hath made me great. (Psalms 18:35)**

Without faith, you have no grasp of truth. Without faith you cannot receive salvation. Without faith you cannot go forth with the Gospel of peace. Without faith you cannot claim the righteousness of Christ and effectively use the sword of the Spirit which is the Word of God.

Faith is not an assumption or presumption. It is a fact based upon God's Word. You can increase your faith by hearing God's Word (Romans 10:17), acting upon your present faith (Romans 1:17), and seeking God (Hebrews 12:2).

The Helmet:

The helmet of salvation is not something you put on when you get saved. Remember, we are dealing with spiritual armor here, and it is assumed that you are a believer and a member of God's army before you start putting on the armor.

The helmet of salvation represents a regenerated mind. It represents a transformed and renewed thought life. You will learn later in this course that Satan desperately fights for control of the mind. An undisciplined mind makes the Christian warrior easy prey to sinful deceptions of the enemy.

Paul speaks of the helmet as the "hope of salvation" in I Thessalonians 5:8. Salvation, when properly experienced and understood, protects your mind. Salvation embraces the past, present, and future. You have been saved from the guilt and penalty of past sin. You are being saved from the power of sin in the present. The "hope of salvation" refers to salvation in the future tense. It is final salvation from the presence of sin when Jesus returns. The hope of this future salvation strengthens your mind against the attacks of Satan. You have a confident hope in the future because God is working out His purpose:

> **...according to His good pleasure, which He hath purposed in Himself;**
>
> **That in the dispensation of the fullness of times He might gather together in one all things in Christ, both which are in Heaven, and which are on earth; even in Him. (Ephesians 1:9-10)**

The Sword Of The Spirit:

The "sword of the Spirit" is the Word of God. It is both a defensive and offensive weapon. You already learned how Jesus used the Word in defense against the attacks of Satan. In the next lesson you will learn how this weapon is used offensively.

Prayer:

After describing the Christian soldier's armor, Paul comments:

> **Praying always with all prayer and supplication in the Spirit, and watching thereunto with all perseverance and supplication for all saints.**
> **(Ephesians 6:18)**

As you learned when you studied "Gods Battle Plan," prayer and its associated practice of fasting are also powerful spiritual weapons. These two weapons can be used both offensively and defensively. Check out the summary of the armor of God and its purposes which follows:

THE ARMOR OF GOD
Ephesians 6:10-18

TRUTH (girdle)
Protects from...DECEPTION ⇐ Sword of the Spirit
   ▽

     RIGHTEOUSNESS (breastplate)
     Protects from... UNRIGHTEOUSNESS
        ▽

          PEACE (shoes)
          Protects from... CONFUSION
             ▽

               FAITH (shield)
               Protects from... UNBELIEF
                   ▽

                    SALVATION (helmet)
                    Protects from... BONDAGE

-The girdle or belt of truth protects from the deception of Satan which can lead to unrighteousness (sin).

-The breastplate of righteousness protects from unrighteousness (sin) which leads to confusion.

-Feet shod with the preparation of the Gospel of peace protects from spiritual confusion which results in unbelief.

-The shield of faith protects against unbelief which results in bondage. The helmet of salvation protects from bondage.

-The sword of the spirit, the Word of God, is used as both an offensive and defensive weapon.

Note the downward progression of one not protected by the armor of God: Deception leads to unrighteousness (sin) which always results in confusion. Confusion results in unbelief, and unbelief always results in spiritual bondage.

INSPECTION

1. Write the Key Verse from the Articles Of War.

   _____

   _____

2. Summarize what you learned about your defensive spiritual weapons:

   _____

   _____

   _____

   _____

3. Give a Scripture reference which lists the armor of God.

   _____

4. List each piece of the armor of God and briefly define its function.

Piece of Armor	Function

(Answers to tests are provided at the conclusion of the final chapter in this manual.)

TACTICAL MANEUVERS

1. Read Psalms 45:3 and Isaiah 59:17. Both passages describe God putting on spiritual armor. What two pieces of armor does God put on that are not included in our spiritual armor? (Isaiah 59:17)

2. David mentions spiritual armor as he recalls how God has helped him in battle. Study Psalms 18:29-50.

3. It is important that you have experience using your spiritual armor. In I Samuel 17 read about what happened when David tried to use armor with which he was not familiar.

4. The Lord uses spiritual armor to protect you from your enemies: Psalms 35:1-3

   David had much to say about his enemies: Psalms 5:8; 6:10; 8:2; 9:3; 11:2; 15:5; 17:9; 18:3, 17, 20, 26, 34, 37; 27:2; 30:1 31:23; 44:5-6; 56:9; 60:12; 61:3; 95:6; 108:13.

   Read what God says about your enemies: Exodus 15:6; Matthew 10:36; 13:39; Luke 1:11; 10:19; Acts 2:35; I Corinthians 15:25-26; Colossians 1:21.

5. God is your shield. See Genesis 15:1; Psalms 3:3; 5:12; 28:7; 33:20; 59:11; 84:9,11; 115:9-11; 119:114; 144:2.

6. Read Exodus 17. Israel was under attack and God told Moses to stretch forth his rod. Previously, Moses had used the rod as a shepherd's staff and to provide water for God's people. Now, for the first time, he stretches forth the rod to resist the principalities and powers of the hosts of wicked spirits responsible for the Amalekite attack. There is a great spiritual lesson in this story. The leaders of God's people are not only responsible to shepherd, feed, and water the flock, but when an attack from the enemy comes it is their responsibility to use the "rod of God" to defend God's people.

7. How do you respond to these fiery darts of Satan? Think about how you would use the shield of faith to defend yourself from each of these attacks. Record your answers to use them in the next attack:

    Selfishness:
    Covetousness:
    Pride:
    Doubt:
    Discouragement:
    Depression:
    Lust:
    Greed:
    Anger:

CHAPTER TWELVE

OFFENSIVE WEAPONS

OBJECTIVES:

Upon completion of this chapter you will be able to:

- Write the Key Verse from memory.
- Identify your offensive weapons.

KEY VERSE FROM THE ARTICLES OF WAR:

> **The Lord hath opened his armory, and hath brought forth the weapons of his indignation: for this is the work of the Lord God of hosts...**
> **(Jeremiah 50:25a)**

INTRODUCTION

Now that you have learned how to defend yourself spiritually, you must also learn how to wage offensive warfare which will help you advance into Satan's territory. With offensive weapons, you will be able to claim new ground as you spread the Gospel and bring deliverance to those held in enemy bondage.

To "war a good warfare" it is evident that you must take offensive action:

> **This charge I commit unto thee, son Timothy, according to the prophecies which went before on thee, that thou by them mightest war a good warfare. (I Timothy 1:18)**
>
> **Fight the good fight of faith, lay hold on eternal life, whereunto thou art also called, and has professed a good profession before many witnesses. (I Timothy 6:12)**

You are to fight this battle intelligently with purpose:

> **I therefore so run, not as uncertainly; so fight I, not as one that beateth the air. (I Corinthians 9:26)**

Knowing your offensive weapons can give you the ability to fight with purpose instead of uncertainty.

OFFENSIVE STRATEGIES

Here are the weapons you use to wage offensive spiritual warfare:

PRAYER:

You already studied prayer and fasting as part of "God's Battle Plan" in Chapter Ten and as a defensive weapon in the last lesson. But prayer is also a powerful offensive weapon. When you use it to wage offensive warfare you do not just pray only for your own personal wants, needs, and problems. You intercede for people, leaders, and nations, pulling down strongholds of Satan and his demonic forces.

All Christians are to intercede at times, but there is a special calling to intercession for some. This powerful ministry brings the intercessor before the Lord to wage mighty battles in the unseen realm.

The value of praise and worship was also mentioned in Chapter Ten. Praise and worship are powerful offensive weapons. In II Chronicles 20 when Israel faced a mighty enemy, they began to sing and praise God and He set an ambush to defeat their army. When you praise and worship God, you are actually setting "ambushments" in the spirit world.

THE SWORD OF THE SPIRIT:

> **Wherefore TAKE unto you the whole Armor of God, that ye may be able to withstand in the evil day...(Ephesians 6:13)**

To "take" something is to get hold of it, grasp it, to draw it to yourself. To take hold of God's armor implies offensive action on the part of the believer.

You studied about the defensive parts of the armor in the last lesson. These included the belt of truth, breastplate of righteousness, helmet of salvation, shoes of the preparation of peace, and the sword of the Spirit.

The "sword of the Spirit," which is the Word of God, is a weapon that can be used both defensively and offensively. The Word is a defensive weapon when you use it to defend against the attacks of Satan. It is offensive when you use it to claim territory for the Lord by sharing the Gospel message and deliverance with others.

There are two different words used in Scripture for the "Word of God." One word is "logos" which refers to the total utterance of God. This refers to the complete revelation of what God has said. The second word, "rhema," refers to a specific saying of God that has special application to a specific situation. This is the word used in this passage calling the "sword of the Spirit" the Word of God.

You will remember that Jesus used specific ("rhema") sayings of God, applicable to the immediate temptation. To be able to do this implies familiarity with the total Word of God.

If you are to use specific Scriptures applicable to immediate battles, you must have knowledge of God's total revelation.

THE MIND OF CHRIST:

> **Forasmuch then as Christ hath suffered for us in the flesh, ARM YOURSELVES likewise with the same mind...(I Peter 4:1)**

> **LET THIS MIND BE IN YOU, which was also in Christ Jesus. (Philippians 2:5)**

To "let" means to permit or embrace. You are to arm yourself with the same mind that Jesus had, a mind set to wage aggressive warfare:

> **...For this purpose the Son of God was manifested, that He might destroy the works of the Devil. (I John 3:8)**

You must "let" or permit this mind to be developed. You must take aggressive action to "arm yourself" with a similar mental attitude:

> **And be not conformed to this world; but be ye transformed by the renewing of your mind, that ye may prove what is that good, and acceptable, and perfect will of God. (Romans 12:2)**

To be "transformed" means to experience a complete change which will be expressed in character and conduct. Renewing and arming your mind with Christlikeness results in such a transformation.

PULLING AND CASTING DOWN:

The goal of offensive warfare is to pull and cast down the strongholds of the enemy:

> **For the weapons of our warfare are not carnal, but mighty through God, to the PULLING DOWN OF STRONG HOLDS; CASTING DOWN imaginations and every high thing that exalteth itself against the knowledge of God, and bringing into captivity every thought to the obedience of Christ. (II Corinthians 10:4-5)**

To "pull down" means to take down by effort or force. To "cast" means to throw or hurl. You are told to cast off the works of darkness (Romans 13:12) and cast out demon powers (Matthew 10:8).

When you pull and cast down strongholds of Satan you are waging offensive warfare. You are not waiting to defend against an attack of Satan but you are attacking strongholds of the enemy's power.

BINDING AND LOOSING:

You have the power to bind the forces of evil and loose the forces of good:

> **And I will give unto thee the keys of the Kingdom of Heaven: and whatsoever thou shalt bind on earth shall be bound in Heaven: and whatsoever thou shalt loose on earth shall be loosed in Heaven. (Matthew 16:19)**

Through delegation of power and authority from Jesus, you can bind and loose spiritual forces. Note that this weapon works together: It is binding and loosing. Whenever you bind something, you should also loose something. For example, if you bind the spirit of lying you should loose the spirit of truth to operate in its place.

THE BLOOD OF JESUS:

When Jesus died on the cross of Calvary, He loosed us from the dominion of sin and the power of the enemy. His blood secures our access to God and release from the bondage of Satan. The Word of God indicates that "they (believers) overcame him (Satan) by the blood of the Lamb (Jesus Christ)" (Revelation 12:11).

Salvation, healing, and deliverance are all available because of the blood of Jesus. His blood enables you to wage offensive warfare for the souls of men and women and bring deliverance in deliverance and healing in the name of Jesus. Your power to "overcome" the enemy is because of the "blood of the lamb."

YOUR TESTIMONY:

Revelation 12:11 indicates the enemy is defeated by the "word of your testimony." The word "testimony" means "evidence or record" like that used in a legal case in a court of law.

You will recall that Jesus often commanded people who had been delivered to go and tell others what God had done for them. As you "testify" or give evidence to the power of God in your life, you wage offensive spiritual warfare. To be effective, your testimony must be based upon the testimony of the Word of God, just as a lawyer in a court bases his arguments on the law of the land.

THE NAME OF JESUS:

You already learned that the name of Jesus is part of God's basic battle plan. The name of Jesus is a powerful offensive weapon also. Jesus said that "in My name" you will cast out demons, heal the sick, and overcome all the power of the enemy (Mark 16:17).

Review the various names of Jesus in Chapter Three of this manual to see how many of His names reflect offensive action against the enemy. Also read through the book of Acts and note the miracles done "in His name."

The name of Jesus is not some magical phrase with which we conclude our prayers. It is a symbol of the authority and power He has given us. You had better be authorized to use His power an authority before you start using His names to war against Satanic powers. Review the story in Acts 19:13-17 and note what happened to the sons of Sceva.

INSPECTION

1. Write the Key Verse from the Articles Of War.

2. Summarize what you have learned about your offensive weapons:

(Answers to tests are provided at the conclusion of the final chapter in this manual.)

TACTICAL MANEUVERS

1. Study these references on the offensive action of "casting":
   Matthew 5:29-30; 7:5; 8:16; Mark 16:17; Romans 13:12; II Corinthians 10:5; I Peter 5:7

2. Study these references on the offensive action of "putting":
   Romans 13:12, 14; I Corinthians 5:13; 13:11; Galatians 3:27; Ephesians 4:22-24; 6:11; Colossians 3:8-14

3. Study these references on the offensive action of "taking":
   I Corinthians 3:10; 8:9; 10:12; Galatians 5:15; Ephesians 6:13,17; I Timothy 4:16; Hebrews 3:12.

4. As you learned in this chapter, you must participate in aggressive warfare to defeat the enemy. You must "let" or permit certain things in your spiritual life if you are to be victorious. Study the following references and complete the chart by recording what the Bible says you are to "let" or permit in your life:

References	**What We Are To "Let"**
Matthew 5:16	
John 4:1,27	
Romans 13:1,12-13	
Romans 14:5,13,16,19	
I Corinthians 3:18-21	
I Corinthians 10:8-9	
II Corinthians 7:1	
II Corinthians 10:17	
Galatians 5:26	
Ephesians 4:26-31	
Ephesians 5:3,6,33	
Philippians 1:27	
Philippians 2:3,5	
Philippians 3:15-16	
Philippians 4:5-6	
Colossians 3:15-16	
Colossians 4:6	
I Thessalonians 5:6-8	
II Timothy 2:19	
Hebrews 4:1,14,16	
Hebrews 6:1	
Hebrews 10:22-24	
Hebrews 12:1	
Hebrews 13:1,5,15	

References   **What We Are To "Let"**

James 1:5-9
James 3:13
James 4:9
James 5:13
I Peter 3:3-4,10-11
I Peter 4:11,15,16,19
I John 2:24
I John 3:7,18
I John 4:7

CHAPTER THIRTEEN

NATURAL PARALLELS OF SPIRITUAL WARFARE

OBJECTIVES:

Upon completion of this chapter you will be able to:

- Write the Key Verse from memory.
- Explain why "warfare" is used to describe the conflict between good and evil.
- Summarize natural principles of warfare applicable to spiritual warfare.
- Apply natural principles of warfare in the spiritual realm.

KEY VERSE FROM THE ARTICLES OF WAR:

> **This charge I commit unto thee, son Timothy, according to the prophecies which went before on thee, that thou by them mightest war a good warfare. (I Timothy 1:18)**

INTRODUCTION

The early Church viewed their spiritual experience in terms of warfare. Protection is described as the "armor of God." The Word of God is compared to a "sword." Satan's attacks are fiery darts and faith is the "good fight." Believers are told to "war a good warfare."

Why did God choose the example of natural warfare to describe what is happening in the spirit world between the forces of good and evil? The answer is found in a basic Biblical principle: Natural principles of spiritual truth. God uses natural principles to explain what is happening in the spirit world. We can understand what we see in the natural world. When parallels are drawn between something in the natural world and the spiritual world, then we can understand the spiritual because of the natural.

Jesus used this principle often. He used the example of a natural harvest to illustrate the great spiritual harvest to which He was calling laborers. There are many parallels between natural harvesting and harvesting in the spiritual world.

The same is true in relation to warfare. There are many principles of natural warfare which have been studied and applied by experts at physical war. These natural principles are applicable in the spiritual world. This chapter presents principles of natural warfare and applies them in the spiritual realm. It reveals why God used natural warfare to describe the ongoing spiritual war in which believers are engaged.

NATURAL PARALLELS OF SPIRITUAL WARFARE

Here are the natural principles of warfare that are parallels of spiritual battle:

THE DEFINITION OF WAR:

A simple definition of war in the natural world is "an act of force intended to compel our opponent to fulfill our will." This definition is applicable also in the spiritual world. Satan is constantly using the forces of evil to compel you to fulfill his will.

A WARTIME LIFESTYLE:

When a nation is at war, the life-style of that nation is affected. Men give up their jobs to fight for their nation. They spend hours in preparation and training. Funds are drawn from the economy to aid in the battle. Residents are alert to invasion and extra guards are posted at national borders.

In the spiritual world many believers are totally unaware of the warfare raging around them and have not adopted a wartime lifestyle. Church fellowships plan programs and parties but they do not have a battle plan. They live in luxury and ease while the enemy is claiming the souls of unnumbered men and women without Jesus Christ. Members of the fellowship are discouraged, depressed, and living in fleshly sins. They are victims of a war they do not even know exists. You must understand: We are at war! We should adopt a wartime life-style in the spirit world. Spiritual warfare should become the focus of our lives. We should spend time in preparation and training. We should learn of and put to use our spiritual weapons.

We should designate material wealth to extending the Gospel message to claim nations being threatened by Satan. We should be alert to invasion from the enemy and post extra guards at the borders of our heart, mind, tongue, soul, spirit, home, community, and church fellowship. We are at war, and our life-style in the spirit world should reflect it.

THE OBJECTIVE OF WAR:

The main objective of warfare in the natural world is victory over the enemy. This is also the main objective in the spiritual world. To achieve victory in natural warfare, there are many short-range objectives that must be met. Individual battles must be won and separate territories claimed. Each of these individual battles contribute to the final goal of victory.

The same is true in the spirit world. Our long-range goal is victory over the enemy. But we must break down this long-range objective into more specific objectives. We must know the objectives God has for us in spiritual warfare in our family, church fellowship, community, and nation. We must identify the specific territory assigned to us for conquest.

Each soldier in a natural army has a different position and responsibility in the battle. The same is true in the spiritual world. You must identify personal objectives which will contribute to the overall goal of victory. The battle commander assigns objectives to soldiers in the natural world. God is your spiritual battle commander and He has set specific spiritual objectives for you as a Christian soldier.

BASIC TRAINING:

Knowing the objectives for war is not enough. A soldier must receive basic training on how to achieve these objectives. In the natural world this training includes learning about the enemy, his tactics, how to use the weapons of warfare, and the battle plan.

In the spiritual world believers often enter the battlefield without this basic training. They do not understand the tactics of the enemy. They are not aware of their spiritual weapons and how to use them and they have not studied the battle plan (God's written Word).

In the natural world, to send a soldier to the battlefield without basic training results in defeat. The same is true in the spirit world. You must be trained in spiritual warfare if you are to experience victory. When a soldier enters basic training in the natural world, he leaves civilian life behind. He is no longer entangled with civilian affairs but is concerned with the army in which he has enlisted.

In the spiritual realm, in order to war a good warfare we must not be entangled in the affairs of life. We are not civilian citizens of this present world. We are warriors of the Kingdom of God:

> **Thou therefore endure hardness, as a good soldier of Jesus Christ.**
> **No man that warreth entangleth himself with the affairs of this life; that**
> **he may please Him who hath chosen him to be a soldier.**
> **(II Timothy 2:3-4)**

PROPAGANDA:

Enemy nations always spread false propaganda (information) about each other. Satan also injects false propaganda into your mind if you allow it. You will learn more about this when you study "The Battle In The Mind" in Chapter Fifteen.

DIPLOMATIC PROPOSALS:

One of the strategies of nations at war is to weaken the enemy by diplomatic proposals. These are suggestions of compromise. Through such proposals each nation tries to gain advantage over the other. In spiritual warfare, Satan attempts to make believers compromise with sin. He knows such "diplomacy" will result in spiritual weakness.

INTELLIGENCE:

When nations are at war, there is always an intricate organization of intelligence. Each side has intelligence forces dedicated to gathering information about the other. The intelligence forces collect and analyze all available information on the enemy. They communicate what they have learned to the soldiers engaged in combat.

In spiritual warfare your knowledge of the enemy and his tactics are vital to victory. The Bible is your "intelligence manual" which reveals information on the enemy. As you learn of Satan's strategies and the Scriptural counter strategies, you should communicate these to other Christian soldiers. Satan gathers information on you too. He learns your points of weakness and targets them with offensive attacks.

OFFENSIVE AND DEFENSIVE WARFARE:

Armies in the natural world use both offensive and defensive strategies. As you have learned, offensive warfare is an aggressive advance against an enemy. Defensive warfare is when the enemy attacks and you must defend your territory.

You have learned that parallels of both offensive and defensive warlike situations exist in the spiritual world. When Satan attacks you must use defensive spiritual warfare. When you are claiming new territory for God, such as sharing the Gospel with those who have never yet heard it, you are conducting offensive warfare. You are claiming new territory in the name of the Lord Jesus Christ.

A great general in the natural world once told his troops, "We are not going to dig foxholes and wait for the enemy to come shooting at us. We are going to move ahead, and move fast." (A foxhole is a hole in the ground in which a soldier can hide). The general said, "When you dig a foxhole, you dig a grave. When you are in that foxhole and fire at the enemy, he knows your exact location...We will keep moving and the enemy will always hit where we have been and not where we are." This general did not believe in defense. His theory was that if the enemy was constantly under attack, there would not be any need to defend. He realized that the force moving in offensive warfare had advantage over the defending forces. He said, "We will fight on our terms and we will win."

In spiritual warfare, he who understands the objective of warfare as the defeat of the enemy will not easily be reduced to a defensive position. To gain total victory, offensive fronts are required.

WEAPONS:

In every war there are weapons which are used. They may be simple weapons such as a spear or bow and arrow, or they may be complex weapons such as a missile system. The soldier must know what weapons are available for use and how to use them. Some weapons are specifically designed for defensive warfare while others are for offensive warfare.
This is also true in the spiritual world. As a Christian soldier you must be aware of your spiritual weapons and know how to use them. As you have learned, there are both defensive and offensive spiritual weapons. The difference is that your weapons are spiritual weapons. Never be reduced to trying to use ineffective natural weapons to fight spiritual battles.

SURPRISE ATTACKS:

Terrorism, sabotage, and ambush are all surprise attacks and are methods used by natural armies at war. These methods have two things in common: First, they are violent offensive methods. Second, they all have an element of surprise. The target at which such assaults are directed is caught unawares and is unprepared. Confusion and defeat usually result.

As terrorists who sabotage and ambush, Satan also uses the methods of violent, offensive, surprise attacks. He will attack when you least expect it in areas of your life left unguarded. Do not assume the enemy will furnish you with warning of his attacks. This does not happen in the natural world of war. Neither will it happen in the spiritual world.

DECISIVE BATTLES:

In every war there are "decisive battles." These are battles which determine the outcome of the entire war. Decisive battles are important because of the territory involved in the fight. If an army wins control of a certain strategic territory he can gain control of surrounding territories. In spiritual warfare there are also decisive battles. For example, if you fail in the battle of the mind and tongue it will affect your soul, spirit, heart, and possibly your entire body.

In the natural world, the greatest concentration of troops are sent to a decisive battlefield. In the spirit world this should be true also. Concentration of your spiritual resources in strategic locations is necessary for successful warfare. This is true also in terms of the spreading of the Gospel. There are times when the spiritual harvest is ripe in key geographic areas of the world and evangelistic forces should be concentrated in that field.

Unfortunately, this is not always so. The greatest concentration of ministers at present is in the United States of America where there is a church in most every community and Christian radio and television programs readily accessible to every home. In the remaining nations of the world there is the greatest concentration of population and many people groups beyond the reach of an effective Christian witness. There are very few trained ministers there to reach them. The enemy is staging decisive battles in many of these nations, warring for the hearts, minds, and souls of men and women. Meanwhile, our spiritual forces are concentrated elsewhere.

COMMUNICATION:

Communication is very important in natural warfare. The troops must be able to communicate with their commander to receive instructions and encouragement. The enemy will try to sever communication between the front line troops and their leader, knowing this will result in failure on the battlefield.

In spiritual warfare, Satan wants to destroy your lines of communication. He will try to prevent you from praying and reading God's Word, as these provide instruction and encouragement for spiritual warfare. If you are so busy at war that you neglect communication with the Commander, you can be easily defeated. Christian ministry is a legitimate means of fighting the enemy. But if you run out of spiritual power, it ceases to be effective. Your power on the front lines comes from communication with the battle Commander. You must constantly receive His instructions and encouragement through prayer and study of His Word.

TARGETS:

In warfare in the natural world there are two kinds of targets: Moving targets (such as a boat, airplane, tank, or troops) and stationary targets (such as a weapons depository, troop headquarters, etc.). The moving targets are the greatest threat in natural warfare because they are offensive. They are on the move to conquer territory.

In the spiritual world, Satan is most concerned about moving targets. He targets the man and woman who is aggressively moving into the battlefield of spiritual warfare to conquer enemy forces. Satan will attack stationary targets also (believers who are not engaged in offensive warfare). But remember, when you are on the move for God, you are a prime target for Satan. He wants to defeat your advances into his territory to claim the souls of captive men and women.

ATTACKS AND COUNTERATTACKS:

In natural warfare when one side attacks, the other side counterattacks. A counterattack is an attempt to stop enemy forces from advancing and to regain lost territory. Satan counterattacks every offensive move made by believers. When you decide to pray more, read the Word of God, or enter a ministry, he will immediately stage a counterattack to prevent you from advancing. If you are aware of this strategy of counterattack you will be prepared and not caught off guard. In military terms, there are basically three forms of attack. Similar attacks are launched by the enemy in the spiritual world.

1. A frontal attack: These are direct, frontal attacks. The temptations of Satan are like a straight forward frontal assaults in the natural world. These direct spiritual assaults should be met by resisting Satan which causes him to flee.

2. A siege or blockade: A siege or blockade in the natural world is when the enemy takes control of territory not belonging to him. Spiritual bondage is similar to a siege or blockade in the natural world. The enemy breaks through your spiritual walls and part of your life is brought under his control. He does not actually possess the area, but he prevents you from functioning properly for God's glory. The way to deal with spiritual siege or blockade is by using the powers of binding and loosing learned in this course. The enemy should be bound and the area of life under his control loosed from his power.

3. Invasion and occupation: When an enemy invades in the natural world, he occupies and controls a territory. This is similar to demonic possession in the spirit world. The unsaved or backslidden person is under the control of an evil spirit which has entered to possess them. The way to deal with this type of attack is to bind the enemy and cast him out.

MOBILITY:

In order to be effective in natural warfare, an army must be mobile. The forces must be able to move to the place where offensive action is to be taken. If they are trapped and held immobile by the enemy, they are ineffective.

Mobility is a requirement in the spiritual world if you are to carry out the orders to "go into all the world and preach the Gospel." Are you a Christian soldier that has been immobilized by the enemy or are you actively pursuing the command to advance with the Gospel message?

A soldier does not put on armor and take up his weapons just to sit comfortably at home in front of a fire. He not only prepares for battle, he goes to the battlefield. Some Christian soldiers prepare for battle, but never leave the security of their home or church fellowship to go to the battlefield. The war is going on in the streets of our cities. It is going on in villages yet unreached with the Gospel message. No matter how prepared we are spiritually, we will never win the battle unless we are mobile for the Lord Jesus Christ.

A soldier does not gain skills as a warrior by just studying the books on warfare. He advances in skill through experience on the battlefield. Study of your spiritual warfare manual (the Bible) is important, but the battle will never be won unless you put what you have studied into practice. Skill in spiritual warfare comes through experience and application, just as it does in the natural world.

COOPERATION:

War is a team effort. Soldiers must cooperate with one another in their effort to defeat the enemy. They must come under the direction of one commander. They move forward as a united front. They do not fight in their own name, but on behalf and in the name of their country. Believers must learn to cooperate in the arena of spiritual warfare. Instead of fighting each other, we need to concentrate our attack against the enemy.

In the natural world when a soldier is wounded, his friends make every effort to rescue him. When the troops move forward, they move as a unit. They do not leave the weak behind, but place them in the center with strong warriors ahead and behind until the weak have recovered from their wounds.

The Christian army tends to shoot its own wounded. When a believer falls in battle we gossip about him or give up on him. Instead, we should rescue these spiritually wounded and surround them with our strength. The forces of God should move ahead as one united front, not as a straggling group trailed by wounded warriors who fall and die by the wayside.

We are not fighting in our own name. We are fighting in the name of the Lord Jesus Christ. We are not fighting in our own behalf. We are fighting on behalf of our spiritual nation, the Kingdom of God.

OBEDIENCE:

A soldier on the battlefield in the natural world does not do as he pleases. He follows orders from the commander. Total obedience is required. There is nothing in war of greater importance than obedience. The same is true in the spiritual realm. If you are to be effective in spiritual warfare, you must follow the instructions of your Commander. You must be in total obedience to Him.

COURAGE:

A great general in the natural world once said, "If you are afraid of being shot at, you are whipped before you start...Fear kills more people than death." Do not fear failure in spiritual warfare. If you are afraid of being shot at by the enemy, you are defeated before you start.

The brave general also said, "There can never be defeat if man refuses to accept defeat. Wars are lost in the mind before they are lost on the ground. No nation was ever defeated until the people accepted defeat."

As in the natural world, there can never be defeat if you refuse to accept it. Spiritual battles are lost in the mind first. Refuse to accept defeat in your mind.

CONQUERING THE LEADERSHIP:

One important general frequently expressed his personal wish that he could fight the highest enemy leader and the victor of the personal fight would settle the war. This has already been done in the spiritual realm by our Commander. Through His death and resurrection, Jesus conquered the power of the enemy. The final outcome of the war is already revealed in God's Word. But the rebel forces of resistance are still in the land. Jesus conquered the leadership, but to us is given the task of overcoming these pockets of resistance.

COMMITMENT:

In speaking about commitment, a famous general said:

> "We are lucky people. We are at war! We have a chance to fight and die for something. Many people never get that chance. Think of all those poor people you know that have lived and died for nothing...Total lives spent doing nothing but eating, sleeping, and going to work..."

As believers, we are at war in the spirit world. We have an opportunity to fight and die for something. We do not have to spend our lives in routine monotony of eating, sleeping, and working. We fight for a Kingdom to which there will be no end. We fight for a Commander who has already conquered the enemy forces. Our victory is assured. We have something worth living for, fighting for, and if called upon to do so, worth dying for.

INSPECTION

1. Write the Key Verse from the Articles Of War.

   _____

   _____

   _____

2. Why is the example of warfare used to describe the conflict between the spiritual forces of good and evil?

   _____

3. Summarize what you learned in this chapter regarding natural warfare principles which are applicable to spiritual warfare.

   The definition of war.
   A wartime lifestyle.
   The objective of war.
   Basic Training.
   Propaganda.
   Diplomatic proposals.
   Intelligence.
   Offensive and defensive warfare.
   Weapons.
   Surprise attacks.
   Decisive battles.
   Communication.
   Targets.
   Attacks and counterattacks.
   Mobility.
   Cooperation.
   Obedience.
   Courage.
   Conquering the leadership.
   Commitment.

(Answers to tests are provided at the conclusion of the final chapter in this manual.)

TACTICAL MANEUVERS

1. To learn more about objectives of warfare in the spiritual world, read Matthew 28:18-20, Mark 16:15-18; Acts 1:8; Ephesians 3:9-11 and Colossians 1:24-29. Find the answer to these questions:

    Who has assigned our objectives?

    _____

    What are the objectives assigned to us as a local church fellowship?

    _____

    _____

    What are the objectives assigned to you personally?

    _____

    _____

2. It is not enough to learn natural principles of warfare parallel to those in the spiritual world. You must apply these principles in your own spiritual battles. Knowledge without application of that knowledge is ineffective. Review what you learned in this chapter, then write a paragraph summarizing how you plan to apply what you have learned about natural principles to your spiritual battles.

    _____

    _____

    _____

INVASION

ENTERING THE COMBAT ZONE...

During an invasion in the natural world, an army enters the combat zone to conquer its foes and claim territory. Basic training is useless unless what is learned is put into action. Even a mobilized army equipped with weapons is not effective if it stands inactive on the sidelines. To be effective in warfare, you must actually enter the combat zone.

CHAPTER FOURTEEN
ENTERING THE COMBAT ZONE:
BATTLING THE WORLD, THE FLESH, AND THE DEVIL

OBJECTIVES:

Upon completion of this chapter you will be able to:

- Write the Key Verses from memory.
- Define the word "strategy."
- Define the word "counterstrategy."
- Explain the strategies of Satan which combine the evil forces of the world and the flesh.
- Identify spiritual counterstrategies for victory over the world and the flesh.

KEY VERSES FROM THE ARTICLES OF WAR:

> **Knowing this, that our old man is crucified with Him, that the body of sin might be destroyed, that henceforth we should not serve sin. For he that is dead is freed from sin. (Romans 6:6-7)**

INTRODUCTION

You have answered the call to arms and been inducted in God's army. You have studied about enemy strategy and territory. You learned about God's battle plan and been armed with defensive and offensive weapons. With this lesson, you actually enter the combat zone and begin to fight!

This chapter is the first in a series which focus on Satan's strategies and Scriptural counterstrategies for overcoming his deceptive tactics. "Strategies" are the science of forming and carrying out military operations. They are the methods or plans which lead to victory.

SATAN'S STRATEGIES:

Satan has organized methods aimed at gaining victory over believers. This is what Paul means when he refers to the "wiles" of the Devil:

> **Put on the whole armor of God, that ye may be able to stand against the wiles of the Devil. (Ephesians 6:11)**

The word "wiles" means crafty or deceitful. Satan's "wiles" are his crafty, deceitful strategies of attack.

GOD'S COUNTERSTRATEGIES:

The believer is not left defenseless in the face of enemy attack. In His written Word God has provided a manual of strategies for spiritual warfare:

> **Lest Satan should get an advantage of us: for we are not ignorant of his devices. (II Corinthians 2:11)**

The word "devices" means thoughts or purposes. The Bible contains counterstrategies for overcoming all the power of the enemy.

The word "counter" means "to act in opposition to, to hinder, defeat, or frustrate." In the spirit world, a counterstrategy is an organized plan and method of opposition to Satan. It is designed to hinder, defeat, and frustrate his "wiles" and "devices."

The next few chapters are organized by strategies and counterstrategies. The strategies of Satan in specific areas of spiritual warfare are discussed first in each chapter. Specific spiritual counterstrategies for victory are then presented. In this lesson you will study how the world and the flesh function together in spiritual warfare and counterstrategies for overcoming these evil forces.

STRATEGIES OF SATAN:
THE WORLD AND THE FLESH

You learned in Chapter Seven that the world and the flesh are enemy territory:

SATAN WORKS THROUGH THE WORLD:

> **And we know that we are of God, and the whole world lieth in wickedness. (I John 5:19)**

Satan is the prince of this world and as its prince he influences the governments of nations. He is described as a "deceiver of nations" in Revelation 20:3 and 7. Daniel chapter 10 identifies a demonic power over the nation of Persia working to prevent Daniel's prayer.
Satan is as a roaring lion in the world:

> **Be sober, be vigilant; because your adversary the Devil, as a roaring lion, walketh about, seeking whom he may devour. (II Peter 5:8)**

The picture of a roaring lion illustrates the open terror tactics Satan uses. But Satan is also described as "an angel of light":

> **And no marvel for Satan himself is transformed into an angel of light. Therefore it is no great thing if his ministers also be transformed as the ministers of righteousness; whose end shall be according to their works. (II Corinthians 11:14-15)**

This describes Satan as alluring and appealing in a more subtle, secret type of attack. So Satan works both openly and secretly in the world.

Satan's activities are varied in the world, but they are always directed against God, His plan, and His people. Satan opposes God's work in the world. This is quite evident in his rebellion and fall from Heaven which you already studied (Ezekiel 28:12-19). Satan opposes the work of Jesus in the world. He is behind the "anti-Christ" spirit of the world:

> **For many deceivers are entered into the world, who confess not that Jesus Christ is come in the flesh. This is a deceiver and an antichrist. (II John 7)**

Satan also opposes the work of the Holy Spirit in the world. One of the purposes of the Holy Spirit is to guide men and women into the truth of the Word of God. Satan tries to keep the Word of God from influencing the hearts and lives of men and women:

> **In whom the god of this world hath blinded the minds of them which believe not, lest the light of the glorious gospel of Christ, who is the image of God, should shine unto them. (II Corinthians 4:4)**

Satan afflicts and tempts believers in the world:

> **For this cause, when I could no longer forbear, I sent to know your faith, lest by some means the tempter have tempted you, and our labor be in vain. (I Thessalonians 3:5)**

> **And the Lord said unto Satan, Behold, all that he hath is in thy power... (Job 1:12)**

Satan deceives the world through "spiritual wickedness in high places." This is how he works in the religious structure of the world. He deceives through false doctrine, ministers, teachers, apostles, and religions.

Satan also wages warfare against believers who are in, but not of, the world. You can read about this warfare in Ephesians 6:10-18. Satan accuses and slanders believers:

> **And the great dragon was cast out, that old serpent, called the Devil, and Satan, which deceiveth the whole world: he was cast out into the earth, and his angels were cast out with him.**
>
> **And I heard a loud voice saying in Heaven, Now is come salvation, and strength, and the Kingdom of our God, and the power of His Christ; for**

the accuser of our brethren is cast down, which accused them before our God day and night. (Revelation 12:9-10)

He plants doubt in the minds of believers. This was part of the first temptation of man in the Garden of Eden (see Genesis 3:1-5).

Satan incites persecution of believers by the world:

Fear none of those things which thou shalt suffer: behold, the devil shall cast some of you into prison, that ye may be tried... (Revelation 2:10)

Satan tries to prevent the believer from effective Christian service:

Wherefore we would have come unto you, even I Paul, once and again; but Satan hindered us. (I Thessalonians 2:18)

Satan uses the appeal of the world to entice believers to sin. He tempts through the worldly atmosphere, environment, and system around you. He encourages a love of the world in your heart:

Love not the world, neither the things that are in the world. If any man love the world, the love of the Father is not in him.

For all that is in the world, the lust of the flesh, and the lust of the eyes, and the pride of life, is not of the Father, but is of the world. (I John 2:15-16)

Satan wars against the mind, the tongue, the spirit, the body, and the spiritual walls of believers. He attacks through family and associates, finances, and circumstances. You will learn more about each of these specific areas of attack in other chapters.

The names of Satan also reveal his strategies in the world. You studied the names of Satan in Chapter Five of this course. Review these and think about how each name reflects strategies of Satan in the world today.

SATAN WORKS THROUGH THE FLESH:

The body, soul, and spirit of man are closely related. Because of this, Satan accesses the soul and spirit through the flesh. This strategy is evident in the first temptation of man. Eve "SAW the tree was good for food (TASTE), and that it was pleasant to the eyes, and a tree to be DESIRED to make one wise" she took of it and gave it to her husband also (Genesis 3:6). Satan used fleshly senses and desires to gain access to Eve's soul and spirit.

If Satan cannot "blind your mind" and keep you from accepting the truth of the Gospel, then he tries to keep you in bondage to the flesh after you receive the Gospel. Fleshly lusts war against the soul:

> **...Abstain from fleshly lusts which war against the soul. (I Peter 2:11)**

Satan uses the flesh to affect the mind:

> **But I see another law in my members, warring against the law of my mind, and bringing me into captivity to the law of sin which is in my members. (Romans 7:23)**

"My members" refers to the flesh. Satan uses the flesh to affect the spirit:

> **Having therefore these promises, dearly beloved, let us cleanse ourselves from all filthiness of the flesh and spirit, perfecting holiness in the fear of God. (II Corinthians 7:1)**

Satan uses the flesh to cause you to reap corruption (rottenness, perversion) in your life:

> **For he that soweth to his flesh shall of the flesh reap corruption... (Galatians 6:8)**

In Ephesians 4 where Paul deals with the sins of the flesh in the context of the old man and the new man, he inserts this warning:

> **Neither give place to the Devil. (Ephesians 4:27)**

This warning indicates that when you commit these fleshly sins, you give place (literally a claim) to Satan in your life. Continued willful indulgence in fleshly sins can result in bondage to Satan:

> **And that they may recover themselves out of the snare of the Devil, who are taken captive by him at his will. (II Timothy 2:26)**

SATAN WORKS THROUGH DEMONS:

As you will learn later in this course, a born-again believer cannot be "possessed" by Satan as long as he remains a true believer. Possession by Satan involves control of body, soul, spirit, conduct, and thought. But if a believer continues to practice fleshly sins there comes a time where the practice may move from a sin of the flesh to a sin controlled by Satanic, demonic activity.

HOW THEY WORK TOGETHER

The world, the flesh, and the Devil with his demons combine their evil forces to war against believers. Each force can operate independently against the believer, but these forces of evil are most often combined in their attack upon believers. Satan uses the world, with its illusions, charms, philosophies, and ungodly systems, to gain access to the flesh. He uses the flesh to gain access to the soul mind, and spirit. Then he tries to conform you to the world rather than to God.

SPIRITUAL COUNTERSTRATEGIES: OVERCOMING THE FLESH

The world, the flesh, and the Devil certainly create a threatening combat zone! But here are some powerful scriptural counterstrategies for overcoming these forces:

PRESENT YOUR BODY AS A SACRIFICE:

In the military forces of the natural world, a man who enlists for service comes under the complete control of his superiors. They give him instructions on how to conduct himself, how to dress, and how to combat the enemy. To be effective in spiritual warfare the same type of control must be put into action:

> **I beseech you therefore, brethren, by the mercies of God, that ye present your bodies a living sacrifice, holy, acceptable unto God, which is your reasonable service.**
>
> **And be not conformed to this world, but be ye transformed by the renewing of your mind, that ye may prove what is that good and acceptable, and perfect, will of God. (Romans 12:1-2)**

You must present yourself to God as an act of your own will. In the Old Testament when a sacrifice was given to God, the person who offered it had no further control over it. It was given totally to the Lord. Instead of conforming to the world and the flesh, you must be transformed (changed) by the renewing of your mind. You will study more about the battle in the mind in Chapter Fifteen.

ARM YOURSELF WITH THE MIND OF CHRIST:

The renewing of your mind is done by "arming" yourself with the same mind as Jesus.

> **Forasmuch then as Christ hath suffered for us in the flesh, arm yourselves likewise with the same mind: for He that hath suffered in the flesh hath ceased from sin;**
>
> **That he no longer should live the rest of his time in the flesh, to the lusts of men, but to the will of God. (I Peter 4:1-2)**

DEVELOP THE PROPER ATTITUDE TOWARDS YOUR FLESH:

We are told that we should "hate even the garment spotted by the flesh" (Jude 23). You should understand that the lust of the flesh is not of the Father but of the world:

> **For all that is in the world, the lust of the flesh, and the lust of the eyes, and the pride of life, is not of the Father, but is of the world. (I John 2:16)**

You should have no confidence in the flesh:

> **...and have no confidence in the flesh...(Philippians 3:3)**

You must understand that life in the flesh brings corruption, while life in the spirit brings life:

> **For he that soweth to his flesh shall of the flesh reap corruption; but he that soweth to the spirit shall of the Spirit reap life everlasting. (Galatians 6:8)**

REALIZE YOU DO NOT HAVE TO BE IN BONDAGE TO THE FLESH:

In times past, you were in bondage to the flesh when you were a sinner:

> **Among whom also we all had our conversation in times past in the lusts of our flesh, fulfilling the desires of the flesh and of the mind; and were by nature the children of wrath even as others. (Ephesians 2:3)**

> **For when we were in the flesh, the motions of sins, which were by the law, did work in our members to bring forth fruit unto death.**

> **But now we are delivered from the law, that being dead wherein we were held; that we should serve in newness of spirit, and not in the oldness of the letter. (Romans 7:5-6)**

Study Ephesians chapter 2 and Romans 8. You will discover you no longer have to be in bondage to the flesh. Your freedom comes through Jesus Christ:

> **For the law of the Spirit of life in Christ Jesus hath made me free from the law of sin and death. (Romans 8:2)**

TRAIN YOUR FLESH TO OBEY:

In the military world, the soldier must obey all orders. He goes through basic training to learn the rules of warfare. He is given trial situations where he must put these strategies into action and he learns through failure and success. He is in training for war.

This is also true in the spiritual world. You must train your flesh to obey. You must learn God's rules. Through trials God permits in your life you will have opportunity to put these rules into action:

> **Beloved, think it not strange concerning the fiery trial which is to try you, as though some strange thing happened unto you. (I Peter 4:12)**

> **And the Lord said unto Satan, Behold all that he hath is in thy power... (Job 1:12)**

In the natural world, a soldier learns the right and wrong responses in military strategy through repeated troop exercises. You can train through study of your warfare manual, the Bible. As you exercise or train your spiritual senses, you will learn to discern between good and evil:

> **For every one that useth milk is unskillful in the word of righteousness: for he is a babe.**
>
> **For strong meat belongeth to them that are of full age, even those who by reason of use have their senses exercised to discern both good and evil. (Hebrews 5:13-14)**

You must train your flesh to obey God's Word. You do not conquer your flesh by giving in to it. As God reveals fleshly areas of your life, you must take action:

> **...abstain from fleshly lusts, which war against the soul. (I Peter 2:11) Having therefore these promises, dearly beloved, let us cleanse ourselves from all filthiness of the flesh and spirit, perfecting holiness in the fear of God. (II Corinthians 7:1)**
>
> **But put ye on the Lord Jesus Christ and make not provision for the flesh, to fulfill the lusts thereof. (Romans 13:14)**

Note that YOU must take action. YOU must abstain from fleshly lusts. YOU must cleanse yourself of filthiness of the flesh. YOU must not make provisions for the flesh.

PUT OFF THE OLD MAN:

The "old man" refers to the flesh nature. Paul writes:

> **That ye put off concerning the former conversation the old man, which is corrupt according to the deceitful lusts; And be renewed in the spirit of your mind;**
>
> **And that ye put on the new man, which after God is created in righteousness and true holiness. (Ephesians 4:22-24)**

PUT YOUR FLESH TO DEATH:

The flesh must be crucified. It will not die a natural death. You must crucify it by refusing to be controlled by it:

> **Knowing this, that our old man is crucified with Him, that the body of sin might be destroyed, that henceforth we should not serve sin. For he that is dead is freed from sin. (Romans 6:6-7)**
>
> **For I am crucified with Christ; nevertheless I live; yet not I, but Christ liveth in me; and the life which I now live in the flesh I live by the faith of the Son of God, who loved me, and gave Himself for me. (Galatians 2:20)**

> **And they that are Christ's have crucified the flesh with the affections and lusts. (Galatians 5:24)**

WALK IN THE SPIRIT:

Your daily walk (how you live) can be controlled by Satan working through your flesh, the world, or demon powers if you permit it. You do not have to be controlled by the world, the flesh, or the Devil. You can learn to walk in the Spirit:

> **This I say then, Walk in the Spirit, and ye shall not fulfill the lust of the flesh. (Galatians 5:16)**

> **If we live in the Spirit, let us also walk in the Spirit. (Galatians 5:25)**

To walk in the Spirit means to let God's Holy Spirit control your conduct and life. The flesh is not more powerful than the spirit. If you let the Holy Spirit manifest His power in you, He will quicken your mortal body of flesh. To "quicken" means to endue with life.

You do not have to live in the death of sin. God can quicken your spirit to new life:

> **And if Christ be in you, the body is dead because of sin; but the Spirit is life because of righteousness.**
>
> **But if the Spirit of Him that raised up Jesus from the dead dwell in you, He that raised up Christ from the dead shall also quicken your mortal bodies by His Spirit that dwelleth in you.**
>
> **Therefore, brethren, we are debtors, not to the flesh, to live after the flesh. For if ye live after the flesh, ye shall die: but if ye through the Spirit do mortify the deeds of the body, ye shall live.**
>
> **For as many as are led by the Spirit of God, they are the sons of God. (Romans 8:10-14)**

To be led by the Spirit you must have the Holy Spirit within you. You must be born again by the Spirit:

> **That which is born of the flesh is flesh; and that which is born of the Spirit is spirit.**
>
> **Marvel not that I said unto thee, Ye must be born again. (John 3:6-7)**

You must also be filled with the Holy Spirit. It is the Holy Spirit who gives you power to walk in the spirit rather than the flesh. An entire Harvestime International Institute course is devoted to the Ministry of the Holy Spirit in the life of the believer. If you are studying the Institute courses in suggested order, this is the next course you will take when you complete this manual. We cannot emphasize enough the importance of the Holy Spirit in overcoming the world, the flesh, and the Devil. Through the Holy Spirit you can be led by the Spirit instead of the flesh.

LET YOUR SPIRIT SPEAK BY THE HOLY SPIRIT:

God communicates to your spirit by the Holy Spirit:

> **For as many as are led by the Spirit of God, they are the sons of God. (Romans 8:14)**

The Holy Spirit can also communicate directly to God from your spirit:

> **For he that speaketh in an unknown tongue speaketh not unto men, but unto God: for no man understandeth him; howbeit in the spirit he speaketh mysteries. (I Corinthians 14:2)**

When you speak in the unknown language, which is the physical evidence of the baptism of the Holy Spirit (Acts 2), your spirit is communicating directly to God. When this happens, one of the important functions of the Holy Spirit is to pray according to the will of God:

> **Likewise the Spirit also helpeth our infirmities; for we know not what we should pray for as we ought: but the Spirit itself maketh intercession for us with groanings which cannot be uttered.**
>
> **And he that searcheth the hearts knoweth what is in the mind of the Spirit, because He maketh intercession for the saints according to the will of God. (Romans 8:26-27)**

DEVELOP THE FRUIT OF THE HOLY SPIRIT:

In contrast to the works of the flesh, develop the fruit of the Holy Spirit. This includes...

> **...love, joy, peace, longsuffering, gentleness, goodness, faith. Meekness, temperance... (Galatians 5:22-23)**

The fruit of the Holy Spirit is discussed in detail in the Harvestime International Institute course "Ministry Of The Holy Spirit."

DO NOT LIVE IN CONDEMNATION:

Satan uses the weaknesses of the flesh to make you live in condemnation. But Paul said:

> **There is therefore now no condemnation to them which are in Christ Jesus, who walk not after the flesh, but after the Spirit. (Romans 8:1)**

If you fail and engage in fleshly conduct, do not remain in condemnation. Repent and ask forgiveness:

If we confess our sins, He is faithful and just to forgive us our sins and to cleanse us from all unrighteousness. (I John 1:9)

SPIRITUAL COUNTERSTRATEGIES: OVERCOMING THE WORLD

Here are some guidelines for overcoming the world:

DEVELOP A PROPER ATTITUDE TOWARD THE WORLD:

Recognize you are not of the world:

> **I have given them thy word: and the world hath hated them, because they are not of the world, even as I am not of the world.**
>
> **I pray not that thou shouldest take them out of the world, but that thou shouldest keep them from the evil.**
>
> **They are not of the world, even as I am not of the world. (John 17:14-16)**
>
> **If the world hate you, ye know that it hated me before it hated you. If ye were of the world, the world would love his own: but because ye are not of the world, but I have chosen you out of the world, therefore the world hateth you. (John 15:18-19)**

Understand that you will experience tribulation in the world:

> **These things I have spoken unto you, that in Me ye might have peace. In the world ye shall have tribulation: but be of good cheer; I have overcome the world. (John 16:33)**

Realize that gaining the world is not worth losing your soul:

> **For what shall it profit a man, if he shall gain the whole world, and lose his own soul. (Mark 8:36)**
>
> **For what is a man advantaged, if he gain the whole world, and lose himself, or be cast away? (Luke 9:25)**

Realize that if you love the world, you are an enemy of God:

> **Love not the world, neither the things that are in the world. If any man love the world, the love of the Father is not in him.**
>
> **For all that is in the world, the lust of the flesh, and the lust of the eyes, and the pride of life, is not of the Father, but is of the world. (I John 2:15-16)**

> **...know ye not that the friendship of the world is enmity with God? Whosoever therefore will be a friend of the world is the enemy of God. (James 4:4)**

Recognize the temporal nature of the world:

> **And the world passeth away, and the lust thereof: But he that doeth the will of God abideth forever. (I John 2:17)**

> **...for the fashion of this world passeth away. (I Corinthians 7:31)**

> **Seeing then that all these things shall be dissolved, what manner of persons ought ye to be in all holy conversation and godliness. (II Peter 3:11)**

RECOGNIZE YOU ARE NOT IN BONDAGE TO THE WORLD:

As a believer, you do not have to be in bondage to the world system. Although in the past you were governed by the present world (Ephesians 2:2), you are no longer in this bondage:

> **Wherein in times past ye walked according to the course of this world, according to the prince of the power of the air, the spirit that now worketh in the children of disobedience:**

> **Among whom also we had our conversation in times past in the lusts of our flesh, fulfilling the desires of the flesh and of the mind: and were by nature the children of wrath, even as others.**

> **But now in Christ Jesus ye who sometimes were far off are made nigh by the blood of Christ.**

> **Now therefore ye are no more strangers and foreigners, but fellow citizens with the saints, and of the household of God. (Ephesians 2:2-3,13,19)**

Romans 12:1-3 teaches that you no longer need be conformed to the world. You can be transformed (changed). You are part of a new kingdom now. You are a resident of the Kingdom of God. You are no longer under the power of the world:

> **Now we have received not the spirit of the world, but the spirit which is of God. (I Corinthians 2:12)**

Study more about your liberty in Galatians 4:1-7.

GUARD AGAINST THE WORLD:

Now that you are free from the world, set a guard against its influence in your life. Do not pattern your life after the rudiments or basic principles of the world:

> **Beware lest any man spoil you...after the rudiments of the world, and not after Christ. (Colossians 2:8)**

Do not love the world:

> **Love not the world, neither the things that are in the world... (I John 2:15)**

Do not let yourself be spoiled by the philosophies of the world:

> **Beware lest any man spoil you through philosophy and vain deceit, after the tradition of men, after the rudiments of the world, and not after Christ. (Colossians 2:8)**

Deny worldly lusts:

> **Teaching us that denying ungodliness and worldly lusts, we should live soberly, righteously, and godly, in this present world. (Titus 2:12)**

Keep yourself unspotted from the world:

> **Pure religion and undefiled before God and the Father is this...to keep himself unspotted from the world. (James 1:27)**

Crucify the power of the world:

> **But God forbid that I should glory, save in the cross of our Lord Jesus Christ, by whom the world is crucified unto me and I unto the world. (Galatians 6:14)**

Crucifixion is an unnatural death. Like the flesh, the power of the world in your life will not die a natural death. You must forcibly crucify it.

RECOGNIZE YOU CAN OVERCOME THE WORLD:

You are not to be overcome by the world. Do not let the cares of the world destroy the work of the Word in your life (Matthew 13:22; Mark 4:19). This "wearing away" with the cares of the world is one of the strategies of the antichrist spirit (Daniel 7:25). Jesus said:

> **...but be of good cheer, I have overcome the world. (John 16:33)**

You can overcome the world because Jesus dwells within you:

> **Ye are of God, little children, and have overcome them: because greater is He that is in you, than He that is in the world. (I John 4:4)**

You can escape the corruption of the world:

> **Whereby are given unto us exceeding great and precious promises: that by these ye might be partakers of the divine nature, having escaped the corruption that is in the world through lust. (II Peter 1:4)**

You overcome the world by the new birth and your faith:

> **For whatsoever is born of God overcometh the world: and this is the victory that overcometh the world, even our faith. (I John 5:4)**

You overcome the world by the blood of Jesus and your testimony:
> **And they overcame him by the blood of the Lamb, and by the word of their testimony... (Revelation 12:11)**

UNDERSTAND YOUR MISSION IN THE WORLD:

You are not to be affected by the world, but you are to affect the world. The believer should be a light in a world of darkness, reflecting the glory of God and sharing the good news of the Gospel:

> **Ye are the light of the world... (Matthew 5:14)**

The impact of the early believers on the world was so great that it was said of them that they "turned the world upside down" (Acts 17:6).

As soldiers in an army sent on a mission in a foreign nation, believers are on a special mission of God in the world. They have been instructed:

> **...Go ye into all the world, and preach the Gospel to every creature. (Mark 16:15)**

INSPECTION

1. Write the Key Verses from the Articles Of War.

   _____

   _____

   _____

2. Define the word "strategy".

   _____

   _____

   _____

3. Define the word "counterstrategy".

   _____

   _____

   _____

4. Summarize what you have learned about Satan's strategies in the world and the flesh.

   _____

   _____

   _____

5. Summarize the counterstrategies given in this chapter for overcoming the world, the flesh, and the Devil.

   _____

   _____

   _____

(Answers to tests are provided at the conclusion of the final chapter in this manual.)

TACTICAL MANEUVERS

1. Crucifixion was one of the worst possible forms of death. Read about the crucifixion of Jesus in Matthew 27. This is what must be done spiritually speaking to both the world and the flesh, spiritual forces of evil which are operating against believers.

2. Examine your own life and ministry. In what areas do you see the affects of the world? The flesh? The Devil? How can you apply what you have learned in this lesson to these problem areas?

3. Study Daniel 7:25. The wearing away of the cares of the world is one of the main tactics of the antichrist. These are the small situations that are tiring and irritating upon which Satan builds one after another, until you are overcome and entangled in earthly rather than spiritual things. Is this happening in your life? Remember, effective warriors do not entangle themselves with the things of the world. Think and pray about how you can become less involved in the cares of the world.

4. The Bible describes the Christian life as:

    -A conquering life: Romans 8:37
    -A victorious life: I Corinthians 15:57
    -An abundant life: John 10:10
    -A triumphant life: II Corinthians 2:14
    -A holy life: Ephesians 1:3-5; 5:25-27; I Peter 1:13-16

    These are the ideals by which you must continually evaluate your Christian walk. The Bible records Paul's personal struggles in this area (Philippians 3:12-17; James 1:2-4; Hebrews 12:10- 16).

    Always remember that a Christian is still a believer even if he is struggling with a problem with sin (I Corinthians 5:1-5; 11:30-32; I John 2:1-2); the world (II Timothy
    4:10); or demonic influences (Acts 5:1-10; I Timothy 5:9-15; 3:6-7).

5. In Ephesians 4:22 and 24 Paul speaks of the old man which must be put off, and the new man which should be put on. Read Ephesians 4:22-6:18. Make a list of things that should be "put off." List things that should be "put on," ie., attitudes, conduct, etc.

Things To Put Off   **Things To Put On**

CHAPTER FIFTEEN
THE BATTLE IN THE MIND

OBJECTIVES:

Upon completion of this chapter you will be able to:

- Write the Key Verses from memory.
- Identify the main battleground of spiritual warfare.
- Explain what is meant by the "fiery darts" of Satan.
- Recognize mental strategies used by Satan to attack the mind.
- Use spiritual counter strategies to quench these "fiery darts" of Satan.

KEY VERSES FROM THE ARTICLES OF WAR:

> **For though we walk in the flesh, we do not war after the flesh:**
> **For the weapons of our warfare are not carnal, but mighty through God**
> **to the pulling down of strong holds;**
>
> **Casting down imaginations, and every high thing that exalteth itself**
> **against the knowledge of God, and bringing into captivity every thought**
> **to the obedience of Christ. (II Corinthians 10:3-5)**

INTRODUCTION

When Paul warned the Corinthians not to be ignorant of the Devil's "wiles," the Greek word for wiles means "schemes" and is from the same word used for "mind." In other words, Satan's primary assaults occur in our thought life. The mind is the main battlefield in spiritual warfare. Every attack of Satan involves the human mind.

This chapter focuses on the battle for the mind. It discusses the strategies of Satan and gives spiritual counter strategies for victory over his attacks. The battle for the mind is easily summarized:

> **For to be carnally minded is death; but to be spiritually minded is life**
> **and peace.**
>
> **Because the carnal mind is enmity against God: for it is not subject to**
> **the law of God, neither indeed can be. (Romans 8:6-7)**

Satan wants to make your mind carnal (sinful, worldly, fleshly). God wants you to be spiritually minded.

WHY SATAN ATTACKS THE MIND

The greatest commandment includes loving God with all your mind. This is one of the main reasons why Satan battles for your mind:

Jesus said unto him, Thou shalt love the Lord thy God with all thy heart, and with all thy soul, and with all thy MIND; This is the first and great commandment. (Matthew 22:37-38)

Satan battles for your mind because it is closely tied spiritually to your heart and mouth:

But those things which proceed out of the mouth come forth from the heart; and they defile the man.

For out of the heart proceed evil thoughts...(Matthew 15:18-19)

Satan battles for the mind because the way you think affects the way you act:

For as he thinketh in his heart, so is he...(Proverbs 23:7)

Satan knows if he can control your mind, he can control your body, your actions, and, if left unchallenged, your spirit.

FIERY DARTS FROM THE ENEMY

In Old Testament times, fiery darts were used as weapons of warfare. They were hollow reeds filled with material which would burn easily. They were set on fire and then shot from bows. They were excellent weapons against the walled cities of the time because they could be shot over the walls to ignite the thatched roofs of the houses within.

In Ephesians 6:11-17 Paul discusses the spiritual battle with Satan. He speaks of "the fiery darts of the wicked." The enemy continuously hurls "fiery darts" at you in the spirit world. Most of these "darts" are aimed at the mind.

The Apostle Paul warns that you should not be "soon shaken in mind" (II Thessalonians 2:2). In the Greek translation, "shake" means to "agitate, disturb, topple, (by implied) to destroy." If you can take hold of something and shake it, you have control over it. Satan wants to "shake" or exert control over your mind.

SATAN'S STRATEGY:
BATTLES IN THE MIND

The mind is one of the most complex and least understood parts of the human body. Because it is so complex, Satan has many subtle methods of attacking the mind. Though it would be impossible to list them all, the following list summarizes the main strategies of attack Satan uses in the battle for the mind:

QUESTIONING THE AUTHORITY OF GOD:

The first temptation of man started in the mind. It started with this strategy: Questioning the authority of God. Satan said to Eve, "Yea, hath God said?..." Did God really say that you could not eat of the tree of knowledge of good and evil? Questioning God and His Word leads to doubt, unbelief, and skepticism.

DECEPTION AND SEDUCTION:

Deception was also part of the enemy's strategy. When Satan confronted Eve, he was disguised as a beautiful serpent. Satan uses lies, cults, and "religious spirits" to deceive millions in our world today. Some of the deceptions Satan advances include the following appeals:

- "You can become a god."
- "You can know the future."
- "You future, including eternity, is predestined. There is nothing you can do about it."
- "Everyone is a child of God."
- "There are more ways to Heaven than by Jesus."
- "God is too good to send anyone to Hell."
- "All God expects you to do is live a good life and do the best you can."
- "The Bible should not be taken literally."
- "The Bible contains many errors."

Seducing spirits of Satan attack the mind to distort the truth of God's Word:

Now the Spirit speaketh expressly, that in the latter times some shall depart from the faith, giving heed to seducing spirits and doctrines of devils. (I Timothy 4:1)

Satan used this attack on Jesus in Luke 4:9-12. He tried to get Jesus to throw himself off a high point of the temple since God had promised to...

...give His angels charge over thee, to keep thee, And in their hands they shall bear thee up...(Luke 4:10-11)

THE FLESH:

You previously studied about the flesh as a spiritual force of evil. Satan uses the flesh to war against the mind:

But I see another law in my members, warring against the law of my mind, and bringing me into captivity to the law of sin which is in my members. (Romans 7:23)

Satan uses your own mouth, your eyes, ears, and even your senses of touch and smell to foster wicked thoughts in your mind.

BLINDING MINDS OF UNBELIEVERS:

Satan works in the minds of unbelievers to blind them to the truth of the Gospel:

> **In whom the god of this world hath blinded the minds of them which believe not, lest the light of the glorious gospel of Christ, who is the image of God, should shine unto them. (II Corinthians 4:4)**

DEPRESSION:

To be depressed is to be downcast, sad, discouraged, or in low spirit. It includes feelings of despair, despondency, and dejection. Depression can lead to suicidal thoughts or actual suicide because of the hopeless feelings which produces uncontrollable mental grief, sorrow, heartache, and crying.

Sometimes Satan uses circumstances of life to lead to depression. For examples, a great loss or fear of loss, suppressed anger, a low self concept, unfulfilled expectations, and a negative attitude can all be used to cause depression. In Proverbs 24:10 we are warned about "fainting in the day of adversity" (troubled or distressed circumstances).

Sometimes depression is caused by the negative attitudes of those around us through which Satan works. In Deuteronomy 1:28 God's people admitted, "our brethren have discouraged our hearts."

We read in Numbers 21:4 that the soul of God's people was much discouraged. King David often reflected discouragement in his Psalms (see Psalms 69 for an example). The Apostle Paul also had times of deep depression:

> **For we would not, brethren, have you ignorant of our trouble which came to us in Asia, that we were pressed out of measure, above strength, insomuch that we despaired even of life... (II Corinthians 1:8)**

If you do not conquer depression it can also lead to oppression by Satanic spirits. This is a deeper form of depression where Satan gains more restrictive power over the mind.

DISCOURAGEMENT:

Discouragement means to be "without courage." Satan wants to discourage you because if you are "without courage," you are ineffective in warfare.

WITHDRAWAL:

Another way Satan attacks the mind is through withdrawal. The purpose of this strategy is to isolate you from the rest of the Body of Christ. Since believers function together in ministry as a body, withdrawal makes you non-functional. Examples of men of God who were attacked mentally by Satan and withdrew are Elijah (I Kings 19) and Jonah (Jonah 4:5-11).

IMPROPER MOTIVES:

A motive is your reason for doing something. Motives are important because although man looks on the outward appearance (actions), God looks on the heart:

> **But the Lord said unto Samuel, Look not on his countenance, or on the height of his stature; because I have refused him; for the Lord seeth not as man seeth; for man looketh on the outward appearance, but the Lord looketh on the heart. (I Samuel 16:7)**

But Jesus did not commit Himself unto them, because He knew all men.

> **And needed not that any should testify of man; for He knew what was in man. (John 2:24-25)**

Many people enter Christian ministry for the wrong reasons. God is more concerned with motive than ministry. This is where you should place your concern also, for when motives are proper then ministry will naturally follow. Your motives for ministry must be right:

> **Feed the flock of God which is among you, taking the oversight thereof, not by constraint, but willingly; not for filthy lucre, but of a ready mind; Neither as being lords over God's heritage, but being ensamples to the flock. (I Peter 5:2-3)**

You must enter the ministry willingly, not because of the advantages and benefits of the office, not as a dictator but as an example. Satan will try to create wrong motives for Christian service by putting them subtly in your mind. Satan causes wrong motives for desiring God's power. You can find an example of this in Acts 8:18-23 in the story of a man named Simon.

You can have vindictive motives for your actions. (Vindictive means that you want to get even with someone who has done you wrong or who you do not like). Biblical examples include the disciples wanting to call down fire from heaven (Luke 9:54) and Jonah wanting Ninevah destroyed (Jonah 4).

David also had a wrong motive in the numbering of the people:

> **Satan (an adversary) stood up against Israel, and stirred up David to number Israel. (I Chronicles 21:1 The Amplified Version)**

WRONG ATTITUDES AND EMOTIONS:

Satan causes wrong attitudes towards others. He inserts fiery darts of envy, jealousy, suspicion, unforgiveness, distrust, anger, hatred, intolerance, prejudice, competition, impatience, judging, criticism, covetousness, and selfishness.

He also tries to cause wrong attitudes of greed, discontent, pride, vanity, ego, importance, arrogance, intellectualism, and self-righteousness. Wrong attitudes lead to wrong emotions and both stem from your thoughts.

These attitudes and emotions render you ineffective in spiritual warfare. For example, James 4:6 indicates that "God resists the proud." When you are filled with pride, you are actually arrayed in battle against God.

REBELLION:

Satan also inserts rebellious thoughts into your mind. Rebellion is willful disobedience against God's authority. Rebellion includes self-will, stubbornness, and disobedience. Remember that rebellion was the original sin of Satan. His five statements of "I will" demonstrated his rebellion (Isaiah 14:12-14). The "I will" spirit is a way to recognize the operation of Satan through rebellion.

ACCUSATION AND CONDEMNATION:

Satan is called "the accuser of the brethren" (Revelation 12:10). He sends fiery darts of accusation into your mind, makes you feel inferior, and condemns you. He will give you guilty feelings of shame, unworthiness, and embarrassment.

One good way to tell the difference between the conviction of the Holy Spirit and the condemnation of Satan is to remember that Satan always generalizes. For example, he speaks into your mind like these: "You are no good," "You can never live a Christian life," "God couldn't love you because you are too great of a sinner."

When the Holy Spirit is convicting you, it is specific. For example, He brings to you attention that you have a problem with anger or dishonesty, etc.

SEXUAL IMPURITY:

Satan will insert thoughts of sexual impurity, lust, and mental sexual fantasies. Jesus said:

> **But I say unto you, That whosoever looketh on a woman to lust after her hath committed adultery with her already in his heart.**
> **(Matthew 5:28)**

CONFUSION:

Satan also causes indecision, confusion, and frustration in your mind. When you are confused, indecisive, and frustrated, you obviously cannot be a good Christian soldier.

TORMENTING THOUGHTS:

There is a whole category of tormenting thoughts Satan sends into your mind including worry, anxiety, dread, apprehension, and nervousness. Mental torment can also come through an overactive mind that will not "shut off" or an under active mind that cannot function properly.

Tormenting thoughts also include fear. Paul speaks of the "spirit of fear" in II Timothy 1:7 and the "fear of death" in Hebrews 2:15. Tormenting thoughts also include bitter memories of events that should be forgiven and forgotten.

COMPROMISE:

To "compromise" is to settle conflicting principles by adjustment. The principles of God and Satan are in opposition. Satan tries to get you to compromise and lower your spiritual principles. For example, he will tell you it is not necessary to be so holy, to believe the Bible literally, etc.

WRONG MENTAL FOCUS:

Satan will constantly try to get your focus on things of the world rather than things of eternal nature:

> **Do not love or cherish the world or the things that are in the world. If any one loves the world, love for the Father is not in him.**
> **(I John 2:15 The Amplified Version)**

The cares of the world can actually cause the Word of God to be ineffective in your life. (See the parable of the sower in Matthew 13, Mark 4, and Luke 8). Cares of the world can make you unaware of the short time before the return of Jesus:

> **And take heed to yourselves, lest at any time your hearts be overcharged with...cares of this life, and so that day come upon you unawares. (Luke 21:34)**

Satan will occupy your thoughts with materialism rather than with eternal values. Read the parable of the rich fool in Luke 12:16-21:

> **For the love of money is the root of all evil; which while some coveted after, they have erred from the faith, and pierced themselves through with many sorrows. (I Timothy 6:10)**

Paul warns there are many who "mind worldly things" (Philippians 3:18-19).

MENTAL CONDITIONS:

If you allow Satan to persist with thoughts of depression, suicide, torment, accusation, etc., it can lead to mental illness. This could include a nervous or mental breakdown and various medically recognized mental conditions. Satan can actually possess the mind of unbelievers and backsliders; those who have once known God, then turned away from Him. (You will learn more about this Chapter Twenty-One.)

SPIRITUAL COUNTER STRATEGIES: VICTORY IN THE MIND

What an arsenal of weapons Satan has targeted for the mind! Left unconquered, these thoughts lead to sinful actions. For example, hatred can lead to murder. Adulterous thoughts can lead to the act of adultery. Divorce starts in the mind. Covetousness can lead to stealing.

There is no doubt...the greatest arena of spiritual warfare is the mind. But do not fear! God has given some tremendous counter strategies for overcoming attacks of Satan on the mind:

LET THE HOLY SPIRIT SEARCH YOUR MIND:

First, ask God to search your mind and reveal to you any wrong attitudes, motives, and thinking which has been inserted by the enemy:

> **Search me, O God, and know my heart; try me, and know my thoughts: And see if there be any wicked way in me, and lead me in the way everlasting. (Psalms 139:23-24)**

As the Holy Spirit reveals things to you, act upon the revelation. Ask forgiveness for wrong thought patterns and use the Word of God to develop new thought patterns.

USE YOUR SPIRITUAL ARMOR:

Two pieces of spiritual armor defend you from attacks in the mind. These are listed in Ephesians 6:16-17. One piece of armor is the helmet of the hope of salvation. A helmet is worn on the head and implies protection to the mind.

Paul is not only speaking of your present salvation in Jesus Christ which can cleanse your mind, he is speaking of the future salvation:

> **...for now is our salvation nearer than when we believed. (Romans 13:11)**

Salvation is also your hope for the future. The believer who has the "helmet of salvation" in place understands God is working out His eternal purpose of salvation. He is not disturbed by the attacks of the enemy. He has hope not only for the present, but for the future.

The other piece of armor for mental protection is the shield of faith. As you learned when you studied about your weapons, a shield was a piece of heavy material which a soldier held in front of himself to keep arrows from hitting him. The arrows bounced off the shield and fell harmlessly to the ground.

The shield for the Christian soldier is called the "shield of faith." The word "faith" not only refers to the basic truths of the Christian Gospel but to your confidence in God. Another piece of spiritual armor is the girdle of truth (Ephesians 6:14). The truth of God's Word will defeat any false accusations the enemy brings to your mind.

USE GOD'S WORD:

In the temptation of Jesus when Satan misused God's Word, Jesus met the attack with the Word of God. When Satan comes with accusations of guilt, use this Scripture:

> **There is therefore now no condemnation to them which are in Christ Jesus, who walk not after the flesh, but after the Spirit. (Romans 8:1)**

When Satan comes with tormenting feelings such as fear, use these Scriptures:

> **There is no fear in love; but perfect love casteth out fear; because fear hath torment. He that feareth is not made perfect in love. (I John 4:18)**

> **For God hath not given us the spirit of fear; but of power, and of love, and of a sound mind. (II Timothy 1:7)**

When Satan tries to discourage you, use this verse:

> **Have not I commanded thee? Be strong and of a good courage; be not afraid, neither be thou dismayed: for the Lord thy God is with thee whithersoever thou goest. (Joshua 1:9)**

When Satan brings false guilt to your mind, remember...

> **If we confess our sins, He is faithful and just to forgive us our sins, and to cleanse us from all unrighteousness. (I John 1:9)**

...and use all the other verses about the mind given in this lesson to war against the attacks of Satan in your mind.

CLAIM A SOUND MIND:

Claim a sound mind as God's will for you. To eliminate tormenting thoughts, claim the peace that is rightfully yours:

> **Peace I leave with you, my peace I give unto you: not as the world giveth give I unto you. LET NOT your heart be troubled, NEITHER LET IT be afraid. (John 14:27)**

> **And the peace of God, which passeth all understanding, shall keep your hearts and MINDS through Christ Jesus. (Philippians 4:7)**

These are examples of how you can develop a whole "arsenal" of Scriptures applicable to the various mental attacks of Satan. As you study God's Word, continue to identify specific verses to defend your mind against the invasion of the enemy.

LET CHRIST'S MIND BE IN YOU:

Paul wrote under the inspiration of the Holy Spirit:

Let this mind be in you, which was also in Christ Jesus. (Philippians 2:5)

The word "let" means to permit or embrace. You are to let your mind become like the mind of Jesus. What was the mind of Jesus like? A project for study of this question is provided in the "Tactical Maneuvers" section of this chapter. It is possible to achieve this, because Paul wrote...

...But we have the mind of Christ. (II Corinthians 2:16)

GIRD UP THE LOINS OF YOUR MIND:

Wherefore gird up the loins of your mind... (I Peter 1:13)

In the natural body, the loins are the central portion of the body below the waist. The loins are the strongest parts of the body. Peter is saying you should prepare your mind to be strong. Again, it is something YOU do.

TAKE WRONG THOUGHTS CAPTIVE:

We are told to bring "into captivity every thought to the obedience to Christ" (II Corinthians 10:5). If thoughts were not enemies, then there would be no need to take them captive. Think about how a soldier takes an enemy captive in the natural world. Apply these ideas spiritually as you "take captive" every thought.

CAST DOWN WRONG THOUGHTS:

One of the main defensive counter strategies to protect the mind is that of casting down. To cast something means to hurl it with great force. Paul said:

For though we walk in the flesh, we do not war after the flesh: For the weapons of our warfare are not carnal, but mighty through God to the pulling down of strong holds;

Casting down imaginations, and every high thing that exalteth itself against the knowledge of God, and bringing into captivity every thought to the obedience of Christ. (II Corinthians 10:3-5)

You are to cast down evil imaginations Satan puts into your mind. You are to cast down thoughts that exalt themselves against God. You are to bring every thought into captivity and obedience to the Lord.

You "cast down" by consciously taking control of your mind and refusing to dwell on the thoughts Satan inserts. Note that YOU are told to cast down...It is not something God does for you.

THINK ON THESE THINGS:

One way to "gird" up the loins of your mind is to think on proper subject matter. Paul said:

> **Finally, brethren, whatsoever things are true, whatsoever things are honest, whatsoever things are just, whatsoever things are pure, whatsoever things are lovely, whatsoever things are of good report; if there by any virtue, and if there be any praise, think on these things. (Philippians 4:8)**

RENEW YOUR MIND:

> **And be renewed in the spirit of your mind. (Ephesians 4:23)**

> **And be not conformed to this world; but be ye transformed by the renewing of your mind... (Romans 12:2)**

You renew your mind by prayer and meditation on God's Word.

ENCOURAGE YOURSELF IN THE LORD:

David encouraged himself in the Lord:

> **And David was greatly distressed; ...but David encouraged himself in the Lord his God. (I Samuel 30:6)**

Again, YOU must take action. You must encourage yourself in God. Do not wait for others to do it. Do it yourself with God's help!

RECOGNIZE THE SOURCE OF CONFUSION:

Recognize that confusion is not of God:

> **For God is not the author of confusion, but of peace...(I Corinthians 14:33)**

Since confusion is not of God, refuse to accept the spirit of confusion in your mind.

CONTROL THE GATES:

In Old Testament times cities were surrounded by walls for defense against enemy forces. The walls had gates where guards controlled the entrance. Whoever controlled the gates of the city controlled the city.

A similar situation exists in terms of controlling the mind. The "gates" to your innermost being are the five senses. It is important that you do not allow anything to enter that has the ability to destroy from within. This means you must control your fleshly nature.

Avoid things that would open the gates to your mind. These include things like drugs and alcohol which reduce your ability to think and respond. Pornography inspires sinful relationships and sex crimes. Certain kinds of music, witchcraft, cultist activity, and mind control all open the "gates" to your mind.

Put off all the works of the flesh and let God develop in you the fruit of the Holy Spirit (See Galatians 5:19-26). NEVER GIVE IN to the mental attacks of the enemy. If you give in, God may give you up. See Romans 1...God sometimes gives people up to what they have given in to. Ask Jesus to help you. Remember that one of the Old Testament prophecies concerning Jesus said He would "control the gates of His enemy." Let Him exert this control over your spiritual "gates."

KEEP YOUR MIND STAYED ON GOD:

Keep your mind "stayed" or centered on God:

> **Thou wilt keep him in perfect peace, whose mind is stayed on thee; because he trusteth in thee. (Isaiah 26:3)**

This is a great promise! If you keep your mind centered on God, you can have peace despite every attack of the enemy.

INSPECTION

1. Write the Key Verses from the Articles Of War.

2. Where is the main battleground of spiritual warfare?

3. What is meant by the "fiery darts" of Satan?

4. Summarize the strategies Satan uses to war against the mind.

5. Summarize spiritual counter strategies presented in this chapter which will overcome mental attacks of Satan.

(Answers to tests are provided at the conclusion of the final chapter in this manual.)

TACTICAL MANEUVERS

1. In the battle for the mind, Satan tries attempts to cause:
   -A carnal mind: Romans 8:6-7
   -A mind alienated from God by wicked works: Colossians 1:21
   -A defiled mind: Titus 1:15
   -A fleshly mind: Ephesians 2:3
   -A hardened mind: Daniel 5:20
   -A doubtful mind: Luke 12:29
   -A vain mind: Ephesians 4:17
   -A blinded mind: II Corinthians 3:14
   -A seared mind and conscience: Titus 1:15
   -A despiteful mind: Ezekiel 36:5
   -An evil mind: Acts 14:2
   -An unbelieving mind: II Corinthians 4:4
   -A fainting mind: Hebrews 12:3
   -A reprobate mind: II Timothy 3:8
   -Double mindedness: James 1:8; 4:8
   -A corrupt mind: I Timothy 6:5; II Timothy 3:8; II Corinthians 11:3

2. Positive mental qualities you should develop:
   -A ready mind: II Corinthians 8:19; I Peter 5:2; Acts 17:11
   -A pure mind: II Peter 3:1
   -A stayed mind: Isaiah 26:3
   -A renewed mind: Ephesians 4:23; Romans 12:2
   -A humble mind: Colossians 3:12; Acts 20:19
   -A sober mind: Titus 2:6
   -A sound mind: II Timothy 1:7
   -A mind of love: Matthew 22:37
   -A serving mind: Romans 7:25
   -A fully persuaded mind: Romans 14:5
   -A fervent mind: II Corinthians 7:7
   -A willing mind: II Corinthians 8:12

3. Because of continued sin, men can be turned over to a reprobate mind. See Romans 1:28-32. A reprobate mind is the most evil kind of mind you can imagine.

4. As you learned in this chapter, one of the strategies for victory in the mind is to let the same mind that was in Jesus be in you. Study the New Testament further to discover just what the mind of Jesus was like. What mental attitudes were reflected in His actions? How did His ministry reflect His thought life? How did His words reflect His thoughts?

5. Jesus knows even the thoughts of your mind: See Luke 5:22; 6:8; 11:17.

6. Compare II Samuel 13:28 with Joshua 1:9. Note that the passage in Samuel is similar to that in Joshua where God is speaking. But the Samuel passage is misapplied. Absalom spoke these words to the assassins of his brother, Amnon. The Devil echoes some of the greatest Biblical words as he misuses and misapplies Scripture. Satan is never more dangerous than when he is quoting the Bible. This is a chief strategy he uses in attacking the mind.

CHAPTER SIXTEEN
THE BATTLE WITH THE TONGUE

OBJECTIVES:

Upon completion of this chapter you will be able to:

- Write the Key Verse from memory.
- Identify the tongue as an important battleground of spiritual warfare.
- Summarize strategies Satan uses to control the tongue.
- Summarize spiritual counter strategies for victory over the tongue.

KEY VERSE FROM THE ARTICLES OF WAR:

> **But the tongue can no man tame; it is an unruly evil, full of deadly poison. (James 3:8)**

INTRODUCTION

In the previous chapter you studied one of the main battlefields of spiritual warfare, the mind. What happens in the mind affects the tongue and the tongue affects the spirit, soul, heart, and body. This chapter concerns another major arena of spiritual warfare, the battle with the tongue.

WHAT THE BIBLE SAYS ABOUT THE TONGUE

Before you examine Satan's strategies for control of the tongue, read what the Bible says about the tongue in James 3:1-13. These verses reveal that although the tongue is a little member of your body, it is very powerful. Through the tongue the whole body can be defiled. The tongue can never be tamed by man. Only when you yield your tongue to God can control be maintained over it. But even then, it will never be tamed. You can never relax your guard over the tongue believing you have totally conquered it.

The Bible compares the tongue to:
- A fire: James 3:5
- A burning fire: Proverbs 16:27
- A world of iniquity: James 3:6
- A beast that needs taming: James 3:7-8
- A fountain of either fresh or bitter water: James 3:11
- A tree bearing either good or evil fruit: James 3:12
- An unruly evil: James 3:8
- Deadly poison: James 3:8
- A sharp razor: Psalms 52:2
- A sharp sword: Psalms 57:4; 59:7
- A poisonous serpent: Psalms 140:3
- A deep pit: Proverbs 22:14

The Bible says the tongue is powerful because of the effect it has on others. The tongue actually has the power to bring death or life:

> **Death and life are in the power of the tongue...**
> **(Proverbs 18:21)**

The tongue is powerful because of the effect it has on you. You can snare yourself with your own
words:

> **Thou art snared with the words of thy mouth; thou art taken with the words of thy mouth. (Proverbs 6:2)**

The tongue is powerful because your words can separate you from God:

> **Who have said, With our tongue will we prevail; our lips are our own: who is lord over us? (Psalms 12:4)**

STRATEGIES OF SATAN: THE BATTLE FOR THE TONGUE

Your tongue is closely related to your heart, body, soul, and spirit. For example, if Satan has control of your heart, he has control of your tongue:

> **But those things which proceed out of the mouth come forth from the heart; and they defile the man.**
>
> **For out of the heart proceed evil thoughts, murders, adulteries, fornications, thefts, false witness, blasphemies;**
>
> **These are the things which defile a man...(Matthew 15:18-20)**
>
> **A good man out of the good treasure of his heart bringeth forth that which is good; and an evil man out of the evil treasure of his heart bringeth forth that which is evil; for of the abundance of the heart his mouth speaketh.**
> **(Luke 6:45)**

Satan uses the things you say to cause a breach (opening) into your spirit:

> **A wholesome tongue is a tree of life: but perverseness therein is a breach in the spirit. (Proverbs 15:4)**

By evil communication you create a breach through which Satan enters to war against your spirit. Satan also uses your lips to affect your soul:

> **A fool's mouth is his destruction, and his lips are the snare of his soul.**
> **(Proverbs 18:7)**

> **Whoso keepeth his mouth and his tongue keepeth his soul from troubles. (Proverbs 21:23)**

Through the tongue, Satan affects your whole body:

> **And the tongue is a fire, a world of iniquity; so is the tongue among our members, that it defileth the whole body, and setteth on fire the course of nature; and it is set on fire of Hell. (James 3:6)**

Your tongue affects your whole life:

> **He that keepeth his mouth keepeth his life; but he that openeth wide his lips shall have destruction. (Proverbs 13:3)**

Satan seeks control of your tongue by tempting you to speak:

COVETOUS WORDS:

> **Let your conversation be without covetousness; and be content with such things as ye have; for He hath said, I will never leave thee, nor forsake thee. (Hebrews 13:5)**

IDOL WORDS:

> **But I say unto you, That every idle word that men shall speak, they shall give account thereof in the day of judgment. (Matthew 12:36)**

FOOLISH WORDS:

> **The heart of him that hath understanding seeketh knowledge; but the mouth of fools feedeth on foolishness. (Proverbs 15:14)**

UNPROFITABLE WORDS:

> **Of these things put them in remembrance, charging them before the Lord that they strive not about words to no profit, but to the subverting of the hearers. (II Timothy 2:14)**

FABLES AND COMMANDMENTS OF MEN:

> **Not giving heed to Jewish fables, and commandments of men, that turn from the truth. (Titus 1:14)**

EVIL ABOUT THINGS YOU DO NOT KNOW:

> **But these speak evil of those things which they know not... (Jude 10)**
> **But these, as natural brute beasts, made to be taken and destroyed, speak evil**

of the things that they understand not; and shall utterly perish in their own corruption. (II Peter 2:12)

FLATTERING WORDS:

For neither at any time used we flattering words, as ye know, nor a cloak of covetousness; God is witness. (I Thessalonians 2:5)

ENTICING WORDS:

And this I say, lest any man should beguile you with enticing words. (Colossians 2:4)

MURMURING, COMPLAINING, AND BOASTING WORDS:

These are murmurers, complainers, walking after their own lusts; and their mouth speaketh great swelling words, having men's persons in admiration because of advantage. (Jude 16)

For when they speak great swelling words of vanity, they allure through the lusts of the flesh, through much wantonness, those that were clean escaped from them who live in error. (II Peter 2:18)

VAIN WORDS:

They speak vanity every one with his neighbor..(Psalms 12:2)

PROUD WORDS:

...with their mouth they speak proudly. (Psalms 17:10)

BOASTFUL WORDS:

How long shall they utter and speak hard things? And all the workers of iniquity boast themselves. (Psalms 94:4)

WORDS WHICH TAKE GOD'S NAME IN VAIN:

Thou shalt not take the name of the Lord thy God in vain; for the Lord will not hold him guiltless that taketh His name in vain. (Exodus 20:7)

CURSING AND BITTER WORDS:

Whose mouth is full of cursing and bitterness. (Romans 3:14)

LIES:

The wicked are estranged from the womb: they go astray as soon as they be born, speaking lies. (Psalms 58:3)

Let the lying lips be put to silence, which speak grievous things proudly and contemptuously against the righteous. (Psalms 31:18)

SLANDERING WORDS:

Thou sittest and speakest against thy brother; thou slanderest thine own mother's son. (Psalms 50:20)

MALICIOUS WORDS AGAINST OTHERS:

Wherefore, if I come, I will remember his deed which he doeth, prating against us with malicious words...(III John 10)

WHISPERING WORDS (GOSSIP):

A froward man soweth strife; and a whisperer separateth chief friends. (Proverbs 16:28)

TALEBEARING WORDS:

A talebearer revealeth secrets; but he that is of a faithful spirit concealeth the matter. (Proverbs 11:13)

BACKBITING WORDS:

He that backbiteth not with his tongue..(Psalms 15:3)

DISSEMBLING WORDS:

Dissembling words cause division:

He that hateth dissembleth with his lips, and layeth up deceit within him. (Proverbs 26:4)

CONTENTIOUS WORDS:

A fool's lips enter into contention, and his mouth calleth for strokes. (Proverbs 18:6)

WORDS OF STRIFE:

> Thou shalt hide them in the secret of thy presence from the pride of man: thou shalt keep them secretly in a pavilion from the strife of tongues. (Psalms 31:20)

WORDS OF DISCORD:

> ...he that soweth discord among brethren. (Proverbs 6:19)

DEVOURING WORDS:

> Thou lovest all devouring words, O thou deceitful tongue. (Psalms 52:4)

FROWARD AND PERVERSE WORDS:

> Put away from thee a froward mouth and perverse lips put far from thee. (Proverbs 4:24)

EVIL AND DECEITFUL WORDS:

> Thou givest thy mouth to evil, and thy tongue frameth deceit. (Psalms 50:19)

> Let not an evil speaker be established in the earth...(Psalms 140:11)

MISCHIEVOUS WORDS:

> They also that seek after my life lay snares for me: and they that seek my hurt speak mischievous things, and imagine deceits all the day long. (Psalms 38:12)

FILTHY WORDS:

> But now ye also put off all these; anger, wrath, malice, blasphemy, filthy communication out of your mouth. (Colossians 3:8)

SPIRITUAL COUNTER STRATEGIES: VICTORY OVER THE TONGUE

When David realized the great battle with the tongue, he cried out:

> What shall be given unto thee? Or what shall be done unto thee, thou false tongue? (Psalms 120:3)

The only way to win the battle with the tongue is by application of spiritual counter strategies given in God's Word.

GET YOUR HEART RIGHT WITH GOD:

The first step in gaining victory over the tongue is to get your heart right with God:

> **But those things which proceed out of the mouth come forth from the heart; and they defile the man.**
>
> **For out of the heart proceed evil thoughts, murders, adulteries, fornications, thefts, false witness, blasphemies;**
>
> **These are the things which defile a man...(Matthew 15:18-20)**

Your mouth will speak what is in your heart. If your heart is not right, your tongue will reveal it. Use your tongue to get your heart right with God:

> **That if thou shalt confess with thy mouth, the Lord Jesus, and shalt believe in thine heart that God hath raised Him from the dead, thou shalt be saved.**
>
> **For with the heart man believeth unto righteousness; and with the mouth confession is made unto salvation. (Romans 10:9-10)**

RECOGNIZE YOUR RESPONSIBILITY:

Recognize you will be held responsible for the words that come out of your mouth:

> **But I say unto you, That every idle word that men shall speak, they shall give account thereof in the day of judgment.**
>
> **For by thy words thou shalt be justified, and by thy words thou shalt be condemned. (Matthew 12:36-37)**
>
> **And he saith unto him, Out of thine own mouth will I judge thee, thou wicked servant... (Luke 19:22)**

REALIZE YOUR WORDS REFLECT ON THE GOSPEL:

As long as you believe your tongue is not important, you will not gain control of it. You must realize your conversation reflects on the Gospel of Jesus:

> **Only let your conversation be as it becometh the Gospel of Christ... (Philippians 1:27)**

Because of this, you should set a good example by your conversation:

> **Let no man despise thy youth; but be thou an example of the believers, in word, in conversation, in charity, in spirit, in faith, in purity. (I Timothy 4:12)**

What comes out of your mouth is noted by the heathen:

> **Then was our mouth filled with laughter, and our tongue with singing: then said they among the heathen, The Lord hath done great things for them. (Psalms 126:2)**

You can actually win others to the Lord Jesus Christ by your conversation:

> **Likewise, ye wives, be in subjection to your own husbands; that, if any obey not the word, they also may without the word be won by the conversation of the wives;**
>
> **While they behold your chaste conversation coupled with fear. (I Peter 3:1-2)**

KEEP YOUR WORDS FEW AND SIMPLE:

> **In the multitude of words there wanteth not sin: but he that refraineth his lips is wise. (Proverbs 10:19)**
>
> **But let your communication be, Yea, yea; Nay, nay; for whatsoever is more than these cometh of evil. (Matthew 5:37)**

THINK BEFORE YOU SPEAK:

> **Wherefore, my beloved brethren, let every man be swift to hear; slow to speak, slow to wrath. (James 1:19)**
>
> **If thou hast done foolishly in lifting up thyself, or if thou hast thought evil, lay thine hand upon thy mouth. (Proverbs 30:32)**
>
> **The heart of the righteous studieth to answer: but the mouth of the wicked poureth out evil things. (Proverbs 15:28)**
>
> **Even a fool, when he holdeth his peace, is counted wise: and he that shutteth his lips is esteemed a man of understanding. (Proverbs 17:28)**

SEPARATE YOURSELF:

Separate yourself from those who cannot control their tongue:

> **Go from the presence of a foolish man, when thou perceivest not in him the lips of knowledge. (Proverbs 14:7)**

LEARN THE POWER OF PEACEFUL WORDS:

Peaceful words are more powerful than words of anger:

> **By long forbearing is a prince persuaded, and a soft tongue breaketh the bone. (Proverbs 25:15)**

RECOGNIZE YOUR TONGUE IS A WEAPON:

Your tongue is a weapon you can use to overcome the enemy instead of being defeated by him:

> **And they overcame him (Satan) by the blood of the Lamb and by the word of their testimony... (Revelation 12:11)**

If you control your tongue, it will put to shame those who falsely accuse you:

> **Having a good conscience; that, whereas they speak evil of you, as of evildoers, they may be ashamed that falsely accuse your good conversation in Christ. (I Peter 3:16)**

TAKE CONTROL OF YOUR TONGUE:

With God's help, you can control the tongue. But YOU must take action to control your own tongue. The following verses indicate action from YOU:

> **For he that will love life, and see good days, LET HIM refrain his tongue from evil, and his lips that they speak no guile. (I Peter 3:10)**

> **...SPEAK evil of no man...(Titus 3:2)**

> **SPEAK NOT EVIL one of another, brethren. He that speaketh evil of his brother, and judgeth his brother, speaketh evil of the law, and judgeth the law; but if thou judge the law, thou art not a doer of the law, but a judge.**

> **There is one lawgiver, who is able to save and to destroy: who art thou that judgest another? (James 4:11-12)**

> **LET YOUR conversation be without covetousness; and be content with such things as ye have... (Hebrews 13:5)**

> **Only LET YOUR conversation be as it becometh the Gospel of Christ... (Philippians 1:27)**

> **That YE PUT OFF concerning the former conversation the old man, which is corrupt according to the deceitful lusts;**

> **And be renewed in the spirit of your mind;**

And that YE PUT ON the new man, which after God is created in righteousness and true holiness.

Wherefore PUTTING AWAY lying, speak every man truth with his neighbor...(Ephesians 4:22-25)

But now YE also PUT OFF...filthy communication out of your mouth. (Colossians 3:8)

LET no corrupt communication proceed out of YOUR mouth, but that which is good to the use of edifying, that it may minister grace unto the hearers. (Ephesians 4:29)

LET all...evil speaking be put away from YOU...(Ephesians 4:31)
...BE YE holy in all manner of conversation; Because it is written, BE ye holy; for I am holy. (I Peter 1:15-16)

PUT AWAY from thee a froward mouth, and perverse lips put far from thee. (Proverbs 4:24)

KEEP thy tongue from evil, and thy lips from speaking guile. (Psalms 34:13)

I said, I WILL TAKE HEED to my ways, that I sin not with my tongue: I will keep my mouth with a bridle, while the wicked is before me. (Psalms 39:1)

Whoso offereth praise glorifieth me; and to HIM THAT ORDERETH his conversation aright will I shew the salvation of God. (Psalms 50:23)

THOU shalt not take the name of the Lord thy God in vain; for the Lord will not hold him guiltless that taketh His name in vain. (Exodus 20:7)

THOU shalt not bear false witness against thy neighbor. (Exodus 20:16)

PATTERN YOUR CONVERSATION AFTER JESUS:

Jesus spoke gracious words:

> **And all bare Him witness, and wondered at the gracious words which proceeded out of His mouth, And they said, Is not this Joseph's son? (Luke 4:22)**

He spoke words of authority about God:

> **And they were astonished at His doctrine: for He taught them as one that had authority and not as the scribes. (Mark 1:22)**

There was no guile (sinful speaking) found in His mouth:

> **Who did no sin, neither was guile found in His mouth; Who, when He was reviled, reviled not again; when He suffered, He threatened not; but committed Himself to him that judgeth righteously. (I Peter 2:22-23)**

USE YOUR TONGUE FOR GOOD:

Speak words of wisdom and kindness:

> **She openeth her mouth with wisdom; and in her tongue is the law of kindness. (Proverbs 31:26)**

> **My mouth shall speak of wisdom; and the meditation of my heart shall be of understanding. (Psalms 49:3)**

Talk about God:

> **I will speak of the glorious honor of thy majesty, and of thy wondrous works. (Psalms 145:5)**

> **My mouth shall shew forth thy righteousness and thy salvation all the day... (Psalms 71:15)**

> **My tongue also shall talk of thy righteousness all the day long... (Psalms 71:24)**

Speak of God's Word:

> **My tongue shall speak of thy Word; for all thy commandments are righteousness. (Psalms 119:172)**

> **With my lips have I declared all the judgments of thy mouth. (Psalms 119:13)**

> **I will speak of thy testimonies also before kings, and will not be ashamed. (Psalms 119:46)**

Speak words of comfort from God's Word:

> **Wherefore comfort one another with these words. (I Thessalonians 4:18)**

Speak of the Kingdom of God:

> **They shall speak of the glory of thy Kingdom, and talk of thy power. (Psalms 145:11)**

Let your lips be filled with praise to God:

> **My mouth shall speak the praise of the Lord; and let all flesh bless His holy name for ever and ever. (Psalms 145:21)**
>
> **Let the high praises of God be in their mouth, and a two-edged sword in their hand. (Psalms 149:6)**
>
> **I will sing of the mercies of the Lord for ever; with my mouth will I make known thy faithfulness to all generations. (Psalms 89:1)**
>
> **I will greatly praise the Lord with my mouth; yea, I will praise Him among the multitude. (Psalms 109:30)**
>
> **My lips shall utter praise, when thou hast taught me thy statutes. (Psalms 119:171)**
>
> **Because thy loving kindness is better than life, my lips shall praise thee. (Psalms 63:3)**
>
> **...and my mouth shall praise thee with joyful lips. (Psalms 63:5)**
>
> **I cried unto Him with my mouth, and He was extolled with my tongue. (Psalms 66:17)**
>
> **Let my mouth be filled with thy praise and with thy honor all the day. (Psalms 71:8)**
>
> **My lips shall greatly rejoice when I sing unto thee; and my soul, which thou hast redeemed. (Psalms 71:23)**
>
> **I will bless the Lord at all times; His praise shall continually be in my mouth. (Psalms 34:1)**

BEFORE YOU SPEAK, ASK THESE QUESTIONS:

1. Will what I am about to say bring glory to God?
   And whatsoever ye do in WORD or deed, do ALL in the name of the Lord Jesus, giving thanks to God and the Father by Him. (Colossians 3:17)
2. Is it the truth?
3. Is it fair to all concerned?
4. Will it be beneficial to all concerned?
5. Will it edify others (result in good will and better friendships)?
6. If you are talking about another person, have you said the same thing to him or her?
7. Do you know that what you are saying is a fact or have you arrived at your own conclusions after hearing rumors?

8. If you have something against your brother or sister, have you attempted to be reconciled to them before discussing it with others?
9. Is it absolutely necessary that you say this?

REMEMBER THESE VERSES:

For there is not a word in my tongue, but, lo, O Lord, thou knowest it altogether. (Psalms 139:4)

...the sweetness of the lips increaseth learning. (Proverbs 16:21)

The heart of the wise teacheth his mouth, and addeth learning to his lips. (Proverbs 16:23)

A man hath joy by the answer of his mouth; and a word spoken in due season, how good is it! (Proverbs 15:23)

Seeing then that all these things shall be dissolved, what manner of persons ought ye to be in all holy conversation and godliness. (II Peter 3:11)

A word fitly spoken is like apples of gold in pictures of silver. (Proverbs 25:11)

Whoso keepeth his mouth and his tongue keepeth his soul from troubles. (Proverbs 21:23)

He that keepeth his mouth keepeth his life; but he that openeth wide his lips shall have destruction. (Proverbs 13:3)

CLAIM THESE PROMISES:

Hear; For I will speak of excellent things; and the opening of my lips shall be right things.

For my mouth shall speak truth; and wickedness is an abomination to my lips. All the words of my mouth are in righteousness; there is nothing froward or perverse in them. (Proverbs 8:6-8)

PRAY THESE PRAYERS:

Set a watch, O Lord, before my mouth; keep the door of my lips. (Psalms 141:3)

Let the words of my mouth, and the meditation of my heart, be acceptable in thy sight, O Lord, my strength, and my redeemer. (Psalms 19:14)

ESTABLISH THIS PURPOSE:

Thou hast proved mine heart; thou hast visited me in the night; thou has tried me, and shalt find nothing: I AM PURPOSED THAT MY MOUTH SHALL NOT TRANSGRESS. (Psalms 17:3)

INSPECTION

1. Write the Key Verse from the Articles Of War.

   _____

   _____

   _____

2. What was the subject of spiritual warfare discussed in this chapter?

   _____

   _____

   _____

3. Identify some ways Satan wants to use your tongue to defeat you in spiritual warfare.

   _____

   _____

   _____

4. Summarize spiritual counter strategies for victory over Satan's control of the tongue.

   _____

   _____

   _____

(Answers to tests are provided at the conclusion of the final chapter in this manual.)

TACTICAL MANEUVERS

The books of Psalms and Proverbs in the Bible have much to say about the tongue.

1. Look up each verse listed in the book of Proverbs. Write the comparisons on the chart. The first one is done for you as an example to follow.

Reference In Proverbs	Good Tongue	Evil Tongue
10:6	blessings	violence
10:11		
10:14		
10:20		
10:21		
10:31		
10:32		
11:9		
11:11		
11:13		
12:6		
12:13		
12:17		
12:18		
12:19		
12:22		
13:3		
14:3		
14:5		
14:25		
15:2		
15:4		
15:7		
15:14		
15:28		
17:9		
19:1		

2. In Proverbs 6:16-19 there is a list of seven things which God especially hates. Which three things are done by the tongue?

3. Read the books of Psalms and Proverbs and do the following:

   A. Make a list of all the verses that refer to wrong use of the tongue. Make your list according to the following pattern:

Reference	Wrong use of tongue
Psalms 5:9	Flattery
Psalms 10:7	Cursing and deceit
(continue this list)	

   B. Make another list showing the proper use of the tongue. Make your list according to the following pattern:

Reference	Proper use of tongue
Psalms 19:14	Acceptable words
Psalms 34:1	Blessing and praising God continually
(continue this list)	

4. "Thou shalt not raise a false report" (Exodus 23:1). The word "raise" in this verse means receive or utter. We are not to listen to or spread false reports. Philippians 4:8 indicates we are to think on only good reports. Here are some ways to recognize if someone is bringing you an evil report.

   AN EVIL REPORT WILL...

   -Raise questions about the motives or actions of other brothers and sisters in the Lord.
   -Discredit spiritual leadership.
   -Cause division and strife. When we are busy fighting between ourselves, we cannot aggressively fight the true enemy, Satan.
   -Always focus on the negative.

   AN EVIL REPORT ARISES FROM MOTIVES OF...
   -Pride: To exalt themselves, a person puts down someone else.
   -Envy and covetousness: A person secretly desires what others have so criticizes them.
   -Guilt: A person transfers his guilt to others. He feels guilty about his own sins and failures so point out those of others.
   -Rebellion: The rebellious spirit targets leadership. Read the story of Absalom in the Bible. (II Samuel 15) One way to recognize an evil report motivated by rebellion is by the statement used by Absalom: "If I were the leader I would....."
   -Bitterness: A person has been hurt, so they hurt others with their words.

HOW TO RECOGNIZE AN EVIL REPORT...

-The person may test you first. They may ask "How do you feel about_____?" They are testing your feelings before proceeding with the evil report.
-The person will create curiosity. They may say "You won't believe what I heard about_____"or "Did you hear the latest about_____". They are trying to motivate your curiosity to ask what they know.
-They will claim to know the true story or have access to secret, inside information. This appeals to your pride. You want to become part of this select group with such knowledge.
-They may disguise it as a request for counsel. "I need your opinion on a matter....", and then proceed to share an evil report under the guise of seeking spiritual counsel.
-An evil report can even be shared through a prayer request. "We really need to pray for _because_____" and they proceed to share what is actually gossip about the individual.
-An evil report is often shared under the guise of concern. The person begins by saying "I am deeply concerned about _____". This serves as an introduction to the evil report which follows.

HOW TO STOP AN EVIL REPORT...

Ask the person bringing you the report the following questions:

-"Why are you telling ME this?"
-"Where did you get this information?" (A person giving an evil report usually will not want to tell you their source.)
-"Have you gone to the person you are talking about according to the principles of Matthew 18:15-17"?
-"Have you checked the facts, or are you just repeating the story?"
-"Can I quote you when I check out the facts on this?"
-"Do you think this qualifies as that which we are to focus on according to Philippians 4:8?"

Or you may just simply say..."I really do not want to hear this."

CHAPTER SEVENTEEN
THE BATTLE OVER THE WALLS

OBJECTIVES:

Upon completion of this chapter you will be able to:
- Write the Key Verse from memory.
- Explain what is meant by "spiritual walls."
- Explain why spiritual walls are destroyed.
- Recognize strategies Satan uses to attack spiritual walls.
- Identify spiritual counter strategies to assure victory at the walls.

KEY VERSE FROM THE ARTICLES OF WAR:

> **Then answered I them, and said unto them, the God of Heaven, He will prosper us; therefore we His servants will arise and build: but ye have no portion, nor right, nor memorial, in Jerusalem.**
> **(Nehemiah 2:20)**

INTRODUCTION

The book of Nehemiah in the Old Testament relates the story of a battle to rebuild the walls of Jerusalem which had been destroyed by an enemy. Walls were an important defense in cities in ancient Israel. They protected against enemy invasion. The natural walls of Jerusalem are symbolic of our spiritual walls:

> **...thou shalt call thy walls Salvation and thy gates Praise. (Isaiah 60:18)**

The natural gates of Jerusalem mentioned in Nehemiah 3 each have symbolic meaning which apply to your spiritual walls:

The Sheep Gate represents the work of the cross in your life, the foundation of spiritual construction: 3:1; John 10:11

The Fish Gate represents Christian witness: 3:3; Matthew 4:19

The Old Gate represents the old nature changing to the new: 3:6; Romans 6:1-23

The Valley Gate speaks of suffering and testing: 3:13; II Corinthians 1:3-5

The Dung Gate represents the works of the flesh which must be eliminated: 3:14; Galatians 5:16-21

The Fountain Gate represents the work of the Holy Spirit: 3:15; John 7:37-39

The Water Gate represents the Word of God: 3:26; John 4:10-14

The Horse Gate represents the believer's warfare: 3:28; Ephesians 6:10-17

The Eastern Gate speaks of the believer's hope in the return of Jesus: 3:29; Ezekiel 43:1-2

The Miphkad Gate speaks of self-examination and the judgment seat of Jesus: 3:31; I Corinthians 3:9-15; II Corinthians 5:10

So your spiritual walls include:
- Walls of salvation, gates of praise
- Work of the cross in your life
- Christian witness
- The old nature changed to the new nature
- Suffering and testing
- Elimination of works of the flesh
- Work of the Holy Spirit
- The Word of God
- Spiritual warfare
- The hope of the return of Jesus
- Self-examination

These are the spiritual walls Satan has targeted to destroy in your life. He wants to destroy your praise and Christian witness. He wants to destroy the work of the cross, suffering, and the Holy Spirit in your life. He tries to keep you from studying God's Word and acting upon its truths. Satan wants to defeat you in spiritual warfare, prevent self-examination, and entrap you in the works of the flesh and the old sinful nature. He wants to destroy your hope in the return of Jesus. These are your spiritual walls, and Satan attacks them with strategies identical to those used in the battle over the walls in Jerusalem. This chapter focuses on the battle over the walls of your spiritual life. It uses the story of Nehemiah to draw powerful parallels of spiritual warfare.

THE SITUATION IN JERUSALEM

Before continuing with this lesson, read Nehemiah chapters 1 through 7:3. Chapters 1 and 2 of Nehemiah describe the condition of the walls around Jerusalem. They were in ruin, destroyed by enemy invasion, and the gates had been burned with fire. Without walls and gates, a city was open to invasion on every side from enemy forces. If your spiritual walls are destroyed, you too are open to attack by the enemy.

THE REASON FOR THE PROBLEM

Nehemiah recognized the walls had been destroyed and the city was in its present condition because of sin. (Nehemiah 1:5-7) When your spiritual walls are in ruin it is also because of sin. Nehemiah felt an intense burden from God to rebuild the walls of Jerusalem to provide protection for the inhabitants. His preparation and plan are described in chapters 1 and 2. He and his workers were determined to "arise and build" the walls (Nehemiah 2:18).

STRATEGIES OF SATAN:
THE BATTLE OVER THE WALLS

When Nehemiah determined to rebuild the wall around Jerusalem, he met powerful opposition from his enemies. When you determine to rebuild spiritual walls, you will face similar opposition from your enemy, Satan. The strategies of the enemies of Nehemiah are identical to the strategies Satan uses to attack spiritual walls. The attacks are divided into two main categories: External attacks and internal attacks.

EXTERNAL ATTACKS:

These are attacks the enemy launches from without through others who are not part of the body of Christ. Such attacks include:

1. Direct criticism: Nehemiah 2:19

The enemies criticized, "What do you think you are doing?" They were against the reconstruction project and tried in every way to prevent it.

2. Mocking and scorn: Nehemiah 4:1-3

Nehemiah became a "target for tongues." The enemy tried to defeat him through the mocking and scorn of others. Satan will use the tongue of others to discourage and defeat you.

3. False accusations: Nehemiah 6:5-7

The enemy attacked Nehemiah personally with false accusations. They accused him of being a rebel. Satan is called "the accuser of the brethren." He will use others to accuse you as well as putting accusing thoughts in your mind.

4. Diversion: Nehemiah 6:2

The enemy tried to get Nehemiah to join them for a meeting. This meeting was a diversion tactic to call Nehemiah away from the work of rebuilding the wall. Diversion from the things of God and the work He has given you to do is still a chief strategy of Satan.

5. Popular influence: Nehemiah 6:2

The enemy said let "us" meet together, trying to influence Nehemiah with popular opinion. Popular opinion said Nehemiah was a rebel and the wall could not be built. Trying to get believers to conform to popular opinion, majority rule, and the principles of the world is a key strategy of Satan. A false prophet claiming to be of God was even used by the enemy to attack Nehemiah (Nehemiah 6:10-13). Popular opinion would say to listen to a "prophet of God." We are warned of false prophets who would divert us from God.

6. Compromise: Nehemiah 5:14-19

Nehemiah refused to compromise. He did not conform to wrong life styles and principles around him. His motto was, "So did not I, because of the fear of God" (Nehemiah 5:15). Satan promotes compromise. He tries to convince believers that something is all right because others are doing it or that such things really are not wrong.

7. Threats and fear: Nehemiah 6:5-9

The enemy made fearful threats against Nehemiah and his workers. Satan knows that fear paralyzes but faith energizes believers to be effective for God. When Nehemiah was offered a way to escape from the enemy, he refused to be fearful and retreat (Nehemiah 6:10-13). He did not take the easy way out. Satan tries to make believers flee in the face of opposition. When you are running you are retreating, and when you retreat you do not gain or hold spiritual ground. When you walk by faith you will encounter opposition of those who walk by sight.

8. Fighting and hindering: Nehemiah 4:8

Open tactics of fighting and hindering were also used. The enemy is not always subtle in his attacks. Sometimes he comes right out in the open to fight and hinder.

9. Conspiracy: Nehemiah 4:8; 6:2

A conspiracy or plot was made against Nehemiah by the enemy. The enemy plots against your life also:

> **The thief cometh not, but for to steal, and to kill, and to destroy... (John 10:10)**

10. Attacks at vulnerable times: Nehemiah 4:6

The greatest attack of the enemy came when the wall was half finished because this was a strategic (important) time. The enemy invades at strategic times when you are vulnerable (most open and affected by his attacks).

- The Prophet Jonah became despondent after the greatest revival ever experienced (Jonah 3-4).
- David fell into sin at a time of great victory in his life. Up until that time he had not known military defeat.
- Samson fell into sin when he "began" to deliver Israel from the hands of the Philistines.

When you are being effective for God, you are vulnerable to enemy attack. Satan is concerned most with those who are advancing in the spirit world.

INTERNAL ATTACKS:

Internal attacks of Satan are those made from within the Body of Christ. They include:

1. Discouragement: Nehemiah 4:10-11

The workers became discouraged which resulted in:
- Loss of strength.
- Loss of vision because of "too much rubbish."
- Loss of confidence

2. Dissension: Nehemiah 5

Nehemiah 5 opens with dissension among God's people. If Satan divides the Body of Christ, he makes us ineffective. We are busy battling each other instead of building. Wrong motives are always behind dissension. In Nehemiah chapter 5 the wrong motive was greed.

3. Weak believers: Nehemiah 4:12

The enemy used weak workers (symbolic of weak believers in the Body of Christ) to try to defeat the construction project.

SPIRITUAL COUNTER STRATEGIES:
VICTORY AT THE WALL

The following strategies were used by Nehemiah to rebuild the wall of Jerusalem. You can use the same strategies to assure victory at your spiritual walls:

EXAMINE THE WALLS:

As Nehemiah did in the natural world, examine the walls of your spiritual life. (Nehemiah 2) Has the enemy crept into your personal life, your home, church fellowship, business, etc.?

> **But let a man examine himself... (I Corinthians 11:28)**
>
> **Examine yourselves, whether ye be in the faith; prove your own selves... (II Corinthians 13:5)**

Remember that self-examination is one of the symbolic gates of your wall in the spirit world. Satan will try to prevent you from self-examination because it will result in recognition of areas in your life where you have let him destroy the walls and invade.

CONFESS YOUR SIN:

As Nehemiah, recognize that the reason walls are destroyed is because of sin. Then like he did (Nehemiah 1:5-7), confess your sin and ask forgiveness:

> **If we say that we have no sin, we deceive ourselves, and the truth is not in us. If we confess our sins, He is faithful and just to forgive us our sins, and to cleanse us from all unrighteousness. (I John 1:8-9)**

RECOGNIZE THAT YOU CANNOT BUILD ALONE:

When Nehemiah's workers said, "We ourselves are unable to build the wall," it was a true statement. By themselves they were unable. They needed the power of God to equip them for the task...So will you!

ARISE AND BUILD:

As Nehemiah, determine to rise and rebuild your spiritual walls:

> **Then answered I them, and said unto them, the God of Heaven, He will prosper us; therefore we His servants will arise and build: but ye have no portion, nor right, nor memorial, in Jerusalem. (Nehemiah 2:20)**

Be prepared...You will face opposition from the enemy.

DO NOT BE DIVERTED:

Nehemiah refused to be diverted by enemy tactics (Nehemiah 6:2-3). Do not let the enemy divert or distract you from rebuilding your spiritual walls.

DO NOT BE SWAYED BY POPULAR OPINION:

Popular opinion was that Nehemiah was a rebel (Nehemiah 2:19). Popular opinion held that the walls could not be properly rebuilt (Nehemiah 4:3). Nehemiah was not swayed by popular opinion. Rather than conform to popular opinion, Nehemiah set an example. He said, "So did not I, because of the fear of God" (Nehemiah 5:14-19. Become an example in spiritual warfare. Do not become part of the crowd that says victory is impossible.

IDENTIFY THE ENEMY AND HIS STRATEGIES:

Nehemiah identified the enemy and his strategies. He discovered that the enemy planned a surprise attack (Nehemiah 4:8 and 11). You must identify your spiritual enemy and his strategies in order to be effective in spiritual warfare. This will help you be prepared for surprise attacks. Recognize that the enemy has conspired against you to kill, steal, and destroy but realize God has greater power and wants to give you life more abundantly (John 10:10).

DEVELOP SPIRITUAL COUNTER STRATEGIES:

Nehemiah developed a counter strategy when he heard the enemy planned to attack. He set some workers as a guard to watch for the enemy. Every worker built the wall but also had his sword and was prepared to fight (Nehemiah 4:13-18). A signal was arranged (a trumpet blast) to alert the warriors of an invasion. Because they were prepared to fight and knew the strategy of the enemy, they prevented an invasion. They knew if they had to war with the enemy, God would fight for them:

>**...our God shall fight for us. (Nehemiah 4:20)**

If you develop proper spiritual counter strategies, you can prevent many invasions of the enemy into your life. When Satan does break through and invade, be assured that God will fight for you!

FACE THE ENEMY:

When Nehemiah was offered refuge from the enemy, he refused. He said, "Should such a man as I flee?" (Nehemiah 6:11). Nehemiah faced the enemy in God's power. When the enemy threatens you, do not flee or take the easy way out or your spiritual walls will never be secure. When internal dissension and discouragement arose and the enemy worked through weak believers, Nehemiah did not ignore the attacks. He confronted and conquered them.

PROTECT YOUR WALL AT VULNERABLE TIMES:

In the story of Nehemiah, the greatest attack of the enemy came when the wall was half finished. When you start building in the spirit world, when you enter the arena of effective spiritual warfare, be prepared. It is a vulnerable time. You are a target for an attacks of Satan.

BUILD THE WALL:

Nehemiah's response to direct criticism, mocking, scorn, false accusations, threats, and fear, was simply to continue building the wall:

>**So we labored in the work: and half of them held the spears from the rising of the morning till the stars appeared. (Nehemiah 4:21)**

Nehemiah stayed with the task. He did not stop building:

>**So the wall was finished in the twenty and fifth day of the month of Elul, in fifty and two days. (Nehemiah 6:15)**

Nehemiah did in a short time what the enemy said could not be done.

If the walls are down around your life, the enemy may tell you the task is hopeless. But, with God's help, you can rebuild the wall. With His strength you do not have to take a long time to do so:

I can do all things through Christ which strengtheneth me. (Philippians 4:13)

When the enemy attacks your spiritual reconstruction project do not quit! Just keep building your spiritual walls.

SET A WATCH:

When Nehemiah completed rebuilding the walls around Jerusalem, he set a guard to watch over the walls and gates of the city (Nehemiah 7:1-3). Set a watch over your spiritual walls. Always be alert for attacks of the enemy.

INSPECTION

1. Write the Key Verse from the Articles Of War.

_____

_____

_____

2. What is meant by our spiritual walls?

_____

_____

_____

3. Why had the walls of Jerusalem been destroyed (the same reason spiritual walls are destroyed)?

_____

_____

_____

4. List strategies Satan uses in the battle over spiritual walls.

_____

_____

_____

5. List spiritual counter strategies which assure victory at the wall.

_____

_____

_____

(Answers to tests are provided at the conclusion of the final chapter in this manual.)

TACTICAL MANEUVERS

1. Are there spiritual walls in your life which have been destroyed by the enemy? Examine your "spiritual walls" which include...
    - Walls of salvation, gates of praise
    - Work of the cross in your life
    - Christian witness
    - The old nature changed to the new nature
    - Suffering and testing
    - Elimination of works of the flesh
    - Work of the Holy Spirit
    - The Word of God
    - Spiritual warfare
    - The hope of the return of Jesus
    - Self-examination

2. Believers are often defeated in spiritual warfare because of lack of proper spiritual preparation. Study how Nehemiah prepared himself before rebuilding the wall and confronting the enemy:

    - He saw conditions as they were: Chapter 1-2
    - He recognized the root problem as sin and confessed his part in it: Nehemiah 1:5-7
    - He fasted, wept, mourned, and prayed: Nehemiah 1:4
    - He prepared properly before starting the task and facing the enemy: Chapters 1 and 2
    - He had a strategy for rebuilding: Chapter 3

3. Ready to rebuild your spiritual walls? Review and apply the strategies learned in this lesson.

CHAPTER EIGHTEEN
BATTLES OVER STRATEGIC TERRITORY

OBJECTIVES:

Upon completion of this chapter you will be able to:

- Write the Key Verse from memory.
- Identify Satan's strategies against the physical body.
- Summarize spiritual counter strategies for victory in the physical body.
- Explain Satan's strategies of using human personalities to war against believers.
- Summarize counter strategies for victory over human personalities which war against believers.
- Identify Satan's strategies against the family.
- Summarize spiritual counter strategies for victory in the family.
- Identify Satan's strategies in the financial and material realm.
- Summarize spiritual counter strategies for victory in the financial and material realm.

KEY VERSE FROM THE ARTICLES OF WAR:

> **The thief cometh not, but for to steal, and to kill, and to destroy: I am come that they might have life, and that they might have it more abundantly. (John 10:10)**

INTRODUCTION

Previous chapters focused on major attacks of the enemy on the mind, the tongue, your spiritual walls, and the combat zone of the world and the flesh. This chapter continues the study of

specific targets of the enemy focusing on the strategic territories of the physical body, the family, finances, and attacks through human personalities.

STRATEGIES OF SATAN: PHYSICAL ATTACKS

Your body is the temple of the Holy Ghost:

> **Know ye not that ye are the temple of God, and that the Spirit of God dwelleth in you?**
>
> **If any man defile the temple of God, him shall God destroy; for the temple of God is holy, which temple ye are. (I Corinthians 3:16-17)**

Because your body is the temple of God's Spirit, it will be attacked by Satan through:

SICKNESS:

Sickness is in the world because of the original sin of Adam and Eve. Although all sickness is in the world because of sin, it does not mean everyone who is suffering is sick because of their own sin.

The Bible reveals various reasons for sickness. The first, and perhaps most obvious, is illness caused by Satan. Satan attempts to afflict the body just as he attempts to afflict the soul and spirit. Your body is no more immune to his attacks than your spirit is to discouragement, condemnation, etc. But illness can also be used as chastisement to deal with sin. For an example see the story of Miriam in Numbers 12.

In one healing Jesus performed during His earthly ministry He said to the recipient:

> **...Behold, thou art made whole: sin no more, lest a worse thing come unto thee. (John 5:14)**

The illness of this man was apparently a result of sin. In another case, Jesus made it clear that the illness was not the result of sin but for the glory of God:

> **And as Jesus passed by, He saw a man which was blind from his birth. And His disciples asked Him, saying, Master, who did sin, this man, or his parents, that he was born blind?**
>
> **Jesus answered, Neither hath this man sinned, nor his parents; but that the works of God should be made manifest in him. (John 9:1-3)**

An illness for the glory of God is one caused by Satan but which God uses for His glory when physical healing comes through prayer. This type of illness is a direct physical attack by Satan. When counter strategies for victory are applied, this physical attack can actually bring glory to God.

All illness is not caused by sin or Satan or as chastisement. Illness may result from the breaking of natural laws. For example, you may become ill because you do not eat properly or you probably will break your leg if you jump from the top of a coconut tree. Tempting you to break natural laws is an indirect attack of Satan on your body. He tempts you to eat improperly and not take care of your body because he knows that it can result in an illness which will hinder your effectiveness for God.

EXHAUSTION:

Satan also attacks the body through exhaustion which results from being too busy or working too hard. When you are extremely tired physically, Satan takes advantage and launches spiritual attacks. Satan came to Jesus when He was exhausted from 40 days of fasting (Matthew 4:2). When Elijah was tired from great spiritual exploits he became so discouraged that he wanted to die (I Kings 19:4).

DEATH:

Although physical death must come to all men until the return of the Lord Jesus Christ, Satan attempts to cause premature death. He will tempt people to commit suicide. He will also make you fearful of illness or accidents which could result in death.

ABUSE:

Satan also tempts people to abuse their physical bodies by putting toxic substances into them such as drugs and alcoholic beverages. He knows such toxic substances can result in illness, mental damage, and death.

SPIRITUAL COUNTER STRATEGIES: VICTORY OVER PHYSICAL ATTACKS

When you are ill, seek the Lord to determine the cause of your illness. Have you violated a natural law which resulted in your illness? For example, have you been eating improperly or drinking bad water? Have you been abusing your body by putting toxic substances such as cigarette smoke into your system?

If you have violated natural laws, God can still heal you. But you should use more wisdom in the future. Remember that your body is the temple of God's Holy Spirit. Stop breaking natural laws and take better care of your body. This is also important to remember in case of exhaustion. Jesus called His disciples to rest when they were exhausted from their busy ministry (Mark 6:31).

When Elijah was tired and depressed he rested under a tree and God sent an angel to him with physical food. Elijah waited until he received a new touch from God and his physical strength had been renewed before going on to new challenges of ministry (I Kings 19:4-8).

When illness results as chastisement for sin it is not caused by Satan and binding the power of the enemy will do no good. Only repentance and return to God will bring relief:

> **Come, and let us return unto the Lord; for He hath torn, and He will heal us; He hath smitten and he will bind us up. (Hosea 6:1)**

> **For I will restore health unto thee, and I will heal thee of thy wounds... (Jeremiah 30:17)**

> **...If thou wilt diligently hearken to the voice of the Lord thy God, and wilt do that which is right in His sight, and wilt give ear to His commandments, and keep all His statutes, I will put none of these diseases upon thee, which I have brought upon the Egyptians: for I am the Lord that healeth thee. (Exodus 15:26)**

> **Who forgiveth all thine iniquities; who healeth all thy diseases. (Psalms 103:3)**

In regards to physical attacks caused by Satan it is important to remember that as a believer, God is in control of your life. Satan cannot touch you physically nor take your life without the knowledge of God. Read Job chapters one and two which verify these facts. The power of God is greater than that of Satan. The God who made the human body has the power to heal that body. Claim these promises for healing when you experience physical attacks from Satan:

> **But unto you that fear my name, shall the Sun of righteousness arise with healing in His wings... (Malachi 4:2)**
>
> **Who His own self bare our sins in His own body on the tree, that we, being dead to sins should live unto righteousness; by whose stripes ye were healed. (I Peter 2:24)**
>
> **But He was wounded for our transgressions, He was bruised for our iniquities; the chastisement of our peace was upon Him, and with His stripes we are healed. (Isaiah 53:5)**
>
> **Beloved, I wish above all things that thou mayest prosper and be in health, even as thy soul prospereth. (III John 1:2)**

When Satan attacks you physically, call for the prayers of other believers, including elders in the church and those with the spiritual gift of healing:

> **...to another the gifts of healing by the same Spirit. (I Corinthians**
>
> **12:9) And God hath set some in the church...then gifts of healings... (I Corinthians 12:28)**
>
> **Is any sick among you? Let him call for the elders of the church; and let them pray over him, anointing him with oil in the name of the Lord:**
>
> **And the prayer of faith shall save the sick, and the Lord shall raise him up; and if he have committed sins, they shall be forgiven him. (James 5:14-15)**

Physical death is part of the process of life until the end of time as we know it. It should not be feared by believers, for we have the promise of eternal life:

> **O death, where is thy sting? O grave, where is thy victory? (I Corinthians 15:55)**
>
> **We are confident, I say, and willing rather to be absent from the body, and to be present with the Lord. (II Corinthians 5:8)**

Satan cannot take the life of a believer before the set time for his death, as illustrated by the story of Job. God does not overrule the human will, however. If a person is tempted by Satan to commit suicide and yields to that temptation, God will not overrule the act of his will.

STRATEGIES OF SATAN:
ATTACKS THROUGH HUMAN PERSONALITIES

Another way Satan attacks you is through human personalities. Satan can use people around you to attack you spiritually. The attack may come from family, friends, enemies, business associates, or even strangers. Human personalities can be disguised as "angels of light," apostles, and ministers of righteousness. But Satan is actually working through them:

> **For such are false apostles, deceitful workers, transforming themselves into the apostles of Christ.**
>
> **And no marvel for Satan himself is transformed into an angel of light. Therefore it is no great thing if his ministers also be transformed as the ministers of righteousness; whose end shall be according to their works. (II Corinthians 11:13-16)**

The strategy of transference of spirits has already been covered in a previous chapter. But Satan also has other ways of using human personalities. Satan will use people to give you wrong counsel. Read the book of Job and note the wrong counsel given by his friends and his wife. Prophecy is one of the gifts of the Holy Spirit, but Satan also has his prophets. Personal prophecies through human personalities are not always God-inspired. Study the tragic example of this in I Kings 13. Attacks of Satan will come through trusted friends as well as enemies or unbelievers:

> **For it was not an enemy that reproached me; then I could have borne it; neither was it he that hated me that did magnify himself against me; then I would have hid myself from him;**
>
> **But it was thou, a man mine equal, my guide, and mine acquaintance. We took sweet counsel together, and walked unto the house of God in company. (Psalms 55:12-14)**

Satan uses human personalities to exalt you and tempt you to take God's glory for yourself:

> **And the people gave a shout, saying, it is the voice of a god, and not of a man. And immediately the angel of the Lord smote him, because he gave not God the glory and he was eaten of worms, and gave up the ghost. (Acts 12:22-23)**

People are used by Satan to get you to stray from the plan of God for your life. Read how Peter was used of Satan to attack Jesus in this way (Mark 8:31-33). Satan will try to get your eyes on others instead of God. Peter was distracted from God's plan by concern with what He had planned for John (John 21:20-23).

Satan will tempt you to "emulation" which is a work of the flesh (Galatians 5:19-21). Emulations is trying to imitate, equal, or excel others, to copy, rival, or compete with them. As long as you are busy doing this, you will not follow the pattern of ministry God has for your own life.

Satan will use people to deceive you. Read how this happened to Joshua (Joshua 9). People will desert you (II Timothy 4:16-17; Acts 15:37- 38; John 6:66). Satan will try to hinder your spiritual objectives in relation to others (I Thessalonians 2:18), and will cause confusion and disharmony (I Corinthians 14:33; James 3:16). Satan also will use others to affect the circumstances in your life Read how this happened to Joseph in Genesis chapters 37 and 39.

SPIRITUAL COUNTER STRATEGIES: VICTORY OVER HUMAN PERSONALITIES

In a previous chapter on transference of spirits the importance of carefully selecting friends and associates was stressed. This is an important counter strategy in gaining victory over attacks of Satan launched through others. Choosing close associates carefully will eliminate much deception, desertion, disagreement, wrong counsel, and hindering of spiritual progress. But two

other important counter strategies bring victory over human personalities.

First: Obey God rather than man.

> **Then Peter and the other apostles answered and said, We ought to obey God rather than men. (Acts 5:29)**

Second: Follow others only as they follow God.

> **Be ye followers of me, even as I also am of Christ. (I Corinthians 11:1)**

> **Be ye therefore followers of God... (Ephesians 5:1)**

Do not accept counsel or prophecies from anyone when they do not agree with God's written Word. Do not admire or follow the leadership of those whose lives do not line up with God's Word. Recognize you will only be successful as long as you follow God's plan for your life. You will not be successful in emulating others. You must not be diverted by those around you. You must rely on revelation, not imitation.

Although those around you may manipulate circumstances that affect you, remember that God is still in control. Although Joseph experienced such an attack through human personalities, God turned it for his good:

> **So now it was not you that sent me hither, but God... (Genesis 45:8)**
>
> **But as for you, ye thought evil against me; but God meant it unto good, to bring to pass, as it is this day, to save much people alive. (Genesis 50:20)**

STRATEGIES OF SATAN: ATTACKS ON THE FAMILY

The family is the basic unit of society established by God in the beginning of the world when He first created man. God has always emphasized the family. He raised up a nation of chosen people from the family of one man, Abraham. He selected the physical union of a man and his wife to describe the spiritual union between Christ and the church. Throughout the Scriptures, God stressed the importance of the family in His plan of the ages.

The family is the basic structure from which all other structures stem. Government and religious leaders are raised in families. Communities and nations consist of many families grouped together. Because of the importance of this basic unit of society, the family is a target for attack by Satan.

Satan attacks the union between a man and his wife. He tries to cause improper sexual relationships which will result in sin (I Corinthians 7:5). He leads men and women into the sin of adultery (Galatians 5:19). He tries to get one partner to influence the other to turn away from God (Job 2). Satan promotes division in the home. This can range from arguments through divorce. Satan tries to bring division because he knows....

> **...Every kingdom divided against itself is brought to desolation; and every city or house divided against itself shall not stand. (Matthew 12:25)**

If Satan can bring division and destroy the homes of a nation, he can eventually destroy the nation itself.

God established a chain of command in the home. The man is to be the head of the home and love his wife. The wife is to follow his leadership and the children are to be in submission to their parents (I Corinthians 7; Ephesians 5:1-6:1). Satan targets the man of the home and tempts him to act in unloving ways. This results in a loss of respect and obedience from the wife and children. Satan tempts the wife to act in rebellion against the husband. Satan targets the children in a home. He creates an atmosphere of lack of discipline which results in rebellion. Read the story of Eli's sons in I Samuel 2 and of David's son, Absalom, in II Samuel 13-19.

Jesus warned of the attacks of the enemy in the home:

> **For from henceforth there shall be five in one house divided, three against two, and two against three.**

The father shall be divided against the son, and the son against the father; the mother against the daughter, and the daughter against the mother; the mother in law against her daughter in law, and the daughter in law against her mother in law. (Luke 12:52-53)

SPIRITUAL COUNTER STRATEGIES: VICTORY IN THE FAMILY

Many problems in the family unit can be avoided if believers choose their mate properly. The Bible warns that believers are not to marry unbelievers:

Can two walk together, except they be agreed? (Amos 3:3)

Be ye not unequally yoked together with unbelievers; for what fellowship hath righteousness with unrighteousness? and what communion hath light with darkness? (II Corinthians 6:14)

When a family unit is composed of believers and unbelievers, spiritual division exists. This division is not a conflict between flesh and blood. It is a spiritual conflict. It cannot be won by harsh words or through debate and argument.

Satan fights the unity of the family because it is a natural parallel of the unity between Christ and the church. Believers must recognize this and declare:

...but as for me and my house, we will serve the Lord. (Joshua 24:15)

As heir of the promise of Abraham, you can also claim the promise "In thee shall all the families of the earth be blessed" (Genesis 12:3). Because you are a spiritual heir of Abraham, your family will be blessed.

To protect against attacks of Satan, the family must grow together spiritually. Prayer and study of God's Word will bind the family together:

And these words, which I command thee this day, shall be in thine heart: And thou shalt teach them diligently unto thy children, and shalt talk of them when thou sittest in thine house, and when thou walkest by the way, and when thou liest down, and when thou risest up.

And thou shalt bind them for a sign upon thine hand, and they shall be as frontlets between thine eyes.

And thou shalt write them upon the posts of thy house, and on thy gates. (Deuteronomy 6:6-9)

The family must be in proper order before you assume leadership in ministry. New Testament requirements for leadership are that the home of leaders be in order. (See Titus 1 and I Timothy 3). Wrong emphasis on ministry has resulted in division in many Christian homes. To defeat Satan's strategy in this area, the home must be in scriptural order before a believer engages in ministry leadership positions.

Parents have a responsibility to discipline their children. The home problems of Eli and David resulted because of lack of discipline. The Bible instructs believers regarding this responsibility:

> **Train up a child in the way he should go: and when he is old, he will not depart from it. (Proverbs 22:6)**
>
> **He that spareth his rod hateth his son: but he that loveth him chasteneth him betimes (early). (Proverbs 13:24)**

STRATEGIES OF SATAN: FINANCIAL ATTACKS

Finances and material possessions of believers are another area Satan targets for attack. His attacks are launched in two major areas:

> **One**: Financial loss through no fault of the believer. This is a direct attack of Satan on the finances or material possessions of believers.
>
> **Two:** Attacks on finances or material possessions through violation of Scriptural guidelines.

The first type of attack is illustrated by the example of Job in chapters 1 and 2. Satan attacked Job's finances by destroying his herds (which was his business) and his home. The roof literally fell in! The Bible declares Job was a righteous man, so we know he was not in violation of Scriptural principles.

The second type of attack is illustrated by any violation of Scriptural guidelines. Satan knows if he can lead believers to violate Biblical principles, their finances will not be blessed. Without material possessions and finances they will not be able to support the spread of the Gospel to the nations of the world.

Study the following references to discover how Satan attacks in our finances:

> -Improper business partnerships with unbelievers: II Corinthians 6:14-18 (This verse is often only applied to the marriage relationship, when in fact it is applicable to any union of believers with non-believers).
> -Debt: Romans 13:8
> -Co-signing for debts of others: Proverbs 6:1-2
> -Withholding payment when funds are readily available: Proverbs 3:27-28
> -Withholding tithes and offerings: Malachi 3:1-12; Proverbs 11:24
> -Dishonesty: Proverbs 16:8; Acts 5:3-4
> -Fraud: James 5:3-4
> -Unfair wages: Jeremiah 22:13
> -Greed: Proverbs 28:22

-Intemperance: Proverbs 23:21
-Violation of government laws regarding money: Romans 13:6-7
-Laziness which results in poverty: Proverbs 20:13
-"Get-rich-quick" schemes: Proverbs 20:21; 28:22
-Love of money: I Timothy 6:10
-Business and financial situations creating "weights": II Timothy 2:4.
-Regarding offerings lightly and receiving inordinate funds for personal gain: I Samuel 2:29

SPIRITUAL COUNTER STRATEGIES: VICTORY IN FINANCES

Satan can attack the finances and material possessions of believers through no fault of their own. You read about this in the example of Job. But remember, Satan did not touch the finances or possessions of Job without the permission of God. This was an attack permitted by God to try Job's faith. Because Job was faithful, God blessed him with more than he had in the beginning.

When you experience financial difficulties through no fault of your own, you can be assured it is an attack launched by the enemy. If faith in God is maintained and you continue to govern their financial affairs according to Scriptural principles, God's blessing of restoration will follow this temporary trial:

So the Lord blessed the latter end of Job more than his beginning...(Job 42:12)

If you are experiencing financial difficulties because of the violation of Scriptural principles then you must repent and correct the violation. You must dissolve partnerships with unbelievers (II Corinthians 6:14-18). You must correct dishonesty (Proverbs 16:8, Acts 5:3-4) and violation of government laws (Romans 13:6-7). To counteract the strategies of Satan you must refrain from fraud (James 5:3-4), unfair wages (Jeremiah 22:13), greed (Proverbs 28:22), intemperance (Proverbs 23:21), and laziness (Proverbs 20:13).

You should remove yourself from business and financial transactions which entangle and prevent you from being a good spiritual warrior (II Timothy 2:4). You should refuse "get-rich-quick" schemes (Proverbs 20:21; 28:22) which are motivated by the love of money (I Timothy 6:10). You must trust in God rather than wealth (Deuteronomy 8:18-19; Psalms 49:6). You should refuse to co-sign debts for others (Proverbs 6:1-2) and get out of debt yourself (Romans 13:8; Proverbs 3:27-28).

If you are withholding offerings and tithes, you must correct this omission (Proverbs 11:24; Malachi 3:1-12). If you are in positions where you receive offerings, you must not use them for personal gain or regard them lightly (I Samuel 2:29). When you give to God, you must give your tithes and offerings:

-Willingly: Exodus 35:5; I Chronicles 29:9
-With A Perfect Heart: I Chronicles 29:9
-Freely: Matthew 6:38
-Secretly: Matthew 6:3

- Regularly: I Corinthians 16:2
- Cheerfully: II Corinthians 9:7
- With Simplicity: Romans 12:8
- According To Your Income: Matthew 5:42
- According To Your Ability: Ezra 2:69
- By Percentage Of Income: Genesis 14:20; 28:22; Leviticus 27:30; II Chronicles 31:5; Malachi 3:10

It is only by correcting these Scriptural violations that you can overcome the attacks of Satan in the area of finances.

INSPECTION

1. Write the Key Verse from the Articles Of War.

2. List some of Satan's strategies against the physical body.

3. Summarize spiritual counter strategies for victory in the physical body.

4. How does Satan use human personalities to war against believers?

5. List some spiritual counter strategies for victory over human personalities which war against believers.

6. What are some strategies Satan uses against the family?

_____

_____

_____

7. List some spiritual counter strategies for victory in the family.

_____

_____

_____

8. What are some of Satan's strategies in the financial and material realm?

_____

_____

_____

9. List some spiritual counter strategies for victory in the financial and material realm.

_____

_____

_____

(Answers to tests are provided at the conclusion of the final chapter in this manual.)

TACTICAL MANEUVERS

1. Read the book of Job. Job was attacked in the physical, material, and family realms. He was also attacked through human personalities. Behind each of these circumstances and areas of attack there was a spiritual reason. See Job.1:6-12; 2:1-6; 42:5.

    REMEMBER: There is a spiritual reason behind every circumstance and problem which you face in life.

2. For further discussion of sickness and divine healing of the body, obtain the Harvestime International Institute course entitled "Battle For The Body." Because sickness and divine healing are covered in detail in the "Battle For The Body" manual, the material is not repeated in this course. It is important that you study further in this area, however, as Satanic attacks the body are a major tactic of the enemy.

3. Are you being attacked physically or financially? How does your attitude and practice of giving line up with what you were taught in this lesson. Do you give...

    -Willingly: Exodus 35:5; I Chronicles 29:9
    -With A Perfect Heart: I Chronicles 29:9
    -Freely: Matthew 6:38
    -Secretly: Matthew 6:3
    -Regularly: I Corinthians 16:2
    -Cheerfully: II Corinthians 9:7
    -With Simplicity: Romans 12:8
    -According To Your Income: Matthew 5:42
    -According To Your Ability: Ezra 2:69
    -By Percentage Of Income: Genesis 14:20; 28:22; Leviticus 27:30

SPIRITUAL WARFARE ADVANCED TRAINING

ADVANCED INSTRUCTION IN SPECIFIC AREAS OF WARFARE

After gaining some experience in warfare, soldiers usually receive more advanced instruction in specific areas of warfare. This portion of the warfare manual is entitled "spiritual warfare advanced training," the initials of which spell "SWAT." In military action, a "SWAT" team is a specialized group of soldiers used for difficult missions.

CHAPTER NINETEEN
TRANSFERENCE OF SPIRITS

OBJECTIVES:

Upon completion of this chapter you will be able to:

- Write the Key Verse from memory.
- Explain the phrase "transference of spirits."
- Give a Biblical example of the transference of a good spirit.
- Give a Biblical example of the transference of an evil spirit.
- Explain counter strategies for defense against transference of an evil spirit.

KEY VERSE FROM THE ARTICLES OF WAR:

And I will come down and talk with thee there: and I will take of the spirit which is upon thee, and will put it upon them; and they shall bear the burden of the people with thee, that thou bear it not thyself alone. (Numbers 11:17)

INTRODUCTION

In this chapter you will study one of the most powerful and influential strategies used by Satan. Recognition of this strategy will answer many questions you have had in the past as you witnessed negative changes in your family, friends, and church fellowship...perhaps even in yourself. The strategy of which we speak is called "transference of spirits."

SOME EXAMPLES FROM LIFE

First, consider the following examples from life:

EXAMPLE ONE:

Your youngest son was raised to be part of a closely knit family with good communication. He respected your rules and you attended church together. Suddenly he does not want to be with the family or attend church. He becomes sullen, withdrawn, and rebellious. He defies your instructions and stays out late at night. You cannot understand the sudden change. You did not have this problem with your older son. You have given them both the same love and guidance. What caused this situation?

EXAMPLE TWO:

An assistant pastor, who was formerly a great spiritual blessing to the church, becomes discontent, critical, and refuses to submit to the leadership of the pastor. He gathers a group of people around him. They develop similar attitudes. The assistant pastor sows discord and splits the fellowship.

WHAT IS THE PROBLEM?

Examine the problem with your son and you will find the change came about after someone else came into his life who he respected and admired. He began to associate closely with this person. He began to tell you what they thought or said and what their parents allowed and he began to pattern himself after their style of behavior and dress.

In the case of the associate pastor, you will find a similar situation. Because families in the church loved and respected him as a spiritual leader, they listened as he sowed the seeds of discord. His critical and rebellious spirit soon spread to others in the church.

TRANSFERENCE OF SPIRITS

Both of these situations occurred because of a strategy of Satan called "transference of spirits." To "transfer" means to convey from one person to another. The word "spirit" as used in this lesson refers to the "character, attitude, or motive behind an action," not a demon.

The actions of each person exhibit a certain "spirit." For example, a person can demonstrate a gentle spirit, a boisterous spirit, or a rebellious spirit by his actions. A person's spirit can be influenced by the spiritual forces of good or evil and he can transfer his spirit to others on a personal or group basis.

IMPORTANCE OF THE SPIRIT

Before you study some Biblical examples of transference of spirits, it is important to understand your own spirit and why it is an important target of Satan's attack. God created your spirit:

> **The burden of the word of the Lord for Israel, saith the Lord, which stretcheth forth the heavens, and layeth the foundation of the earth, and formeth the spirit of man within him. (Zechariah 12:1)**

> **Thus saith God the Lord, He that created the heavens, and stretched them out; He that spread forth the earth, and that which cometh out of it: He that giveth breath unto the people upon it, and spirit to them that walk therein. (Isaiah 42:5)**

It is the spirit that gives life:

> **For as the body without the spirit is dead, so faith without works is dead also. (James 2:26)**

At death, the spirit returns to God:

> **Who knoweth the spirit of man that goeth upward, and the spirit of the beast that goeth downward to the earth. (Ecclesiastes 3:21)**

> **Then shall the dust return to the earth as it was: and the spirit shall return unto God who gave it. (Ecclesiastes 12:7)**

God is the Lord of your spirit:

> **Let the Lord, the God of the spirits of all flesh, set a man over the congregation. (Numbers 27:16)**

> **Furthermore we have had fathers of our flesh which corrected us, and we gave them reverence: shall we not much rather be in subjection unto the Father of spirits, and live? (Hebrews 12:9)**

God weighs or judges your spirit:

> **All the ways of a man are clean in his own eyes; but the Lord weigheth the spirits. (Proverbs 16:2)**

God wants to put His spirit (the Holy Spirit) within you so you will be able to live for Him. This is why Satan attacks your spirit:

> **And I will put my spirit within you, and cause you to walk in my statutes, and ye shall keep my judgments, and do them. (Ezekiel 36:27)**

God wants to preserve your spirit in holiness until the return of Jesus Christ:

> **And the very God of peace sanctify you wholly; and I pray God your whole spirit, and soul, and body be preserved blameless unto the coming of our Lord Jesus Christ. (I Thessalonians 5:23)**

One important reason Satan attacks the spirit of man is because it is the spirit that bears witness with the Holy Spirit and gives assurance of salvation:

> **The Spirit itself beareth witness with our spirit, that we are the children of God. (Romans 8:16)**

Another reason is that God uses your spirit to guide your life. In the natural world a candle gives light so that one has guidance. This is the function of the spirit in the spiritual world:

> **The spirit of man is the candle of the Lord, searching all the inward parts of the belly. (Proverbs 20:27)**

Satan also attacks the spirit because he knows it is a man of right spirit that God uses for His Kingdom:

> **...but to this man will I look, even to him that is poor and of a contrite spirit, and trembleth at my word. (Isaiah 66:2)**

Satan attacks the spirit because God dwells with a man of right spirit. He also sends revival through and to a man of right spirit:

> **For thus saith the high and lofty One that inhabiteth eternity, whose name is Holy; I dwell in the high and holy place, with him also that is of a contrite and humble spirit, to revive the spirit of the humble, and to revive the heart of the contrite ones. (Isaiah 57:15)**

When Satan causes wrong spirits in a church fellowship, he prevents revival. Satan combines his attacks on your spirit with his attack on your tongue. As you previously learned, the tongue is used by Satan to cause a breach in the spirit. A breach is an open place, a hole that provides entrance for the enemy:

> **A wholesome tongue is a tree of life: but perverseness therein is a breach in the spirit. (Proverbs 15:4)**

When Satan causes you to sin with your tongue, he has created a breach which provides access to your spirit.

IS TRANSFERENCE OF SPIRITS SCRIPTURAL?

It is possible to receive "another spirit". Paul mentions transference of "another spirit":

> **For if he that cometh preacheth another Jesus, whom we have not preached, or if ye receive another spirit, which ye have not received... (II Corinthians 11:4)**

Biblical examples also support the concept of transference of spirits. An example of the transference of a good spirit is found in Numbers 11:16-17:

> **And the Lord said unto Moses, Gather unto me seventy men of the elders of Israel, whom thou knowest to be the elders of the people, and officers over them; and bring them unto the tabernacle of the congregation, that they may stand there with thee.**
>
> **And I will come down and talk with thee there: And I will take of the spirit which is upon thee, and will put it upon them; and they shall bear the burden of the people with thee, that thou bear it not thyself alone. (Numbers 11:16-17)**

The powerful anointing of God upon Moses was transferred from him to these selected elders. They came under the influence of Moses. Their spirits were in unity with and submission to his.

SATAN'S STRATEGY: TRANSFERENCE OF AN EVIL SPIRIT

Satan is an imitator, not an originator. He uses the pattern established by God for transferring a good spirit to transfer wrong spirits between men. One example of this is the story of the twelve spies sent by Moses to spy out the land promised by God to Israel. Read the account in Numbers 13:17-14:39.

Ten of these spies returned with a negative report. They told of the great walled cities and the powerful enemy forces in the land. They transferred a spirit of fear and unbelief to God's people:

> **...We are not able to go up against the people; for they are stronger than we. And there we saw the giants, the sons of Anak, which come of the giants, and we were in our own sight as grasshoppers, and so we were in their sight. (Numbers 13:31, 33)**

But two of the twelve spies had a different spirit:

> **But my servant Caleb, because he had another spirit with him, and hath followed me fully, him will I bring into the land where into he went; and his seed shall possess it. (Numbers 14:24)**

> **And Joshua the son of Nun, and Caleb the son of Jephunneh, which were of them that searched the land, rent their clothes;**

> **And they spake unto the company of the children of Israel, saying, The land, which we passed through to search it, is an exceeding good land.**

> **If the Lord delight in us, then He will bring us into this land, and give it us; a land which floweth with milk and honey. (Numbers 14:6-8)**

Here were two contrary spirits seeking to control the people. One was the spirit of unbelief. The other was the spirit of belief:

> **And Caleb stilled the people before Moses, and said, Let us go up at once, and possess it; for we are well able to overcome it. (Numbers 13:30)**

Look how the negative spirit of the ten spies affected the people:

> **And all the congregation lifted up their voice, and cried; and the people wept that night.**
>
> **And all the children of Israel murmured against Moses and against Aaron; and the whole congregation said unto them, Would God that we had died in the land of Egypt! Or would God we had died in this wilderness!**
>
> **And wherefore hath the Lord brought us unto this land, to fall by the sword, that our wives and our children should be a prey? Were it not better for us to return into Egypt?**
>
> **And they said one to another, Let us make a captain, and let us return into Egypt. (Numbers 14:1-4)**

There were spirits of despair, murmuring, and rebellion transferred by the ten spies to God's people. Israel was not kept out of the Promised Land because of an inferior army. They were kept out because of a wrong spirit.

Why were the people affected by the evil spirit instead of the good? Because of the basic sin nature people tend to immediately accept and believe an evil report. There is also a tendency to "follow the crowd" and accept the decision of the majority as the will of God. Also, if Israel had accepted the positive report, it would have meant putting their lives on the line. They would have to expose themselves to great danger. Our human nature always wants to take the easy way out.

This powerful strategy of transference of spirits accounts for many of the spiritual battles fought by believers today. It accounts for the abrupt changes from positive to negative behavior which we witness in those around us. It explains why two children, raised in the same home, who receive the same Christian training, can turn out so differently. It is the reason behind divisions in homes, friendships, and church fellowships. When you maintain close association with or come under the influence of a person with a spirit more powerful than yours, you are open to the transference of that spirit to your own spirit. You are influenced by that spirit and it is transferred to you.

COUNTERSTRATEGIES:
PREVENTING TRANSFERENCE OF AN EVIL SPIRIT

God has given spiritual counter strategies to prevent the transference of an evil spirit:

CONTROL YOUR OWN SPIRIT:

Control your own spirit. Be sure you do not develop a wrong spirit which you can transfer to others:

> **He that hath no rule over his own spirit is like a city that is broken down, and without walls. (Proverbs 25:28)**

> He that is slow to anger is better than the mighty; and he that ruleth his spirit than he that taketh a city. (Proverbs 16:32)

> ...therefore take heed to your spirit, that ye deal not treacherously. (Malachi 2:16)

GUARD YOUR TONGUE:

As you have learned, the tongue can be used to create a breach in the spirit and provide access to the enemy. Watch what you say!

GUARD YOUR AFFECTIONS:

> Keep thy heart with all diligence; for out of it are the issues of life. (Proverbs 4:23)

Guard your affections. Do not give your respect and love to just everyone. You open yourself up emotionally to those you love and respect and this makes you receptive to their spirit.

CAREFULLY SELECT YOUR ASSOCIATES:

The book of Proverbs warns repeatedly of the danger of association with those who have wrong spirits. For examples read Proverbs 1:10-19 and 2:11-22. We are warned:

> Make no friendship with an angry man; and with a furious man thou shalt not go;

> Lest thou learn his ways, and get a snare to thy soul. (Proverbs 22:24-25)

> Enter not into the path of the wicked, and go not in the way of evil men.

> Avoid it, pass not by it, turn from it, and pass away. (Proverbs 4:14-15)

> Go from the presence of a foolish man, when thou perceivest not in him the lips of knowledge. (Proverbs 14:7)

> Be not among winebibbers (drunkards)...(Proverbs 23:20)

> Whoso is a partner with a thief hateth his own soul... (Proverbs 29:24)

If you walk with wise men their spirits will be transferred to you:

> He that walketh with wise men shall be wise; but a companion of fools shall be destroyed. (Proverbs 13:20)

Choose your close associates carefully. If you are a parent, carefully monitor the associates of your children.

GUARD YOUR PHYSICAL SENSES:

You will remember from the study of the flesh that your physical senses are important. Protect your hearing from reports of gossip, accusations, slander, and criticism. They can cause you to develop a wrong spirit. Guard your eyes from violent and pornographic movies or reading materials which can transfer spirits of adultery, lust, and violence.

USE CAUTION IN LAYING ON OF HANDS:

The "laying on of hands" is one of the foundations of the Christian faith spoken of by Paul in Hebrews 6:1-3. It has important spiritual purposes which are covered in detail in another Harvestime International Institute course entitled "Foundations Of Faith."

What is important to recognize here is that, as demonstrated in the story of Moses and the seventy elders, a spirit can be transferred by the "laying on of hands." If a good spirit can be transferred by the laying on of hands, it is probable that an evil spirit can be also. Be careful about who you allow to "lay hands" on you for the purpose of spiritual impartation.

INSPECTION

1. Write the Key Verse from the Articles Of War.

2. What is meant by the phrase, "transference of spirits?"

3. Give a Biblical example of the transference of a good spirit.

4. Give a Biblical example of the transference of an evil spirit.

5. List six strategies of defense against transference of evil spirits.

(Answers to tests are provided at the conclusion of the final chapter in this manual.)

TACTICAL MANEUVERS

1. Study further the transference of a good spirit: The prophet Elisha asked for the "mantle" of Elijah to fall upon him at the time of Elijah's death. This "mantle" symbolized the spirit of God which was upon Elijah. Elisha asked for a "double portion" of the good spirit which rested on Elijah. Read the story in II Kings 2.

2. Study further the transference of an evil spirit: Read the story of Ananias and Sapphira in Acts 5:1-11. This is an example of a husband who transferred a spirit of deception to his wife.

3. Study the following references. They reveal the many ways your spirit can be affected with certain attitudes and emotional responses, both right and wrong. Your spirit can be:

    Jealous: Numbers 5:14
    Hardened: Deuteronomy 2;30
    In Anguish: Exodus 6:9
    Good: Nehemiah 9:20
    Guileless: Psalms 32:2
    Right: Psalms 51:10
    Broken: Psalms 51:17
    Overwhelmed: Psalms 77:3; 142:3; 143:4
    Diligent and searching: Psalms 77:6
    Steadfast: Psalms 78:8
    Failing within: Psalms 143:7
    Faithful: Proverbs 11:13; II Corinthians 4:13
    Hasty: Proverbs 14:29; Ecclesiastes 7:9
    Haughty: Proverbs 16:18
    Humble: Proverbs 16:19
    Wounded: Proverbs 18:14
    Vexed: Ecclesiastes 1:14
    Patient: Ecclesiastes 7:8
    Proud: Ecclesiastes 7:8
    Seeking: Isaiah 26:9
    Judgmental: Isaiah 28:6
    In error: Isaiah 29:24
    Humble and contrite: Isaiah 57:15
    Poor and contrite: Isaiah 66:2
    Quieted: Zechariah 6:8
    Excellent: Daniel 5:12; 6:3
    Grieved: Daniel 7:15
    Wise: Exodus 28:3
    Strong: Luke 2:40
    Wrong: Luke 9:55
    Worshipful: John 4:23-24; Philippians 3:3

Troubled: Genesis 41:8; Daniel 2:3; John 13:21; II Thessalonians 2:2
Persuasive: Acts 6:10
Stirred: Ezra 1:1; Haggai 1:14; Acts 7:16
Pressed: Acts 18:5
Fervent: Acts 18:25; Romans 12:11
Bound: Acts 20:22
Serving: Romans 1:9
Circumcised: Romans 2:29
New: Ezekiel 11:19;18:31; 36:26; Romans 7:6
In bondage: Romans 8:15
Bear witness with God's spirit: Romans 8:16
Slumbering: Romans 11:8
Meek: Galatians 6:1
Meek and quiet: I Peter 3:4
Prayerful: I Corinthians 14:14; One
with God: I Corinthians 6:17
Glorifying God: I Corinthians 6:20
Singing: I Corinthians 14:15
Refreshed: I Corinthians 16:18; II Corinthians 7:13
Restless: II Corinthians 2:13
Filthy: II Corinthians 7:1
United with other believers: II Corinthians 12:18; Philippians 1:27
Preserved: I Thessalonians 5:23
An example of the believers: I Timothy 4:12
Fearful: II Timothy 1:7
Lustful: James 4:5
Willing: Exodus 35:21; Matthew 26:41
Poor: Matthew 5:3
Perceptive: Mark 2:8
Ready: Mark 14:38
Sorrowful: I Samuel 1:15
Sad: I Kings 21:5
Rejoicing: Luke 1:47
Sighing: Mark 8:12

4. Do you feel you have been affected by the transference of an evil spirit? Who do you believe influenced your spirit? What were the results of this negative influence? If you have been affected by the transference of an evil spirit and to defend against being affected by such, follow the counter strategies given in this chapter:
    -Control your own spirit.
    -Guard your tongue.
    -Guard your affections.

- Carefully select your associates.
- Guard your physical senses.
- Use caution in "the laying on of hands."

5. There is a special gift of the Holy Spirit called "discerning of spirits." It enables believers to recognize whether a spirit is good or evil. You can study more about this gift in the Harvestime International Institute course entitled "Ministry Of The Holy Spirit."

CHAPTER TWENTY

SPIRITUAL WICKEDNESS IN HIGH PLACES

OBJECTIVES:

Upon completion of this chapter you will be able to:

- Write the Key Verses from memory.
- Explain what is meant by "spiritual wickedness in high places."
- Summarize the strategies of Satan in this area.
- Identify spiritual counter strategies to overcome spiritual wickedness in high places.

KEY VERSES FROM THE ARTICLES OF WAR:

And no marvel; for Satan himself is transformed into an angel of light. Therefore it is no great thing if his ministers also be transformed as the ministers of righteousness: whose end shall be according to their works. (II Corinthians 11:14-15)

INTRODUCTION

You have learned that spiritual warfare is not with flesh and blood. You studied about the forces of evil and how they are organized. This chapter focuses on a specific division of Satan's evil forces, "spiritual wickedness in high places." The Apostle Paul warns of these forces:

For we wrestle not against flesh and blood, but against principalities, against powers, against the rulers of the darkness of this world, against spiritual wickedness in high places. (Ephesians 6:12)

HIGH PLACES

It seems to be inherent in human nature to think of God as dwelling somewhere in the heights. From earliest times men have chosen high places for worship, both of the true God or false gods and idols invented by man. In Old Testament times these high places became the scenes of evil orgies and human sacrifice connected with the worship of false gods.
God told Israel when they entered the Promised Land to drive out all the inhabitants of the land and destroy their high places:

Then ye shall drive out all the inhabitants of the land from before you, and destroy all their pictures, and destroy all their molten images, and quite pluck down all their high places. (Numbers 33:52)

In the book of Judges we read of Israel's failure to drive the people out of the land. As a result, they fell into idolatrous worship in the high places. After the period of the judges, some of the good kings of Israel destroyed the high places. Others rebuilt them and worshiped false gods.

King Manasseh was one who rebuilt the high places. After he had been punished and repented for this sin, he was restored to his throne and resumed worship of the true God. The people still sacrificed in the high places, but "only unto Jehovah their God" (II Chronicles 33).

When Gideon was called of God to be a mighty warrior, the Lord told him to destroy the altar and cut down the wooden image. Then Gideon was to build an altar to God. A burnt offering could be made only after the high places were torn down. It was then that deliverance came! God still calls today for the "spiritual wickedness in high places" to be torn down by the mighty warriors of God.

STRATEGIES OF SATAN:
SPIRITUAL WICKEDNESS IN HIGH PLACES

When Paul speaks of "spiritual wickedness in high places", he is referring to wicked spirits who have infiltrated the religious systems of the world. They have even crept into the congregations of the righteous. Satan has organized his evil forces to imitate the organization of the true church of God. In some cases he actually has congregations known as "The Church of Satan" or "Spiritualists." He has set up a form of worship in the spiritual high places.

Satan has also prompted the organization of many cults. The word "occult" means to "hide or conceal a thing." Cults are those who are part of the occult, those who hide and conceal evil behind the cloak of religion. But even more dangerous, Satan has set up his system right in the true church through evil people who have "crept in unawares" (Jude 4).

Through "spiritual wickedness in high places" Satan aims for the total allegiance of man. He uses false cults, his own church of Satan, and infiltration into the Body of Christ to accomplish this purpose. This is what the Bible teaches about Satan's religious organization:

SATAN HAS HIS OWN TRINITY:

You previously studied about the Trinity of God, the Father, the Son Jesus Christ, and the Holy Spirit. Satan also has a trinity. It includes Satan himself, the beast and a false prophet. You will study about the latter two in the final chapter of this course. In the book of Revelation, John describes the final destiny of this unholy trio:

> **And the Devil that deceived them was cast into the lake of fire and brimstone, where the beast and the false prophet are, and shall be tormented day and night for ever and ever. (Revelation 20:10)**

SATAN HAS HIS OWN CHURCH:

God established the true church which is known as the "Body of Christ" of which Jesus is the head:

> **Now ye are the Body of Christ, and members in particular...
> (I Corinthians 12:27)**

> **But speaking the truth in love, may grow up into Him in all things, which is the head, even Christ:**
>
> **From whom the whole body fitly joined together and compacted by that which every joint supplieth, according to the effectual working in the measure of every part, maketh increase of the body unto the edifying of itself in love. (Ephesians 4:15-16)**

Satan has his own church which is called "a synagogue of Satan":

> **...I know the blasphemy of them which say they are Jews, and are not, but are the synagogue of Satan. (Revelation 2:9)**

The name "synagogue of Satan" is not always openly used but his synagogue is established anywhere the true Gospel of the Lord Jesus Christ is not preached.

SATAN HAS A DOCTRINE:

The Bible is filled with the true doctrines of God revealed by the Holy Spirit:

> **All Scripture is given by inspiration of God, and is profitable for doctrine... (II Timothy 3:16)**

The doctrine of Satan is called the "doctrine of demons":

> **Now the Spirit speaketh expressly, that in the latter times some shall depart from the faith, giving heed to seducing spirits, and doctrines of devils. (I Timothy 4:1)**

One category of demons is called "seducing spirits." Their specific job is to seduce men into doctrinal error. The "doctrine of demons" is any teaching presented as "truth" which does not agree with the written Word of God.

SATAN HAS A SYSTEM OF SACRIFICE:

In Romans 12:1, we are told to present ourselves to God as a living sacrifice. This means we are to surrender in total allegiance to God. Satan demands sacrifices also:

> **But I say, that the things which the Gentiles sacrifice, they sacrifice to devils, and not to God: and I would not that ye should have fellowship with devils. (I Corinthians 10:20)**

Satan demands total allegiance of body, soul, and spirit. There are actually services of sacrifice carried out where men and women dedicate themselves to the service of Satan. The blood sacrifice of humans and animals is also practiced.

SATAN HAS HIS OWN COMMUNION SERVICE:

The sharing of the communion bread and wine was started by Jesus as a way of remembering His sacrifice for the sins of all mankind on the cross (I Corinthians 11:23-34). Satan counterfeits this by his own communion:

> **Ye cannot drink the cup of the Lord, and the cup of devils; ye cannot be partakers of the Lord's table, and of the table of devils. (I Corinthians 10:20)**

SATAN HAS MINISTERS:

God has called some believers to serve as pastors and minister to His church and proclaim the Gospel (I Corinthians 12:28). Satan also has ministers:

> **And no marvel; for Satan himself is transformed into an angel of light. Therefore it is no great thing if his ministers also be transformed as the ministers of righteousness; whose end shall be according to their works. (II Corinthians 11:14-15)**

SATAN'S MINISTERS PROCLAIM HIS GOSPEL:

The "gospel" of Satan is contrary to the Gospel of the Lord Jesus Christ:

> **Which is not another, but there be some that trouble you and would pervert the Gospel of Christ.**
>
> **But though we or an angel from Heaven preach any other gospel unto you than that which we have preached unto you, let him be accursed. (Galatians 1:7-8)**

SATAN HAS HIS THRONE:

God has a throne in Heaven. Satan also has a throne, although we are not told its exact location:

> **And the beast which I saw was like unto a leopard, and his feet were as the feet of a bear, and his mouth as the mouth of a lion: and the dragon (Satan) gave him his power, and HIS SEAT, and great authority. (Revelation 13:2)**

SATAN HAS WORSHIPERS:

There are many who worship the true God. Satan also has worshipers:

> **...and they worshiped the beast, saying, Who is like unto the beast?... (Revelation 13:4)**

Some worshipers of Satan pretend to be followers of Jesus:

> **The field is the world; the good seed are the children of the kingdom; but the tares are the children of the wicked one;**
>
> **The enemy that sowed them is the devil; the harvest the end of the world; and the reapers are the angels. (Matthew 13:38-39)**

Satan mixes the bad "seed" in with the good "seed" (believers).

SATAN HAS PROPHETS:

God has set in the Church prophets, men who are especially anointed to bring a direct message from Him to the Church (I Corinthians 12:28). Satan has false prophets who deliver false messages:

> **And many false prophets shall rise, and shall deceive many. (Matthew 24:11)**

SATAN HAS TEACHERS:

God has anointed some people as teachers to share and explain His Word to others (I Corinthians 12:28). But all teachers are not from God. Satan has false teachers to spread his evil doctrine:

> **But there were false prophets also among the people, even as there shall be false teachers among you, who privily shall bring in damnable heresies, even denying the Lord that bought them, and bring upon themselves swift destruction.**
>
> **And many shall follow their pernicious ways; by reason of whom the way of truth shall be evil spoken of.**
>
> **And through covetousness shall they with feigned words make merchandise of you... (II Peter 2:1-3)**

Satan's teachers bring in "damnable heresies," teachings which are false and cause division. They speak lies and are experts at mixing truth and error in a way that makes error acceptable. Many such false teachings have resulted in the growth of cults. A cult is any system of religion or worship that is not in complete harmony with the written Word of God. It is a "damnable heresy."

The names, doctrines, and organization of cults vary from nation to nation. There are so many cults that it is not possible to mention them all. But remember, any religious system not in harmony with God's Word is a cult. (The "Tactical Maneuvers" section of this lesson provides additional guidelines for recognizing cults.)

SATAN HAS APOSTLES:

An apostle is a person who spreads the Gospel and establishes churches (I Corinthians 12:28). Satan also has apostles doing his work throughout the world. They deceive people by imitating the true apostles:

> **For such are false apostles, deceitful workers, transforming themselves into the apostles of Christ. (II Corinthians 11:13)**

Satan's apostles become leaders of false cults and infiltrate churches in leadership capacities.

SATAN IMITATES JESUS BY FALSE CHRISTS:

Satan has even imitated the Lord Jesus Christ by raising up false Christs. Jesus warned:

> **...Take heed, that no man deceive you. For many shall come in my name, saying, I am Christ; and shall deceive many. (Matthew 24:4-5)**

SATAN HAS A SYSTEM OF COMMUNICATION:

The Bible is a record of how God spoke to man. God continues to speak to men today. (An entire Harvestime International Institute course is devoted to "Knowing God's Voice"). Satan also speaks to man. His first words to humans resulted in their fall into sin in the Garden of Eden (Genesis chapter 3).

Believers pray to God regarding their needs and God responds to the prayer of the righteous (James 5:16). Satan's followers pray to him and communicate with evil spirits. Sometimes Satan responds with supernatural events such as voices, the moving of objects, noises, etc.

God has communicated to man through His written Word, the Bible. Satan's message is also being communicated through the written word by evil magazines, books, motion pictures, and music. God's communication through His written and spoken Word provides guidance for man in the affairs of life. Satan has a system of false guidance accomplished through methods such as the following:

Astrology and horoscope: Which use stars to predict events and give guidance.

Reading of tea leaves, cards, pictures, bumps on the head, palms of the hand and crystal balls: The formation of the tea leaves, cards, lines in the human hand, crystal balls, and pictures are claimed to give guidance.

Witchcraft: Using spells, potions, charms, magic, rituals, séances, divinations, methods of chance, divining rods, visions, drawings, and similar unscriptural methods to receive guidance.

SATAN HAS SUPERNATURAL POWER:

Jesus promised supernatural power to His followers after they received the baptism of the Holy Spirit (Acts 1:8). Satan also gives supernatural power and authority (Revelation 13:2). His demons can provide supernatural strength and energy. Satan can perform many supernatural signs and miracles:

> **For they are the spirits of devils, working miracles... (Revelation 16:14)**

Jesus said:

> **Many will say to me in that day, Lord, Lord, have we not prophesied in thy name? and in thy name have cast out devils? and in thy name done many wonderful works?**
>
> **And then will I profess unto them, I never knew you: depart from me, ye that work iniquity. (Matthew 7:22-23)**

SPIRITUAL COUNTER STRATEGIES:
TO WAR AGAINST SPIRITUAL WICKEDNESS IN HIGH PLACES

Here are specific counter strategies for overcoming spiritual wickedness in high places.

RECOGNIZE SATAN IS AN IMITATOR:

From your study of this lesson to this point it should be clear that Satan is an imitator. "Imitation" means to copy or counterfeit something. The first step in overcoming wickedness in high places is to recognize that Satan imitates every part of God's religious structure. Be on the look out for imitations!

USE DISCERNMENT:

There is a special gift of the Holy Spirit called "discerning of spirits." It is an unusual ability given by God to immediately discern another person's spirit and know if they are good or evil. If you have this spiritual gift, use it in dealing with spiritual wickedness in high places.

If you do not have this gift, God has provided other methods of detection. In II Peter 2 and the book of Jude He has listed the characteristics of these men with seducing spirits. (Use the "Tactical Maneuvers" section of this lesson for additional study of this subject.) All believers are encouraged to "try the spirits" (I John 4:1) To "try" means to "test" the spirits. If you test the spirits it does not mean you are operating in unbelief. If the spirits are of God, they will pass the test!

STUDY THE WORD OF GOD:

In order to recognize the false doctrines of Satan's teachers, apostles, prophets, and ministers, you must know what is taught in the Word of God. Paul told Timothy:

> **Study to shew thyself approved unto God, a workman that needeth not to be ashamed, rightly dividing the word of truth. (II Timothy 2:15)**

Even though Paul was a great spiritual leader in the early Church, the believers at the city of Berea checked everything he said by God's written Word:

> **These were more noble than those in Thessalonica, in that they received the Word with all readiness of mind, and searched the Scriptures daily, whether those things were so. (Acts 17:11)**

To avoid being deceived by spiritual wickedness in high places, examine everything that is taught in light of God's Word.

REJECT ANYTHING NOT IN THE WORD:

Satan establishes much spiritual wickedness in high places through so-called "special revelation of new truth." People will claim special dreams, appearances by angels, visions, voices, or other supernatural events. But Paul warned:

> **...but there be some that trouble you and would pervert the Gospel of Christ. But though we or an angel from Heaven preach any other gospel unto you than that which we have preached unto you, let him be accursed. (Galatians 1:7-8)**

Reject any teaching, doctrine, manifestation, or revelation that is not in harmony with God's Word. Do not accept any so-called prophecy that is not in right relation to the faith (Romans 12:6) and which does not come to pass (Deuteronomy 18:22). Do not accept any revelation that leads you away from God and the truth of His Word (Deuteronomy 13:1-5):

> **The man that wandereth out of the way of understanding shall remain in the congregation of the dead. (Proverbs 21:16)**

EVALUATE BY SPIRITUAL FRUIT:

Because Satan imitates the power of God through supernatural manifestations of miracles, signs, and wonders, God has provided a special method of evaluating ministries. You are to evaluate the supernatural on the basis of spiritual fruit.

Jesus compared men to fruit trees. He said you would know both the real and the imitators by their spiritual fruit:

> **A good tree cannot bring forth evil fruit, neither can a corrupt tree bring forth good fruit.**
>
> **Wherefore by their fruits you shall know them. (Matthew 7:18, 20)**

Satan can imitate spiritual gifts and God's power, but he has no imitation for a holy life exhibiting the fruit of the Holy Spirit which includes true...

> **...love, joy, peace, longsuffering, gentleness, goodness, faith, Meekness, temperance; against such there is no law. (Galatians 5:22-23)**

Evaluate ministries by spiritual fruit, not by supernatural manifestations of power.

AVOID EVERY SATANIC INFLUENCE:

God warned Israel to avoid every type of Satanic influence:

> **...destroy all their pictures, and destroy all their molten images, and quite pluck down all their high places. (Numbers 33:52)**

Read the additional instructions God gave in Deuteronomy 18:9-14. Israel was to have no contact with the work of Satan in any form. You should destroy anything you own that has to do with witchcraft or the work of the devil. This would include idols, "lucky charms", potions, amulets, crystal balls, games, divining devices, and other similar items. This is what people did in the New Testament when they became believers:

> **Many of them also which used curious arts brought their books together, and burned them before all men, and they counted the price of them, and found it fifty thousand pieces of silver (about $9,300). (Acts 19:19)**

Destroy any evil literature and music that does not glorify God. Do not spend time in places where there is evil influence. The Bible records that God manifested Himself in special places such as the Old Testament temple and the upper room of a house on the Day of Pentecost. It is equally true that Satanic power can be manifested in special places dedicated to evil. This would include places where evil pictures are shown, drinking and riotous behavior is occurring, séances are being held, worship of Satan is occurring.... anywhere sinful practices are going on. Avoid such environments, because Satan's power is especially strong there. You cannot pray the Lord's prayer, "Lead us not into temptation" and then put yourself in such a place:

> **...and I would not that ye should have fellowship with devils.
> (I Corinthians 10:20)**

Do not associate with false leaders, teachers, prophets, ministers or apostles:

> **Abstain from all appearance of evil. (I Thessalonians 5:22)**

EXPOSE THE WICKEDNESS IN HIGH PLACES:

Believers must not ignore this spiritual wickedness in high places. Pastors must preach the whole counsel of God in face of deception (II Timothy 4:1-4). False teachings of the occult and doctrines of demons must be identified. Believers are not to participate in the "unfruitful works of darkness" but rather should expose them (Ephesians 5:11).

EXERCISE THE MINISTRY OF DELIVERANCE:

God's organization, the true Church, is more powerful than that of Satan. You learned that Jesus is the head of the church, and that believers are the body. With that in mind, read the following verses:

> **(God) hath put all things under His feet, and gave Him to be the head over all things to the church. Which is His body... (Ephesians 1:22-23)**
> **To the intent that now unto the principalities and powers in heavenly places might be known by the church the manifold wisdom of God. (Ephesians 3:10)**

Jesus is the head of the Church. Believers are the body. If all things (including Satan and his religious structure) are under the feet of Jesus, then they are also under our feet because we are the body. "Under the feet" means they are under the power and authority which God has delegated to us. Jesus said He has given us power over "all the power of the enemy" (Luke 10:19). This includes spiritual wickedness in high places.

The church is actually to demonstrate His power to these principalities and powers! We must exercise this ministry to bring deliverance from those in bondage to "spiritual wickedness in high places." We must turn men from darkness to light and from the power of Satan to the Kingdom of God (Acts 26:18).

INSPECTION

1. Write the Key Verses from the Articles Of War.

   _____

   _____

   _____

2. How were the "high places" used in the Old Testament?

   _____

   _____

   _____

3. What is meant by "spiritual wickedness in high places"?

   _____

   _____

   _____

4. Summarize what you remember about Satan's strategies for spiritual wickedness in high places.

   _____

   _____

   _____

5. Summarize the counter strategies for overcoming wickedness in high places.

   _____

   _____

   _____

(Answers to tests are provided at the conclusion of the final chapter in this manual.)

TACTICAL MANEUVERS

1. Study the warnings of God to Israel regarding Satan and the occult: Deuteronomy 18:10-12; Leviticus 17:7; 19:31; 20:16.

2. Study more about sacrifices made to devils: Deuteronomy 32:17; II Chronicles 11:15; Psalms 106:37.

3. The following are common characteristics of cults:

    -Dictatorial Leadership: Cults cluster around domineering, charismatic personalities who have absolute authority and are accountable to no one.
    -Exclusive: Cults adopt the attitude that they are the only group with divine truth. They exclude from fellowship others who disagree with them.
    -Legalistic: Cults usually have strict rules of belief and behavior which have no Scriptural basis.
    -Defensive: Cult members are usually led to believe that society, organized religion, and government are against them. This causes a reactionary attitude towards religion, government, and society.
    -Oppressive: Cult members are usually manipulated and oppressed by the leadership.
    -Secretive: Many things about the cult are kept secret from "outsiders".
    -Higher Revelation: Cults often claim "higher revelation" from God. They will always have a source of authority beyond the Scriptures. It may be the writings or revelation of the founder or another person. In some cases it may be the founder's peculiar interpretation of the Bible. Their doctrines will not currently represent Biblical teachings.
    -Anti-church: Cults vigorously oppose organized churches and their pastors.
    -Anti-family: Cults are sometimes anti-family, which means they want their members to break ties with family who are not members. They try to break biological family ties in order to retain their disciples.

4. There are so many cults world-wide that it is impossible to identify them all, but because of the increasing growth of what is called the "new age movement" we felt it important to mention this "doctrine of demons." At the time of writing of this manual new age involves millions of people throughout the world and is growing rapidly! Major publishing houses in the United States now have "new age departments" because there is such a demand for their materials. The new age movement has its roots in the ancient occultism. It has historical ties to Sumerian, Indian, Egyptian, Chaldean, Babylonian, and Persian religious practices. The "new age" is a fresh title, but the occult involved in it is nothing new.

    Jesus is considered just one of many "gods" or revealers of "truth" along with Buddha, Mohammed, Confucius, Zoroaster, Krishna, and many others. The deity of Jesus is denied. While the Bible teaches man was separated from God by sin, the new age movement believes man is born inherently good. They believe he is separated from God only in his consciousness and is the victim of a false sense of separate identity that blinds him to his essential unity with God.

Because of this, the new age movement advocates various methods of altering the consciousness such as yoga, meditation, chanting, ecstatic dancing, drugs, etc. They consider these a means to salvation. Because of these practices and involvement with witchcraft, sorcery, mediums, etc., new age practices open the door to demonic influences.

The new age movement also heavily emphasizes the ancient Hindu doctrines of reincarnation and karma. They believe successive reincarnations help work off bad "karma." Man is considered his own "Satan" as well as his own god and salvation. Thus, the new age movement is rooted in humanism. Values and morals are relevant, which means they vary according to person and culture. You create your own reality by doing what feels good and right to you. The new age movement does not recognize the moral absolutes in God's Word.

Because they believe there is no evil, therefore there is no crime and no victim. Death is considered an illusion and because they believe a person is continually reincarnated, there are no victims of murder or abortion.

The new age methods of spreading propaganda include infiltration (even of the true Church) and unification through world-wide networking. New age members speak of a coming "purging" which will cleanse the world of all those "lesser evolved souls" who do not see themselves as gods. They are working towards the centralizing of power on a global level, an ungodly unity with man as the sole authority. The new age movement may be one of several forces through which Satan will culminate his plans for global unification. It could very possibly could be the platform upon which the antichrist will rise to world-wide domination.

5. Study II Peter chapter 2 and the book of Jude. List characteristics that will help you detect Satan's messengers in the church:

**Characteristics Of False Teachers
II Peter Chapter Two:**

False teachers teach damnable heresies: Verse 1
They deny the Lord: Verse 1

Now...continue the list:

_____
_____
_____
_____
_____
_____
_____
_____
_____

**Characteristics Of "Certain Men"
Who Have Crept Into The Church
The Book Of Jude**

_____
_____
_____
_____
_____
_____
_____

CHAPTER TWENTY-ONE
DEALING WITH DEMONIC POWERS

OBJECTIVES:

Upon completion of this chapter you will be able to:

- Write the Key Verse from memory.
- Identify three major kinds of demons that attack the body, soul, and spirit of man.
- Explain the value of the gift of discerning of spirits in dealing with demonic powers.
- Explain what it means to be demon obsessed.
- Identify characteristics of a demon obsessed person.
- Explain what it means to be demon oppressed.
- Identify characteristics of a demon oppressed person.
- Explain what it means to be demon possessed.
- Identify characteristics of a demon possessed person.
- Summarize the ministry of Jesus in relation to demonic powers.
- Use Scriptural guidelines for overcoming demonic powers.

KEY VERSE FROM THE ARTICLES OF WAR:

How God anointed Jesus of Nazareth with the Holy Ghost and with power: who went about doing good, and healing all that were oppressed of the Devil; for God was with Him. (Acts 10:38)

INTRODUCTION

For too long the work of demons has been dismissed by many as a curious practice in heathen cultures. It has not been considered as a problem which invades lives, homes, churches, and nations.

As you previously learned, demons are an organized force of powers against which believers wrestle (Ephesians 6:12). Demons are the agents through which Satan works to accomplish his purposes in the world.

The following chart summarizes what you have learned about demons and their realms of operation:

Seducing Spirits	Unclean Spirits	Spirits Of Infirmity
▽	▽	▽
Affect the spirit of man	Affect the soul of man	Affect the body of man

▽

These spirits can...

▽

Oppress
Possess
Obsess

If you are to wage effective warfare, you must learn how to deal with demonic powers that obsess, oppress, or possess the body, soul, and spirit. There are people all about you who are tormented, troubled, and even possessed by the powers of darkness known as demons. This chapter presents guidelines for ministering to those affected by demonic powers.

JESUS AND DEMONS

The teaching and ministry of Jesus demonstrated that demonic spirits are a real force of evil. What Jesus taught about demons and how He dealt with them yields valuable information about the strategies of Satan.

Jesus accepted the fact that Satan is the ruler of a host of demons. He taught of the reality and power of demons. He said that the casting out of demonic powers was one of the signs that the Kingdom of God had come. Read Matthew 12:22-30, Mark 3:22-27, and Luke 11:14-23 for a summary of what Jesus taught concerning demons.

A large portion of the ministry of Jesus involved dealing with demons. It is the example of Jesus and the authority of His name that provides the Scriptural basis for dealing with demonic powers. Jesus ministered to "all" who came with demonic problems. Peter said of Jesus:

> **... God anointed Jesus of Nazareth with the Holy Ghost and with power: who went about doing good, and healing all that were oppressed of the devil. (Acts 10:38)**

In the "Tactical Maneuvers" section of this lesson you can study further on specific cases recorded in the Bible where Jesus dealt with demonic powers.

HOW DEMONS OPERATE

As you have learned, demons are used by Satan to oppose God, His plan and purposes, and His people. They also war against unbelievers to keep them from the truth of the Gospel. Demons control specific territories (principalities) such as the prince of Persia mentioned in Daniel 10:12-13. Demons also work through personalities, through men and women, to accomplish Satanic objectives in the world.

Opposition to God's will is Satan's main objective. The word "Satan" means "adversary." Satan is primarily God's adversary (Job 1:6; Matthew 13:39). He is secondarily, man's adversary (Zechariah 3:1; I Peter 5:8).

As you learned, demons have different natures. Remember that one demon identified himself in I Kings 22:23 as a "lying spirit." A "deaf and dumb" spirit is identified in Mark 9:25. Demons of various natures operate as spirits of infirmity, seducing spirits, and unclean spirits. Satan uses them to war against man in body, soul, and spirit:

SPIRITS OF INFIRMITY:

These are spirits that can afflict the bodies of believers as well as unbelievers. Read Luke 13:10-17. This woman was afflicted with a spirit of infirmity. She was present in the Sabbath services and Jesus called her "a daughter of Abraham." Both of these facts indicate she probably was a follower of God, yet her body had been afflicted by Satan for eighteen years. For other examples of demonic powers afflicting the body see Matthew 12:22; 17:15-18; Acts 10:38; II Corinthians 12:7.

SEDUCING SPIRITS:

These spirits afflict the spirit of man, seducing him to believe doctrinal lies and be condemned to eternal punishment. They are the spirits of false doctrine, cults, false Christs, and false teachers:

> **Now the Spirit speaketh expressly, that in the latter times some shall depart from the faith, giving heed to seducing spirits, and doctrines of devils. (I Timothy 4:1)**
>
> **These seducing spirits are deceptive. They actually work miracles which lead some to believe they are of God:**
>
> **For they are the spirits of devils, working miracles, which go forth unto the kings of the earth and of the whole world, to gather them to the battle of that great day of God Almighty. (Revelation 16:14)**

Even him, whose coming is after the working of Satan with all powers and signs and lying wonders.

> **And with all deceivableness of unrighteousness in them that perish; because they received not the love of the truth, that they might be saved. (II Thessalonians 2:9-10)**

Seducing spirits include the "spirit of divination" mentioned in Acts:

> **And it came to pass, as we went to prayer, a certain damsel possessed with a spirit of divination met us, which brought her masters much gain by soothsaying. (Acts 16:16)**

Such spirits of divination or "familiar spirits" operate in fortune tellers, witches, and palm, crystal ball, and tea leaf readers. Through unscriptural methods the spirits of divination foretell the future or discover knowledge which is naturally unknown. Warnings against familiar spirits are given in Leviticus 19:31; 20:6; Deuteronomy 5:9; 18:10; Leviticus 20:27; and I Samuel 28:3.

Seducing spirits sear the conscience, seduce, entice, tempt, allure, interest, fascinate, excite, arouse, attract, and deceive. Seducing spirits are active in causing "spiritual wickedness in high places." They are present and operative in every cult and wherever doctrinal error exists.

Remember that Satan craves worship and he will take it any way he can get it. Seducing spirits entice men and women to worship idols and even Satan himself. You will learn more about "spiritual wickedness in high places" in Chapter Twenty.

UNCLEAN SPIRITS:

These demonic powers afflict the soulish nature of man. They are responsible for immoral acts, unclean thoughts, temptations and other strategies of Satan used to bind men and women. When Satan controls individuals with unclean spirits, he can also operate in homes, churches, and entire nations as these groups are composed of individuals. This is how Satan works in the various levels of structure in society. For examples of unclean spirits see Matthew 10:1; 12:43; and Mark 1:23-26.

OPPRESSION, OBSESSION, POSSESSION

Evil spirits can oppress people. To oppress means to bear down, come against, or bind from the outside. This oppression is accomplished by evil spirits in various ways. They cause depression, create negative circumstances, and insert wrong thoughts into the mind such as thoughts of suicide, immorality, unbelief, fear, etc. Demons create Satanic circumstances and situations which tempt men to sin:

> **How God anointed Jesus of Nazareth with the Holy Ghost and with power: who went about doing good, and healing all that were OPPRESSED of the Devil; for God was with Him. (Acts 10:38)**

Demons can also possess human beings. Demon possession is a condition in which one or more evil spirits (demons) inhabit the body of a human being and take complete control of their victim at will. Some people prefer using the word "demonized" rather than possession, but regardless of the term, the possessed person is host to resident demons. "Possession" does not mean a person is not responsible for his own sin. His responsibility rests with the factors that led to his condition.

Possession can happen willingly. A person may desire to be taken over by spirit powers in order to conduct séances, pronounce curses, become a witch, or secure some other supernatural power. Possession can also occur unwilling. An individual does not ask to be possessed, but through sinful thoughts, actions, or contact with the occult possession results.

Demonic powers operating in parents and the sins of the parents can affect the next generation. (See Exodus 20:5; 34:7; and Deuteronomy 5:9.) This accounts for demon possession or oppression of children such as recorded in Mark 7:24-30 and 9:17-21.

There is also such a thing as demon obsession. This is a condition where one becomes obsessed by an interest in or preoccupation with demons. It is an unusual interest in the occult, demons, and Satan which controls interests and pursuits in a dictating manner. Such obsession with demon powers can lead to possession by them.

CAN DEMONS AFFECT BELIEVERS?

A true believer cannot be possessed by a demon because the Holy Spirit cannot inhabit the same temple as an evil spirit:

> **What? Know ye not that your body is the temple of the Holy Ghost which is in you, which ye have of God, and ye are not your own?**
>
> **For ye are bought with a price: Therefore glorify God in your body, and in your spirit, which are God's. (I Corinthians 6:19-20)**

When you belong to God and are filled with the Holy Spirit, you cannot belong to Satan and be filled with his spirits at the same time. The Holy Ghost will not abide in the same "temple" with Satan.

But this does not mean believers cannot be affected by demonic powers. It is these powers against which we wrestle. Satan uses demonic powers to attack believers from the outside through oppression, the symptoms of which were previously discussed. But he cannot possess the true believer. To "possess" indicates inside occupation. To "oppress" or bind indicates control from the outside. The activities of believers can be Satanically directed if they allow demonic powers to oppress them. Such oppression or binding by evil powers permits Satan to use them for evil purposes.

This is what happened when Peter, a disciple of Jesus, was used of Satan to try to divert Jesus from suffering for the sins of all mankind. When Jesus described the suffering He was to go through, Peter said:

> **...Be it far from thee, Lord: this shall not be unto thee. (Matthew 16:22)**

Jesus said to Peter:

> **...Get thee behind me, Satan: thou art an offence unto me: for thou savourest not the things that be of God, but those that be of men. (Matthew 16:23)**

Jesus did not mean Peter was actually Satan. He recognized that at that moment Peter had allowed Satan to operate through him. He was not demon possessed, but he was allowing Satanic spirits to influence him.

> **Believers, by their own actions, give place or make room for Satan to use them. (Ephesians 4:27)**

When a person is born again, his name is written in a special book in Heaven called the book of life. Only those whose names are in this book will be residents of Heaven for eternity:

> **And whosoever was not found written in the book of life was cast into the lake of fire. (Revelation 20:15)**

It is possible to have your name written in the book of life, but later blotted out because of turning back to sinful living:

> **He that overcometh, the same shall be clothed in white raiment; and I will not blot out his name out of the book of life, but I will confess his name before my Father, and before His angels. (Revelation 3:5)**

If a believer continues in known, unconfessed sin, there is a point at which he can cease to be a Christian. The Apostle Paul expressed his own concern that he not be "cast away" after preaching to others:

> **But I keep under my body, and bring it into subjection: lest that by any means, when I have preached to others, I myself should be a castaway. (I Corinthians 9:27)**

Paul realized that sin, especially continued unconfessed sins of the flesh, could result in the loss of his own soul even though he had preached to others.

By continuing to live in sin you will eventually end up in a backslidden condition. This means you will no longer be a true follower of Jesus Christ. If you continue in known and unconfessed sin, no one can tell you at what point you cease to become a follower of Jesus and again become part of Satan's Kingdom. It is God that determines that point. But at when it does occur, you are opening yourself up to greater attacks of the enemy, including the possibility of demon possession. This is why it is important when you sin to immediately confess your sin and turn from unrighteousness:

If we confess our sins, He is faithful and just to forgive us our sins, and to cleanse us from all unrighteousness.

If we say that we have not sinned, we make Him a liar, and His Word is not in us. (I John 1:9-10)

Jesus is called the Word of God in many places in Scripture. If the Word of God does not dwell in you, then Jesus does not dwell in you.

HOW DEMONS GAIN CONTROL

Demons gain control in several ways:

1. Through generations: Demons may oppress or possess a person because of previous possession or oppression of the parents. This accounts for demonic influence over children (Exodus 20:5; 34:7; Deuteronomy 5:9).

2. Through the mind: The mind is one of the major battlefields of Satan. If Satan can control your thoughts, he will eventually control your actions. Lack of mental control eventually results in lack of use of the will. This leads to sinful actions. Continuing in sinful thoughts and actions can lead from oppression to possession and finally to a reprobate mind such as is described in Romans 1. This is a mind totally controlled by evil thoughts.
Demons also gain access through mind-altering drugs which reduce the ability to resist demons and grant increasing access. "Brain washing" or "mind control" teaching also provides an entrance point.

3. Through sinful actions: Sinful thoughts are soon fulfilled by sinful actions. For example, the thought of adultery is fulfilled in the actual act of adultery. Sin is rebellion, and rebellious thoughts and actions provides an entry point for demonic activity.

When a believer continues in sinful thoughts or actions they "give place" to the Devil (Ephesians 4:27). More spiritual room is given for the operation of the enemy. Sins of involvement with the occult, including objects, literature, séances, etc., are actions which are especially dangerous and attract demonic powers.

An unbeliever who lives in sin is open not only to oppression of demonic powers, but also possession. As you have learned, there is no neutral ground in spiritual warfare. You are either on the side of good or evil. You belong either to God or Satan. If you belong to Satan and have not experienced the new birth in Jesus Christ, then you are his to use, oppress, or possess as he wills.

4. Through desire: Some people desire and request of Satan to be under the control of demons powers. They do this for purposes of having supernatural power or performing supernatural acts.

5. Through an empty "house": Demons consider the body of the person they inhabit as their house (Matthew 12:44). When a person who has been delivered from demonic powers does not fill his spiritual house with the new birth experience and the infilling of the Holy Spirit, reentry may occur.

6. Through permission: Sometimes God grants permission for activities of demonic powers to accomplish special purposes. This can be allowed as a trial of believers as in the case of Job. It can also be judgment for sin as in the case of King Saul.

WHO IS TO DEAL WITH DEMONIC POWERS?

Dealing with demonic powers is not something to be left to professional ministers. Jesus said all believers would have the ability to overcome demonic powers:

> **And these signs shall follow them that believe: In my name shall they cast out devils... (Mark 16:17)**

Jesus has given His followers the ability to deal with demonic powers. He first delegated such power to the disciples:

> **And when He had called unto Him His twelve disciples, He gave them power against unclean spirits, to cast them out, and to heal all manner of sickness and all manner of disease. (Matthew 10:1)**

> **And He called unto Him the twelve, and began to send them forth by two and two; and gave them power over unclean spirits. (Mark 6:7)**

He delegated this same power to all believers:

> **And these signs shall follow them that believe: In my name shall they cast out devils... (Mark 16:17)**

> **Heal the sick, cleanse the lepers, raise the dead, cast out devils: freely ye have received, freely give. (Matthew 10:8)**

There is no Biblical basis for believing God intended this important ministry to be restricted to a particular group of people. A layman named Philip was used by God to cast out evil spirits in Samaria (Acts 8). But this does not mean believers should rush into encounters with demonic powers without proper preparation, as the sons of Sceva discovered (Acts 19).

It is also important that believers do not become overly demon conscious. We are not called to major in demons. There is no spiritual gift of "casting out demons." But you are not to fear demonic powers. When confronted with those affected by demons, you should have the power to bring deliverance from God.

DETECTING DEMONIC PRESENCE

To overcome demonic powers it is important to be able to recognize their presence and tactics. The Holy Spirit has provided a special spiritual gift for this purpose. This gift is called "discerning of spirits" (I Corinthians 12:10).

To discern means "to discover, evaluate, and make a distinction between." The gift of discerning of spirits enables a believer to discern the spirits operating in others. It permits him to discover, evaluate, and identify evil spirits.

The gift of discerning of spirits is very important when dealing with demonic powers. It enables you to immediately discern whether or not a person has an evil spirit operating through or against him. It prevents deception by seducing or lying spirits. One with this gift can recognize the evil tactics and motives of demonic powers.

For example, some deafness and dumbness (according to the Biblical record) is caused by a spirit. Other deafness and dumbness might be the result of an accident or illness. Discernment would enable you to determine the cause behind the condition which would enable specific ministry.

Not all believers have this special spiritual gift of discerning of spirits. If a believer does not have this gift there are signs of demonic presence which can be observed.

When the Syrophenician woman came to Jesus with an appeal that He cast out an unclean spirit from her daughter, she said "My daughter is grievously vexed with a devil" (Matthew 15:22). How did she know this? She knew it by the symptoms. Detection is simply observing what demonic spirits do to a person.

Here are some symptoms of demonic activity:

Demonic obsession is recognized by an uncontrollable and unusual preoccupation with demons, Satan, or the occult. Such a person may dabble in occult practices, constantly credit everything to Satan or demons, or be preoccupied with the study of demons and Satan.

Demonic oppression can be recognized by the following signs:

1. A physical binding: The "daughter of Abraham" who Jesus relieved of a spirit of infirmity was bound physically. See Luke 13:10-17. Chronic sickness may be demonic oppression. All illness is not caused by demonic powers. Some illness is caused by a violation of natural laws, such as not eating properly or drinking bad water. Some illness is also chastisement. One King in the Bible who did not give glory to God was stricken with intestinal worms and died!

2. A mental oppression: Disturbances in the mind or thought life such as mental torment, confusion, doubt, loss of memory, etc. Restlessness, inability to reason or listen to others, abnormal talkativeness or reserve may be exhibited. All mental problems are not caused by Satan. Discouragement, depression, and disorientation can be caused by allergies to certain foods or a wrong chemical imbalance in the brain. God is able to heal mental problems and illnesses not caused by demonic powers as well as bring deliverance in cases caused by demons. But caution should be taken not to class all illness or mental problems as being caused by demonic spirits. Sometimes a simple change in diet or lifestyle will eliminate a problem if it is caused by physical causes.

3. Emotional problems: Disturbances in the emotions which persist or recur, including

resentment, hatred, anger, fear, rejection, self-pity, jealousy, depression, worry, insecurity, inferiority, etc.

4. Spiritual problems: Extreme difficulties in overcoming sin, including sinful habits. Rejection of spiritual solutions to problems. Any type of doctrinal error or deception, including bondage to objects and literature of the cults.

5. Circumstances: Demons can create difficult circumstances which are oppressive. Such circumstances usually involve confusion and can immediately be identified as demonic because God is not the author of confusion (I Corinthians 14:33; James 3:16).

Demonic possession can be recognized by the following signs:

1. Indwelling of an unclean spirit: This is demonstrated by a basic moral uncleanness and filthiness. It might include the desire to go without clothing. For examples see Mark 5:2 and Luke 8:27.

2. Unusual physical strength: A person shows strength beyond normal capabilities. For examples see Mark 5:3 and Luke 8:29.

3. Fits of rage: These fits may be accompanied by foaming at the mouth. See Mark 9:14-29 and Luke 8:26-39.

4. Resistance to spiritual things: In the accounts in Mark 6:7 and 1:21-28, the demons knew Jesus immediately and asked Him to leave them alone. Fear of the name of Jesus, prayer, and the Word and blasphemy of that which is spiritual are all symptoms of demon possession. Excessive blasphemy may be noted or contorted physical features and abrupt behavior changes when spiritual things are mentioned.

5. Changes in personality and/or voice: A person who is normally shy may become aggressive or violent. Actions as well as appearance may be affected. Moral character and intelligence may change. Voice may be altered. See Mark 5:9.

6. Accompanying physical afflictions: In cases of demon possession, these appear most commonly to be afflictions of the mental and nervous system. (See Matthew 9:33; 12:22; Mark 5:4-5). They can also include a general "pining" or wasting away physically. (See Mark 9:14-29).

7. Self-inflicted physical injury: In Matthew 17:14-21 there is the story of a man's son who would cast himself in the fire. In Luke 8:26-39 this demon possessed man cut himself with stones to inflict physical injury.

8. Terrible anguish: Luke 8:28 relates that this man went about crying because of the terrible inner torments caused by his possession.

9. Incapacity for normal living: This man could not live in society but lived in the tombs of the cemetery. See Luke 8:27.

10. Through unscriptural methods, the ability to foretell the future or discover that which is unknown: The woman in Acts 16:16 is said to be "possessed" by a spirit of divination.

The following also may indicate demonic oppression, possession, or obsession:

1. Obsessive immorality such as involvement with pornography, adultery, fornication, masturbation, homosexuality, and other sex sins. Strong compulsions toward eating disorders, suicide, self-mutilation, maiming, and murder.

2. Addiction to drugs or alcohol.

3. Trances, visions, and meditation which are not focused on or from the one true God.

4. Bondage to emotions such as fear, anxiety, depression, hatred, rage, jealousy, backbiting, envy, pride, bitterness, negativism, and criticism.

COUNTER STRATEGIES: FOR DEALING WITH DEMONS

Here are some Scriptural strategies for dealing with demonic powers:

PRELIMINARY PREPARATION IN YOURSELF:

Faith comes by hearing the Word of God, the specific or "Rhema" Word. Begin to build faith in your own heart by reading the New Testament through with a new attitude:

-Whatever Jesus told His followers to do, you begin to do.
-Whatever He said He would do, expect Him to do it.
-If He said you can deliver those afflicted by Satan, then expect to see them delivered.
-If He said to cast out Devils, then do it in His name and expect them to obey you.

Disregard all the teaching of man and personal experiences you have had. Accept that the New Testament means exactly what it says. Accept it as true and act accordingly. You are an ambassador for Christ (II Corinthians 5:20). An ambassador never doubts that the country he represents will back up its Word.

Fast and pray before you go to minister deliverance. Since power and authority for deliverance comes from God, it is well to be in touch! Some demons will come out only by prayer and fasting. Isaiah 58 teaches that God honors the fast which focuses on ministering to the needs of others.

PRELIMINARY PREPARATION IN OTHERS:

Whenever possible, a team of believers should be used when binding or casting out demons. Jesus sent out His disciples in pairs for this ministry:

> **And He called unto Him the twelve, and began to send them forth by two and two: and gave them power over unclean spirits. (Mark 6:7)**

This does not mean you cannot minister alone to a demonically affected person when you encounter them, but there is strength in unity of prayer with another believer. Since strength comes from unity, those who are joining you in the ministry of deliverance should be similarly prepared with prayer and fasting.

In cases of oppression and obsession (such as depression, demonically caused illnesses, etc.), prepare the person who is to receive the ministry. They need to have their faith built through the "Ramah" word of God about deliverance. (This may not be possible in the case of possession).

If you encourage the demonically affected to be prayed for without proper instruction, it is like encouraging the unsaved to accept Jesus as Savior without knowing who He is, recognizing their sin and need for salvation. When sharing the Gospel a wise soul winner does not press for a decision too quickly. There is preliminary ministry to be done. Proper instruction must be given.

The same is true of deliverance. Sometimes, God delivers without such instruction. But in ministering deliverance you want to properly use every channel prescribed by God's Word to see the work done. Faith is one channel for God's delivering power and it comes by hearing God's Word, so instruction is important. Jesus combined preaching and teaching with healing and deliverance and He instructed His followers to do so also.

THE PLACE FOR MINISTRY:

Ministry of deliverance to those affected by demonic powers can be done during a regular part of the church service. Such ministry need not be confined only to private sessions. It is a valid ministry of the church.

Jesus ministered to the demon possessed as part of a regular church service (Mark 1:21-25). However, it is not necessary to wait until a regular service to deal with demonic powers. Jesus brought deliverance when and wherever they were encountered.

THE TIME OF MINISTRY:

When you are ready to minister deliverance...

1. Begin with worship and praise:

We enter His presence (where there is deliverance and healing) through worship and praise. Deliverance can come through worship and praise, even without ministry by prayer because God inhabits the praises of His people. When we praise, He is present to heal and deliver.

2. Create an environment of faith:

You already started to do this when you ministered the Word on deliverance, but you may also need to take additional steps to create an environment of faith.

Unbelief hindered even the ministry of Jesus in Nazareth. Sometimes Jesus put unbelievers out when he ministered (Mark 5:35-40). Other times He led people out of their village (an environment of unbelief) in order to minister to them (Mark 8:23). On occasion as God leads, you may need to ask those struggling with unbelief, fear, etc., to leave.

3. Pray first:

Ask for wisdom and discernment before you begin to minister deliverance. During prayer, God may reveal to you...

> -A word of knowledge: Specific facts and information about a person or condition so you will know how to pray. A "word of knowledge" can include a deep sense of knowing or an impression in your spirit, thoughts, words, or feelings. The Word of knowledge may reveal what the sickness is or why the person has the condition.
>
> -A Scripture verse: The Rhema word for that situation, condition, person, or group.
>
> -A vision: Pictures in the mind's eye pertaining to the one to whom you are ministering.
>
> -Words of faith: Special words of encouragement and faith specifically for that individual.
>
> -A special anointing: A sudden infusion of power, perhaps felt as a tingling, heat, or supernatural confidence.
>
> -A special act of faith, that if the person will perform, will be delivered.

4. Conduct a brief interview:

This is not required. It is optional and should be done according to the leading of the Lord. God may give you specific words of wisdom about the person's condition and you will not need to interview.

But if God does not supernaturally reveal something to you, do not hesitate to use the interview. Jesus used both natural and supernatural methods. On occasions He discerned people's conditions by the Holy Spirit. At other times He asked them what they wanted and how long they had been afflicted.

An interview helps you gain information so you can pray more specifically. It also helps you determine if the person needs further instruction before you pray. Jesus often did this. He asked people questions concerning their faith and then dealt with negative forces of unbelief before ministering. Study the following examples:

-Mark 5:1-20: Jesus questions the demonized man.
-Mark 8:22-26: Questioning the blind man.
-Mark 9:14-27: A boy with an evil spirit.
-Mark 10:46-52: Questioning blind Bartimaeus.

Ask the person, "What is the problem?" Speaking a request for prayer is important. Jesus delivered many who came to Him making known their need. The request is in itself an act of faith that can set in motion the healing processes (James 5:14-15). Ask for a specific statement. You need only brief facts. You do not need the complete history or a life's story.

Do not try to psychoanalyze the information you are given. Your function is to minister deliverance. Some unique cases may require privacy and more time for counseling with a trained counselor. Have counselors available for this purpose.

Ask the person who is to be prayed for, "Do you believe Jesus can deliver you?" If they answer positively, then ask, "Do you believe Jesus will do it now?" If the answer is "no" to either of these questions, further instruction from God's Word is needed.

When you are ministering to a large crowd, you will not be able to talk to each person. God may reveal to you specific demonically caused conditions of people in the audience or may lead you to pray specific prayers for individuals.

If you are ministering deliverance in a crowd, it is best to train others to minister along with you rather than you doing all the ministering yourself. The commission of Jesus was that these signs would follow THEM that believe, not "him." The work of the ministry was to be through the body, not just one or two lone believers or evangelists.

5. Determine the specific problem:

Use the information from the interview and/or the wisdom God has given to you to determine if the problem is in the:

Spiritual realm: Problems related to sin. These require a ministry of spiritual healing (salvation, repentance and forgiveness of sin).

Physical realm: Bodily sickness caused by demonic spirits of infirmity.

Emotional realm: Problems concerning anxiety, fear, anger, bitterness, resentment, guilt, doubt, failure, jealousy, selfishness, confusion, frustration, perfectionism in the energy of the flesh, unforgiveness, past situations.

This is often called "inner healing," but the term has been abused. It is not necessary to go back through a rehearsal of the facts and relive these emotions. It is not necessary to spend weeks, months, years to recover from such traumas. If you do this, you are trying to heal the old person instead of helping them become a new creation in Christ.

Problems in the emotional realm are often related to the social realm of a person's life, ie., they affect and stem from family and social relationships. Deliverance comes through identifying, asking forgiveness, and forgiving the other parties involved.

The greatest barrier to emotional healing is usually forgiveness, so emotional healing includes the healing of social relationships.

We are called to be ministers of reconciliation (II Corinthians 5:18-21). Reconciliation includes both with God and man, and this is where emotional, mental, or inner healing comes in (all similar titles for in essence the same thing).

You may need to instruct the person in forgiveness. It is not:

-Justifying someone else's wrongs which they have done ("They were under a lot of pressure")
-Denying we were hurt in the first place.
-Accepting with resignation what was done to you.
-Waiting for "time" to heal the hurt.

True forgiveness comes by:
-Recognizing what was done to us was wrong, the result of sinful men in a sinful world.
-Confessing the hurt to God and asking Him to heal the harmful emotions (i.e., hate, bitterness, etc.). You may not ever forget the fact of the incident...What you are in need of is healing for the wrong emotions relating to it.
-Asking God to help you forgive others involved, then forgiving even as Christ forgives you.

Recognize that God extends forgiveness to you as you forgive others: "Forgive us our trespasses AS we forgive those who trespass against us." The person may also need to forgive themselves (guilt over their own wrongdoing) and will definitely need to pray for emotional healing:

-Acknowledge the sin causing guilt and/or sinful emotions, confess it to God, and repent.
-Ask Him to forgive your sin and heal your emotions.
-Recognize when God forgives, He forgets (He casts our sins as far as east from west).
-Claim I John 1:8-9 and Romans 8:1.
-By an act of your own will, release yourself from condemnation. Control future thought patterns by casting down "vain imaginations" and "forgetting those things behind."

Mental realm: Problems stemming from negative thinking, attacks of Satan on the mind, mental retardation. Remember: Because man is a triune being, problems in one realm affect the whole person. As you minister, deal with the whole person, not just one area. Man is body, soul, spirit: Wholeness implies dealing with all of these.

6. Determine whether it is time to pray:

Determine whether or not it is time to pray the healing prayer. In most cases, you will pray, but in some, do not be surprised if the Lord directs you not to pray or to delay prayer.

Jesus delayed healing in the case of the Syrophonecian woman's daughter and Lazarus. He did not do many works at all in Nazareth because of unbelief. The Lord may also direct you to delay until further instruction is given, i.e., they may need to deal with a sin problem, need more instruction on deliverance, etc.

7. Pray the prayer of deliverance:

Pray a prayer of deliverance which focuses on the specific problem of demonic influence which you have identified. You do not have to persuade God to deliverance by your prayer. Just as salvation is already available, the same is true of deliverance. Just as salvation is based on the condition of faith, so is deliverance. God wants to deliver, just as He wants to save.

Although the power of God is sometimes present in a special way for deliverance (Luke 5:17), you can still pray without a special anointing to do so because Jesus commanded you to do so just as He told you to spread the Gospel.

Use others to help you minister if you are in a group setting. There is multiplication of spiritual power when more people are praying (Matthew 18:19). "Body ministry" discourages individuals who experience success in deliverance and those who receive it from giving glory to man. Jesus taught that first you should bind the enemy, then you can exercise power over him:

> **Or else how can one enter into a strong man's house, and spoil his goods, except he first bind the strong man? and then he will spoil his house. (Matthew 12:29)**

If demonic powers are binding in oppression from the outside, pray for their hold to be loosed and their powers to be bound. For example, Jesus loosed the woman in the synagogue from the spirit of infirmity. She was not possessed, but oppressed. A casting out was not necessary.

In cases of demon possession, you have the authority to cast demons out in the name of Jesus. It is not authority in your own power or ability, but in His name. It is important to use the name of Jesus in the actual prayer of casting out the demon.

Faith, fasting, and prayer are necessary to cast out demons. (Read the account in Matthew 17:14-21). This is why preliminary preparation is encouraged in these areas. The Word of God (Ephesians 5:17; Hebrews 4:12); the blood of Jesus (Revelation 12:11), and the infilling power of the Holy Spirit (Acts 1:8; 2:38) are also "tools" for deliverance God has given you.

Yelling and screaming at the demons is not necessary. It is your authority in the name of Jesus that will cause them to come out, not the volume of your voice during the prayer of deliverance.

Always forbid the demons to reenter. This is an important part of the prayer of deliverance:

> **When Jesus saw the people came running together, He rebuked the foul spirit, saying unto him, Thou dumb and deaf spirit, I charge thee come out of him, and enter no more into him. (Mark 9:25)**

Do not spend time talking with the demon, should it manifest itself through spoken words. Jesus rebuked demons and told them to be quiet (Luke 4:34-35). Remember that any conversation with demons is dangerous because there are lying spirits.

The Holy Spirit will direct you in the prayer of deliverance, but if you are new to this ministry here is a sample prayer pattern to study:

"In the name of Jesus Christ and on the basis of the authority of His power, His Word, His blood, and the Holy Spirit..."
    ...This establishes the power base for deliverance...

"...I bind you...."
    ...Jesus taught to bind the strong man first before attempting to cast him out...

"...and I command you..."
    ...Ministering deliverance is a prayer of authority, not of entreaty. You can speak quietly, but you must take authority over the forces of evil in the name of Jesus. Look directly into the eyes of the person as you speak.

"...the spirit of _____" or "...you foul spirit of Satan..."
    ...if the spirit has been identified either through spiritual or natural discernment, then name it specifically; otherwise, generally.

"...to depart...."
    ...this is the casting out process...

"...without harming_____(name of person being delivered), or anyone in this house, and without creating noise or disturbance"
    ...Sometimes the demon will try to harm the person or create disturbance.

"I forbid you to reenter this person..."
    ...Remember that Jesus used this command...

"...and I loose the Holy Spirit to fill of this person with the cleansing, delivering power of the blood of Jesus."

    ...We are told to loose as well as bind. If you have identified a specific spirit at work, loose the opposite spirit. For example, bind the spirit of pride and lose the spirit of humility.

Do not make a show of such ministry and try to attract crowds with it. When Jesus saw the actions of a demon attracting a crowd, He immediately stopped the performance being staged by the evil spirit and cast it out:

> **When Jesus saw that the people came running together, He rebuked the foul spirit, saying unto him, Thou dumb and deaf spirit, I charge thee, come out of him, and enter no more into him. (Mark 9:25)**

Do not attempt to cast demons into Hell. Jesus and His disciples did not do this. We have authority only to bind, loose, and cast out. There is a set time for the final judgment of demons in the future. The demons said to Jesus:

> **...What have we to do with thee, Jesus, thou Son of God? Art thou come hither to torment us BEFORE THE TIME? (Matthew 8:29)**

Prayer for those affected by demons can be done with or without the laying on of hands. Jesus used the laying on of hands to minister to the woman oppressed with the spirit of infirmity in Luke 13:11-13. In other cases, He did not lay on hands but simply spoke to the demons (Luke 9:42).

8. Praise God for the answer:

Follow prayer with praise to God for deliverance. Remember that in the Biblical example of the ten lepers, all were healed but only the one who returned to praise was made whole. Praise by faith and not by sight. You have done what God's Word said to do. Believe He has done what He said He would do. Thank Him for it.

RECOGNIZING SIGNS OF DELIVERANCE:

In cases of demonic possession, sometimes the demons come out with a struggle, such as crying out or throwing the person on the floor. When demons have departed (whether in possession or oppression), there will be a sense of release, joy, like the lifting of a weight.

PROVIDING FOLLOW UP CARE:

After deliverance, those who have been possessed by demons should be led in a prayer of confession, repentance, and renouncing any sins or involvements connected with the demonic activities. If the person has any occult items (for example idols, voodoo items, witchcraft equipment, etc.), these should be destroyed.

Additional follow up care is very important for those delivered from demonic possession. When a demon is cast out, he will seek another body through which to operate. Jesus taught that the departure of evil spirits leaves an empty place. There is danger of a demon returning to his former victim accompanied by worse spirits:

> **When the unclean spirit is gone out of a man, he walketh through dry places, seeking rest; and finding none, he saith, I will return unto my house whence I came out.**
>
> **And when he cometh he findeth it swept and garnished.**
>
> **Then goeth he, and taketh to him seven other spirits more wicked than himself; and they enter in, and dwell there; and the last state of that man is worse than the first. (Luke 11:24-26)**

When a demon is cast out it is restless and discontent outside of a human body. It is only by indwelling and controlling a human life that a demon is able to fulfill Satan's evil purposes. This is why casting the demon out is not enough. The spiritual "house" must be filled by the new birth experience and the infilling of the Holy Spirit. Follow up counseling and ministry is necessary. The person should be immersed in the Word of God and prayer and become part of a community of believers.

Those experiencing deliverance from demonic powers also should be encouraged to give their testimony. Jesus told the demoniac of Gadarene:

> **...Go home to thy friends, and tell them how great things the Lord hath done for thee, and hath had compassion on thee.**
>
> **And he departed and began to publish in Decapolis (ten cities) how great things Jesus had done for him; and all men did marvel. (Mark 5:19-20)**

PROTECTION FROM DEMONIC POWERS

There are specific ways to protect yourself from the activities of demonic powers. The most important protection is to receive Jesus Christ as Savior because demons cannot possess a true born-again believer. Keep yourself from sin, for through sin you "give place to the Devil." You provide opportunity for him to use demonic activities of oppression against you.

Be filled with the Holy Spirit. Demonic spirits and the spirit of God cannot inhabit the same spiritual vessel.

Avoid an obsessive interest in demons. It is not wrong to study what God's Word says about them, or courses such as this one which are based on God's Word. But do not read secular books, attend séances, etc., to learn more about demons. Avoid any contact with the occult. Do not consult witches, shaman, astrologers, horoscopes, card, palm, or tea leaf readers. Do not serve false gods or allow idols to come into your home:

> **The graven images of their gods you shall burn with fire; you shall not desire the silver or gold that is on them, nor take it for yourself, lest you be ensnared by it; for IT IS AN ABOMINATION TO THE LORD YOUR GOD.**
>
> **Neither shall you bring an abomination (an idol) into your house, lest you become an accursed thing like it; but you shall utterly detest and abhor it, for it is an accursed thing. (Deuteronomy 7:25-26 The Amplified Version)**

It is important to control your mind, your tongue, and select your associates carefully. It is also important to gain victory over the world and the flesh.

You must also wage both defensive and offensive warfare against demonic powers. Use the weapons and strategies you have learned about in this course.

INSPECTION

1. Write the Key Verse from the Articles Of War.

   _____

   _____

2. What are the three major kinds of demons that attack the body, soul, and spirit of man?

   _____

   _____

3. What is the value of the gift of discernment in dealing with demonic powers?

   _____

   _____

4. What does it mean to be demon possessed?

   _____

   _____

5. What are the characteristics that may be shown by a demon possessed person?

   _____

   _____

   _____

6. What does it mean to be obsessed by demons?

7. What are the characteristics of a person who is demon obsessed?

8. What does it mean to be oppressed by demons?

9. What are the characteristics of a person who is demon oppressed?

10. Summarize Scriptural guidelines given in this lesson for overcoming demonic powers.

(Answers to tests are provided at the conclusion of the final chapter in this manual.)

TACTICAL MANEUVERS

1.   Study the following examples of how Jesus dealt with demonic powers:

Incident: Woman in the synagogue with the spirit of infirmity (Luke 13:10-17).

Summary: This woman was attending Sabbath day services and Jesus called her a "daughter of Abraham". We can assume she was a righteous, God fearing person. Yet a spirit of infirmity had bound her for 18 years.

In His ministry, Jesus distinguished between normal physical illnesses, which were cured by laying on of hands or anointing with oil, and cases of demonic affliction. In cases of a believer being bound from the outside as a result of demonic affliction, the binding spirit was loosed. If it was an unbeliever with physical infirmities resulting from demonic possession, the demons were cast out.

The deliverance of this woman occurred during a regular church service. It raised opposition from the spiritual leaders, including the ruler of the synagogue. Dealing with demonic powers still raises objections from many spiritual leaders. Some deny their existence. Others deny their power to oppress or possess.

In this deliverance, Jesus laid hands on the bound woman. Immediately, she was made straight and glorified God. In all true ministry to demonic oppressed or possessed, God should receive the glory, not the person used of God in the deliverance process.

Incident: The Syrophonenican woman's daughter (Mark 7:24-30; Matthew 15:21-28).

Summary: This young girl and had an unclean spirit which her mother recognized by outward manifestations of the spirit. She described her daughter as being "grievously vexed".
Jesus healed the girl because of the great faith shown by her mother. The daughter was never in the presence of Jesus, which demonstrates actual physical presence is not necessary for effective ministry to those oppressed or possessed by Satan. This and the following incident prove children
can be possessed and oppressed by Satan.

Incident: The deaf mute boy (Mark 9:14-29; Matthew 17:14-21; Luke 9:37-43).

Summary: The father of an only son sought Jesus for the healing of his boy. The demonic possession of this boy included physical deafness and dumbness. The combined descriptions of Matthew, Mark, and Luke reveal that the demon sorely vexed the boy, causing him to fall into the fire and water.

At times the demon would tear him and cause fits with foaming at the mouth and grinding of teeth. He was often bruised (injured) by the spirit, and the demonic presence caused a general pining away physically. His father called him a "lunatic", which indicated there were also mental problems associated with his condition. The disciples of Jesus tried to cast out the demon in the boy, but failed.

Luke records that as the boy was coming to Jesus, the demon caused him to have a fit. Jesus rebuked the spirit and healed the child. Matthew records that Jesus rebuked the devil and he departed and the lad was cured that very hour.

Mark's record of this demonic encounter is more extensive than those of Matthew and Luke. He records that Jesus questioned the father as to how long the boy had been possessed. The father said the condition had existed from early childhood.

Jesus stressed to the father the importance of belief, then spoke to the deaf and dumb spirit and told it to come out and enter no more. The spirit cried and came out leaving him in such a condition that many thought him dead. But Jesus took him by the hand and lifted him up.

When the disciples asked Jesus why they were unable to cast out the demon, Jesus answered:

> **If ye shall have faith as a grain of mustard seed ye shall say unto this mountain, Remove hence to yonder place: and it shall remove; and nothing shall be impossible unto you.**
>
> **Howbeit, this kind goeth not out but by prayer and fasting. (Matthew 17:20- 21)**

His answer reveals the importance of faith, prayer, and fasting in dealing with demonic powers. It also proves some demons are more difficult to cast out than others because Jesus said "THIS KIND goeth not out" without prayer and fasting.

Incident: Demon in the synagogue (Mark 1:23-28; Luke 4:31-37).

Summary: Although this man was present in the synagogue, Jesus does not refer to him as a son of Abraham or indicate He was a follower of God. There can be those present in a church fellowship who are unbelievers and demon possessed. Church attendance does not guarantee a born again experience or freedom from demonic powers. This possession was indicated by "us," revealing the presence of more than one demon. One demon was the spokesman, however, for he said "I." When the demon began to speak, Jesus told it to "hold its peace," which means to be quiet. He rebuked the demons, they tore the man, cried out, threw him down, and came out. The witnesses of this event marveled at the authority and power with which Jesus dealt with unclean spirits.

Incident: The blind and dumb demoniac (Matthew 12:22-29; Mark 3:22-27; Luke 11:14-22).

Summary: Possession here included the physical afflictions of blindness and dumbness. Jesus healed this man by casting the demon out of him. He was able to speak and see after the deliverance. It was in connection with this deliverance that Jesus gave His most extensive teaching regarding the casting out of demons. A summary of this teaching reveals:

>   -A house with division cannot stand. Demons call the bodies in which they
>   reside their "house." It is not possible for demons and the spirit of God to exist
>   in the same house.
>   -Kingdoms or cities divided also cannot stand.
>   -Satan cannot cast out Satan.
>   -Casting out of demons is part of the ministry of God's Kingdom.
>   -Demons are cast out by the Spirit of God.
>   -It is necessary to bind the strong man (Satan) before attempting to cast him out
>   (spoil his works).
>   -There is no neutral ground in this spiritual battle. If you are not with Jesus,
>   you are against Him.
>   -When an unclean spirit is cast out of a person, it seeks reentry into a human body.
>   -If the person from whom the demon has departed does not fill his spiritual
>   house, the demon will return with other demons. The final condition of that
>   person will be worse than in the beginning.

Incident: Demoniac of Gadarene (Mark 5:1-20; Matthew 8:28-34; Luke 8:26-34).

Summary: According to Matthew, two men possessed by demons, so fierce that no man could control them, lived in the tombs. Mark and Luke stress the terrible condition and the deliverance of one of the two, whose condition was perhaps the worst ever encountered during the ministry of Jesus.

Possession here was by many demons. Both men were so affected that they could not live in normal society. They lived in the graveyard. The demons in one man called themselves "Legion" for they were many. They made it impossible to bind him even with chains. The demons tormented him so badly that he went around crying out, cut himself with stones, and did not wear clothing.

The demons recognized Jesus and asked if He had come to torment them before their time. "Their time" refers to their final judgment to the lake of fire (Hell). That they requested not to be sent out of the country indicates demons may be assigned by Satan to specific territories. Jesus permitted them to enter a herd of pigs when He cast them out which resulted in the death of the pigs. The residents of the city asked Jesus to leave. Pigs, which was their livelihood, were more important to them than the deliverance of men from demonic powers.

Other incidents: In addition to these specific encounters of Jesus, the Bible makes general references of His ministry to those affected by demonic powers.

>   -In the following references the term "healed" is used to describe how Jesus dealt with
>   the demons: Matthew 4:24; Luke 6:18.
>   -In the following references the term "cast out" is used to describe His strategy: Mark
>   1:32- 34,39; 6:13.
>   -Luke 4:41 simply records that the devils "came out." Luke 7:21 states that He
>   "cured" them. Matthew 8:16 records that He "cast them out with His word".

-Mark 16:9 and Luke 8:2-3 state that Jesus cast seven devils out of Mary Magdalene.

2. Sometimes God uses demons to accomplish His purposes. See I Samuel 16:14 and II Corinthians 12:7. Wicked Ahab was punished for his sin by a lying spirit which God put in the mouth of his prophets to lead him to disaster. See I Kings 22:23. Demons will lure the armies of Armageddon to a similar fate. (See Revelation 16:13-16).

3. Demonic powers can exercise control over nations as well as men and women. See the example in Daniel 10 of the "prince of the kingdom of Persia." This demonic power seemed to be in charge of the affairs of this region. The book of Revelation also mentions evil spirits and their activities in regards to nations. See Revelation 16:13-16.

4. Joking about demons or Satan is not wise. See II Peter 2:10-11. Neither do we have the power in ourselves to rebuke Satan. See Jude 9.

5. Jesus gave His disciples power to cast out demons. Study the following accounts of their use of this power: Mark 9:38; Luke 10:17; Acts 5:16; 8:7; 16:16-18; 19:11-12.

6. Study the following references where the word "possessed" is used: Matthew 4:24; 8:16,28,33; 9:32; 12:22; Mark 1:32; 5:15-18; Luke 8:36; Acts 8:7; 16:16.

7. Jesus was oppressed, but without sin: Isaiah 53:7. When Hezekiah was oppressed, he asked God to undertake for him: Isaiah 38:14. Jesus Christ healed all who were oppressed of the Devil: Acts 10:38.

   Study further about oppression:
   -By the wicked: Psalms 17:9
   -By our enemies: Psalms 106:42
   -By the proud: Psalms 119:122
   -By the rich: James 2:6

CHAPTER TWENTY-TWO
CASUALTIES OF WAR

OBJECTIVES:

Upon completion of this chapter you will be able to:

- Write the Key Verse from memory.
- Explain how suffering entered the world.
- Identify five ways suffering enters the life of a believer.
- Demonstrate understanding of the proper attitude towards suffering.
- Identify positive benefits of suffering.
- Explain the difference between going through a storm within and without of the will of God.

KEY VERSE FROM THE ARTICLES OF WAR:

**Thou therefore endure hardness as a good soldier of Jesus Christ.
(II Timothy 2:3)**

INTRODUCTION

In every natural war, there are casualties of war, soldiers who are wounded in battle. Some recover from their injuries to return to the battlefield. Others become permanent casualties. The same is true of the spiritual warfare in which we are engaged. Christian soldiers are not immune to the attacks of Satan, nor are they exempt from the effects of suffering.

Many of us do not like to talk about suffering. We do not hear a great deal of preaching on this subject. We prefer to hear messages on victory and prosperity, and these things are good, as they are part of the revelation of God. But we avoid the subject of suffering because there are things about it that are hard to understand and difficult to explain. But the Bible is not just a book of promises concerning the abundant life. It is a record of suffering, both of the righteous and the unrighteous.

When Jesus was here on earth and spoke of the suffering He was to face on the cross, many of His followers deserted Him. (John 6:55-66) They had expected the Messiah to reign in power and glory. Instead, He spoke of suffering. They could not understand this, so they turned away from following Him. If you do not understand suffering, you too may turn from following Jesus when you face difficult circumstances. You will become a casualty of the war instead of a conqueror.

This lesson concerns "casualties of war," those who have been wounded in battle. You will not only learn how to deal with suffering yourself, but how to minister to others experiencing difficulties.

THE SOURCE OF SUFFERING

God did not create suffering. It originally entered the world through the sin of man which was instigated by Satan (Genesis 3). When man yielded to Satan's temptation and sinned, suffering entered the world. Therefore, sin which resulted in all suffering can be traced to its originator, Satan. Although there are different reasons why suffering enters your life, all suffering can be traced back to this original source. But happily, in the life of a Christian soldier, God can take suffering, which Satan intends for evil, and turn it for good to accomplish His purposes. He can make a victim become a victor.

THE REASONS FOR SUFFERING

The Bible has much to say concerning suffering, problems, and afflictions. In summarizing its teaching, we discover five ways that suffering can come into the life of a believer. All suffering you face in life will come through one of these ways:

OTHERS AROUND YOU:

Suffering and difficult circumstances of life may come through others around you. Joseph is an example of this type of suffering. Through no fault of his own, Joseph was sold into Egypt by his brothers, was imprisoned falsely by Potiphar's wife, and was forgotten by those he helped in prison. But listen to his response. Joseph said...

> **Now therefore be not grieved, nor angry with yourselves, that ye sold me hither; for God did send me before you to preserve life...so now it was not you that sent me hither but God. (Genesis 45:5,7)**

One way suffering comes to the Christian soldier from others around him is by what the Bible calls an "evil report" or gossip. Much suffering comes because of what you say about others, and what they say about you. As you have learned in this course, the tongue is the most powerful of weapons, and can create many casualties of war by the words it speaks.

CIRCUMSTANCES OF LIFE:

The second way suffering comes to you is through the circumstances of life. This is illustrated by the experiences of Naomi recorded in the book of Ruth in the Bible. She was bitter with sorrow because of the death of her husband and sons.

Until Jesus returns and the final enemy of death is conquered, death is part of life. Death entered through the original sin of man and it is a natural circumstance which we all will face, for "it is appointed unto man once to die" (Hebrews 9:27).

When Naomi experienced these difficult circumstances of life, she said, "No longer call me Naomi (which means blessed), but call me Mara." The name Mara means "bitter." Naomi was facing bitter waters.

YOUR MINISTRY:

The third reason for suffering is because of your ministry for the Lord. The New Testament speaks of suffering for His name's sake (Acts 9:16), in behalf of Christ, (Philippians 1:29) for the Kingdom of God (II Thessalonians 1:5), for the Gospel (II Timothy 1:11-12), for well-doing (I Peter 2:19-20; 3:17), for righteousness sake (I Peter 3:14), as a Christian (I Peter 4:15-16), and according to the will of God (I Peter 4:19).

The Apostle Paul is an example of suffering resulting from ministry. Some people view suffering as a sign of failure or lack of faith. If this is true, then the Apostle Paul had no faith and was the greatest failure in the history of the church. Paul said that while in Asia he was so utterly crushed that he despaired of life itself (II Corinthians 1:8). He presents a different image than that of the cheerful evangelist who promises believers nothing but peace and prosperity.

When Paul was first called of God to ministry he was told of "great things" he would suffer for the sake of the Lord (Acts 9:16). Paul's response to suffering was to endure "the loss of all things to win some for Christ." He wrote to believers "to you it is given not only to believe, but to suffer for Him" (Philippians 1:29).

Paul was not alone in suffering for the ministry. The whole church suffered in New Testament times (Acts 8). Hebrews chapter 11 records the stories some of the cruel persecutions they endured. Many of these men and women of faith were delivered by the power of God. Prison doors were opened and they walked out. They were sentenced to death in fiery furnaces but emerged unaffected by the flames.

But some of these believers, who are also called men and women "of faith," did not receive such deliverances. They were imprisoned, afflicted, tormented, and even martyred because of their testimony of the Gospel (Hebrews 11:36-40). We focus on living faith but God also reveals His power in dying faith. This is a faith that stands true in the bad times, not just in good times when mighty deliverances are manifested.

DIRECT SATANIC ACTIVITY:

Suffering can also enter your life as a result of direct Satanic activity. This is evident in the story of Job. This book wrestles with the question, "Why do the righteous suffer?"
God's testimony of Job was that he was a righteous man (Job 1-2). Job did not suffer because he had sinned, as his friends claimed. They believed if Job repented, his circumstances would change. These friends tried to make a universal application based on individual experience. It would be similar to saying that because God delivered Peter from prison He will do the same for you. This is not true. Many have been martyred in prison despite their great faith and sinless lives.

We must be careful when we view the suffering of others that we do not accuse them of sin, faithlessness, or unbelief. The Bible does teach that a sinful man reaps a bitter harvest because of sowing in fleshly corruption (Galatians 6:8). But sowing and reaping cannot be used to explain the suffering of the innocent.

Job did not suffer because of anything he had done. Job was a righteous man. This was God's testimony of Job, Job's testimony of himself, and his reputation before man. Behind the scenes in the spiritual world was the true cause of Job's suffering. There was a spiritual battle going on over the heart, mind, and allegiance of Job.

There is a warfare going on in the spiritual world over you. That warfare is manifested in the difficult circumstances you experience in the natural world. An important truth evident in Job's suffering is that nothing can enter the life of a believer without the knowledge of God. God does not cause your suffering. It is inflicted by Satan, but its limits are set by God. God's power is greater than that of Satan, and you will experience victory if you continue to trust Him.

YOUR OWN SIN:

The fifth way suffering enters your life is because of your own sin. Jonah is an example of such suffering. In disobedience to God, Jonah headed the opposite direction from Ninevah where he had been commanded to go and preach repentance. He experienced a terrible storm at sea and ended up in the belly of a great fish because of his own sin (Jonah 1-2).

Trouble should always be treated as a call to consider your ways and examine your heart before God. You may be suffering because of your own sin. The Bible reveals that God chastises those who are living in disobedience to His Word. Chastise means to discipline, reprove, and correct:

> **Now no chastening for the present seemeth to be joyous, but grievous: nevertheless afterward it yieldeth the peaceable fruit of righteousness unto them which are exercised thereby. (Hebrews 12:11)**

God uses suffering to correct you and bring you back to His will for your life:

> **Before I was afflicted I went astray; but now have I kept thy Word...**
> **It is good for me that I have been afflicted; that I might learn thy statutes...**
> **I know, O Lord, that thy judgments are right, and that THOU in faithfulness hast afflicted me. (Psalms 119:67,71,75)**

THE PROPER ATTITUDE TOWARDS SUFFERING

Trouble is not necessarily a sign of being out of God's will. The Bible declares that "many are the afflictions of the righteous" (Psalms 34:19). When you suffer innocently and not because of your own sin, you should maintain a proper attitude towards suffering. The real test of your spirituality is how you respond in the day of distress:

> **If thou faint in the day of adversity, thy strength is small. (Proverbs 24:10)**

The Bible describes the attitude you should have when you suffer as a believer within the will of God. You should not be ashamed:

> **If any man suffer as a Christian let him not be ashamed, but let him glorify God on this behalf...(I Peter 4:16)**

You should commit your soul (your suffering) to God, knowing He works all things for your good:

> **Wherefore let them that suffer according to the will of God commit the keeping of their souls to Him in well doing as unto a faithful Creator. (I Peter 4:19)**

You should be happy when you suffer according to the will of God:

> **And they departed from the presence of the council, rejoicing that they were counted worthy to suffer shame for His name. (Acts 5:41)**

Paul says you should be:

> **Rejoicing in hope; patient in tribulation; continuing instant in prayer. (Romans 12:12)**
>
> **...being reviled, we bless; being persecuted, we suffer it... (I Corinthians 4:12)**
>
> **...in all things approving ourselves as the ministers of God, in much patience, in afflictions, in necessities, in distresses... (II Corinthians 6:4)**
>
> **Be not thou therefore ashamed of the testimony of our Lord, nor of me his prisoner; but be thou partaker of the afflictions of the gospel according to the power of God. (II Timothy 1:8)**
>
> **That no man should be moved by these afflictions: for yourselves know that we are appointed thereunto. (I Thessalonians 3:3)**
>
> **But watch thou in all things, endure afflictions, do the work of an evangelist, make full proof of thy ministry. (II Timothy 4:5)**

You should not think it strange when you experience suffering:

> **Beloved, think it not strange concerning the fiery trial which is to try you, as though some strange thing partaker of Christ's sufferings; that when His glory shall be revealed ye may be glad with exceeding joy. (I Peter 4:12-13)**

Paul summarizes the proper attitude toward suffering when he explains...

> **..though our outward man perish, yet the inward man is renewed day by day. For our light affliction, which is but for a moment, worketh for us a far more exceeding and eternal weight of glory:**

> **While we look not at the things which are seen, but at the things which are not seen: for the things which are seen are temporal; but the things which are not seen are eternal... (II Corinthians 4:16-18)**

Paul viewed suffering as a servant...He said it "worketh for us".

POSITIVE BENEFITS OF SUFFERING

There are many positive benefits of suffering according to God's will. If you understand these, it will help you deal with your own suffering as well as minister to others who are "casualties of war":

YOUR FAITH IS TESTED:

Everything in the spiritual world is based on faith. This is why the strength of your faith must be tested:

> **That the trial of your faith being much more precious than of gold that perisheth though it be tried with fire, might be found unto praise and honor and glory at the appearing of Jesus Christ. (I Peter 1:7)**

It is a trial of faith when you pray as Jesus did, for God to let the cup of bitterness pass, and yet it does not pass. Instead, you are forced to drink deeply of its suffering. But faith will learn that our prayers are not unanswered just because they are not answered the way we want.

YOU ARE EQUIPPED TO COMFORT OTHERS:

> **Blessed be God, even the Father of our Lord Jesus Christ, the Father of mercies, and the God of all comfort;**
>
> **Who comforteth us in all our tribulation that we may be able to comfort them which are in any trouble, by the comfort wherewith we ourselves are comforted of God. (II Corinthians 1:3-4)**

When you share God's comfort with others you...

> **...lift up the hands which hang down, and the feeble knees;**
>
> **And make straight paths for your feet, lest that which is lame be turned out of the way; but let it rather be healed. (Hebrews 12:12-13)**

YOU LEARN NOT TO TRUST IN YOURSELF:

Paul spoke of the purpose of his sufferings in Asia:

> ...In Asia we were pressed out of measure, above strength, insomuch that we despaired even of life;
>
> But we had the sentence of death in ourselves, that we should not trust in ourselves but in God which raiseth the dead. (II Corinthians 1:8-9)

You will come to recognize that...

> ... we have this treasure in earthen vessels, that the excellency of the power may be of God, and not of us. (II Corinthians 4:7)

YOU DEVELOP POSITIVE SPIRITUAL QUALITIES:

> We glory in tribulations, knowing that tribulation worketh patience, and patience experience, and experience hope, (resulting in the love of God being shed abroad in our hearts). (Romans 5:3-4)

> ...after ye have suffered awhile, make you perfect, stablish, strengthen, settle you. (I Peter 5:10)

These qualities conform you to the image of Jesus, which is God's plan for you (Romans 8:28-29; Hebrews 2:10,18).

THE WORKS OF GOD ARE MANIFESTED:

When the disciples saw a man who had been blind from birth, they asked who was responsible for his condition. Was it the sin of his parents or of the man himself? Jesus answered:

> Neither this man sinned nor His parents; but that the works of God should be made manifest in Him. (John 9:3)

THE POWER OF GOD IS PERFECTED:

> And He said unto me, My grace is sufficient for thee; for my strength is made perfect in weakness. Most gladly therefore will I rather glory in my infirmities, that the power of Christ may rest upon me. (II Corinthians 12:9)

THAT WHICH IS UNSTABLE IS REMOVED:

Suffering results in all that is unstable being shaken out of your life. You cease to depend on people, programs, or material things as these all fail in your time of need. God permits this...

> ...removing of those things that are shaken as of things that are made, that those things which cannot be shaken may remain. (Hebrews 12:26-27)

During the storms of life, everything crumbles that is not built upon God and His Word (Psalm 119:89 and Matthew 7:24-27).

YOUR FOCUS IS CHANGED:

When you experience suffering you often focus your attention on cause and effect. You are concerned with what caused the difficult circumstances and the terrible effect it is having in your life. God wants to change your focus from struggling to understand the temporal situation to recognizing the benefits of the eternal:

> **For our light affliction, which is but for a moment, worketh for us a far more exceeding and eternal weight of glory;**
>
> **While we look not at the things which are seen, but at the things which are not seen; for the things which are seen are temporal; but the things which are not seen are eternal. (II Corinthians 4:17-18)**
>
> **Beloved, think it not strange concerning the fiery trial which is to try you, as though some strange thing happened unto you:**
>
> **But rejoice, inasmuch as ye are partakers of Christ's sufferings; that, when His glory shall be revealed, ye may be glad also with exceeding joy. (I Peter 4:12-13)**
>
> **If we suffer, we shall also reign with Him... (II Timothy 2:12)**

THE OLD SELF-NATURE IS CHANGED:

God said of the nation of Moab:

> **Moab hath been at ease from his youth, and he hath settled on his lees, and hath not been emptied from vessel to vessel, neither hath he gone into captivity; therefore his taste remained in him, and his scent is not changed. (Jeremiah 48:11)**

Because Moab had not experienced the troublesome pouring out and stirring similar to that necessary to develop good wine, the nation did not change. Moab was at ease and settled in prosperity and because of this did not develop and mature properly spiritually. Therefore there was no change. His "own scent" remained in him. Suffering rids you of the old self-nature. As you are stirred, troubled, and poured out, your spiritual scent changes from carnal to spiritual.

YOU ARE PREPARED FOR MINISTRY:

You have asked to be used by God. You desire to be more like Jesus and prayed to be a chosen vessel for His use. The answer to your prayer may come through suffering:

> Behold I have refined thee, but not with silver; I have chosen thee in the furnace of affliction. (Isaiah 48:10)

It is through affliction that you move beyond the calling as a child of God to become chosen of God. Affliction according to the will of God refines you for His use just as metals are refined in a furnace in the natural world. God actually prepares you to wage warfare against the enemy by suffering!

YOU ARE PREPARED TO REIGN WITH CHRIST:

> If we suffer, we shall also reign with Him...(II Timothy 2:12)

YOU RECEIVE SPIRITUAL BLESSINGS:

Jesus said:

> Blessed are they which are persecuted for righteousness sake; for theirs is the Kingdom of Heaven.
>
> Blessed are ye, when men shall revile you, and persecute you, and shall say all manner of evil against you falsely, for my sake.
>
> Rejoice, and be exceeding glad: for great is your reward in heaven: for so persecuted they the prophets which were before you. (Matthew 5:10-12)

YOU LEARN OBEDIENCE:

> Though He were a Son, yet learned He obedience by the things which He suffered... (Hebrews 5:8)

THE WORD OF GOD IS TESTED WITHIN YOU:

> The words of the Lord are pure words: as silver tried in a furnace of earth, purified seven times. (Psalms 12:6)

YOU ARE HUMBLED:

> Who led thee through that great and terrible wilderness, wherein were fiery serpents, and scorpions, and drought, where there was no water; who brought thee forth water out of the rock of flint;
>
> Who fed thee in the wilderness with manna, which thy fathers knew not, that He might humble thee, and that He might prove thee, to do thee good at thy latter end... (Deuteronomy 8:15-16)

YOU ARE ENLARGED SPIRITUALLY:

This means you grow spiritually

> **Thou has enlarged me when I was under pressure.
> (Psalms 4:1 Revised Standard Version)**

YOU COME TO KNOW GOD INTIMATELY:

You come to know God on a more intimate basis through suffering. Job, who suffered much, learned this truth and said...

> **I have heard of thee by the hearing of the ear: but now mine eye seeth thee. Wherefore I abhor myself and repent in dust and ashes. (Job 42:5-6)**

Some of us know God only second handedly. When you are experiencing the blessings of life, God is often a luxury instead of a necessity. But when you have a real need, God becomes a necessity. Job came to know God more intimately through suffering. Before he suffered, Job knew God through theology. Afterwards, he knew Him by experience.
Paul expressed a similar desire when he said:

> **That I may know Him, and the power of His resurrection and the fellowship of His sufferings, being made conformable unto His death. (Philippians 3:10)**

You can only come to know God in resurrection power through the intimate fellowship of suffering. Throughout his suffering, Job questioned God as to the cause of his suffering. It is not wrong to question God. Jesus knew the purpose for which He had come into the world was to die for the sins of all mankind. Yet in His hour of suffering He cried out, "My God, My God, WHY hast thou forsaken me?" It is what follows the questioning that is important. Jesus' next words were, "Into thy hands I commit my spirit."

Despite the questions, Job's response was...

> **Though He slay me, yet will I trust in Him...(Job 13:15)**

> **For I know that my Redeemer liveth, and that He shall stand at the latter day upon the earth:**

> **And though after my skin worms destroy this body, yet in my flesh shall I see God. (Job 19:25-26)**

After all the questioning is finished, the emphasis must change from "me" to "Thee." You must commit your suffering, with all its unanswered questions, into the hands of God.

> **Trust in the Lord with all thine heart; and lean not unto thine own understanding. (Proverbs 3:5)**

God may reveal some of the purposes in your suffering, but it is possible you will never fully understand it:

> **It is the glory of God to conceal a thing...(Proverbs 25:2)**

> **The secret things belong unto the Lord our God; but those things which are revealed belong unto us... (Deuteronomy 29:29)**

There are some secret things that belong only to the Lord. As Job, you may never understand all the purposes of your suffering:

> **Since the Lord is directing our steps, why try to understand everything that happens along the way? (Proverbs 20:24 The Living Bible)**

When God finally talked with Job, He used several examples from nature which Job could not explain. God stressed that if Job could not understand what he saw in the natural world, he certainly could not understand that which he could not see in the spiritual world.

When Job faces God, it no longer matters that he does not get an answer to his questions about suffering. He is in the direct presence of God, and that experience leaves no room for anything else. He is no longer controlled and tormented by human reasoning. He replaces questions, not with answers, but with faith.

When you come to know God intimately through suffering, you see yourself as you really are. You no longer know God second-handedly. That face-to-face encounter with God does what arguments and discussions cannot do.

When Job stood before God, he had no new answers. He was given no new facts about his suffering. But he replaced questions with faith. Job had been in the direct presence of God, and that experience left no room for questions or doubts.

THE STORMS OF LIFE

Suffering is sometimes compared to a natural storm. When you suffer, you experience a storm spiritually speaking. This "storm" may affect you spiritually, mentally, physically, materially, or emotionally.

The Bible tells of a storm which the disciples of Jesus experienced. Read the story in your Bible in Mark 4:35-41. Jesus told the disciples to go to the other side and He joined them in the boat. The storm was an attack of Satan who was trying to prevent them from reaching the shore because of the miraculous works that were to be done in Gadarea (see Mark chapter 5).

Immediately Jesus took authority over the storm. He rebuked the powers of the enemy. Calm returned to the sea and they continued their journey unhindered.

Difficulties of life can be compared to natural storms. A "storm" of Satan is anything that tries to hinder you from fulfilling the will of God for your life and being an effective Christian soldier. It is not suffering resulting from your own disobedience. Neither is this kind of suffering is "according to the will of God." God does not want anything to hinder His plan for you and your victory in spiritual warfare! When you face a storm caused by Satan, exercise authority over the enemy. Jesus has given you power over every power of Satan.

There are two other stories of natural storms recorded in the Bible which illustrate storms resulting from chastisement for sin and storms that occur "according to the will of God." Read the story of Jonah and the storm in Jonah chapter 1. Read the story of Paul and the storm in Acts 27. Then study the following chart:

Jonah	**Paul**
Jonah put himself in the storm.	Paul was in the storm through no fault of his own...
He paid the fare	He tried to prevent them from sailing
Jonah was the cause of the storm	Paul was the remedy for the storm
Jonah slept during the storm	Paul fasted and prayed in the storm
God's blessing was not with Jonah	God's blessing was with Paul
The crew was fearful	The crew was told to be of good cheer
To be saved: Jonah must be cast out	To be saved: All must abide in the ship

There are differences between going through a storm of life within God's will and experiencing a storm out of the will of God. When you go through a storm out of the will of God, it is a situation which you have created. For example, a believer who marries an unsaved person will experience trouble because they have violated a Scriptural principle. You are the cause of a storm that results from disobedience. You have violated God's will and His commands. Often you are not even aware of the seriousness of your situation. You sleep spiritually while the storm increases its fury around you.

In a storm caused by your own sin, you are fearful and those around you grow fearful. The storm is not an attack of Satan. It is chastisement from God. You can confess promises of "power over the enemy" but it will not change the situation. When you recognize a "storm" of suffering as one resulting from sin, there is only one remedy: Ask forgiveness from God!

But when you suffer according to the will of God, the situation is different. You suffer through no fault or sin of your own. You can be a remedy to the problems around you instead of a cause. Like Paul, you can assume spiritual leadership because God's blessing is on you. You can bring encouragement to others because you are a solution to the storm instead of the cause. You should not bail out of the ship or run from the trouble. You must abide in the "ship" of this type of suffering for it is the will of God.

THE SUFFERING SOLDIER

When you suffer according to the will of God, you should realize you are not alone. Many others in God's army are experiencing similar battles:

> **...knowing that the same afflictions are accomplished in your brethren that are in the world. (I Peter 5:9)**

"Storms" of life are inevitable and uncontrollable, as illustrated by the parable of the two houses in Matthew 7:24-27. Storms will come to those who have built their lives upon God's Word as well as those who have not. The foundation of a man's life is what will determine the outcome of the storm. Suffering is to be expected as part of the will of God:

> **Yea, and all that will live godly in Christ Jesus shall suffer persecution. (II Timothy 3:12)**

For unto you it is given in the behalf of Christ, not only to believe on Him, but also to suffer for His sake (Philippians 1:29).

> **...that ye may be counted worthy of the Kingdom of God, for which ye also suffer... (II Thessalonians 1:5)**

> **For verily, when we were with you, we told you before that we should suffer tribulation; even as it came to pass and ye know. (I Thessalonians 3:4)**

> **Then shall they deliver you up to be afflicted, and shall kill you: and ye shall be hated of all nations for my name's sake. (Matthew 24:9)**

> **...they shall lay their hands on you, and persecute you, delivering you up to the synagogues, and into prisons, being brought before kings and rulers for my names sake. (Luke 21:12)**

> **Remember the word that I said unto you, The servant is not greater than his lord. If they have persecuted me, they will also persecute you... (John 15:20)**

Now this does not mean that you make yourself suffer believing it would be pleasing to God. God is never pleased when people suffer. To purposefully make yourself suffer (an act called asceticism) is a sin. Many people try to do this to try to appease God's anger and/or make themselves appear holy or religious before men. But God is only appeased by the blood of Jesus Christ. God does, however, take the tragedy of suffering when it does touch your life and redeem it for good.

Part of the follow up plan in establishing early churches was to teach believers that they would experience suffering. This is missing in many churches today:

> **...They returned...confirming the souls of the disciples, and exhorting them to continue in the faith, and that we must through much tribulation enter the kingdom of God. (Acts 14:22)**

The call of Jesus to followers is one of denial and suffering:

> **And he that taketh not his cross, and followeth after me, is not worthy of me. (Matthew 10:38)**

> **Then said Jesus unto his disciples, If any man will come after me, let him deny himself and take up his cross and follow me. (Matthew 16:24)**

> **...Whosoever will come after me, let him deny himself and take up his cross, and follow me. (Mark 8:34)**
>
> **...come, take up the cross, and follow me. (Mark 10:21)**
>
> **If any man will come after me, let him deny himself, and take up his cross daily, and follow me. (Luke 9:23)**
>
> **And whosoever doth not bear his cross, and come after me, cannot be my disciple. (Luke 14:27)**

Spiritual warfare is not a succession of great victories and celebrations of praise. As a soldier in God's army, you are called to endure suffering:

> **Thou therefore endure hardness as a good soldier of Jesus Christ. (II Timothy 2:3)**

One of the principles of natural warfare also applies to the spiritual realm: "Do not stop fighting just because you are wounded!"

INSPECTION

1. Write the Key Verse from the Articles Of War:

   _____

   _____

2. How did suffering enter the world?

   _____

3. Identify five ways suffering enters the life a believer.

   _____

   _____

   _____

4. List three positive benefits of suffering according to the will of God.

   _____

   _____

   _____

5. Identify three attitudes a believer is to have when experiencing suffering.

   _____

   _____

   _____

6. Read the following statements. If the statement is True, write the letter T on the blank in front of it. If the statement is False, write the letter F on the blank in front of it.

   a._____It is never God's will for you to suffer.
   b._____If you experience trouble it means you are out of the will of God.
   c._____Paul was out of the will of God in the storm at sea which he experienced.
   d._____When we suffer out of the will of God we are often the cause of our own problems because of disobedience.

   (Answers to tests are provided at the conclusion of the final chapter in this manual.)

TACTICAL MANEUVERS

1. Are you currently suffering? How? Review the five reasons for suffering given in this chapter.

    -Others around you.
    -Circumstances of life.
    -Your ministry.
    -Direct Satanic activity.
    -Your own sin.

    Which reason(s) might be behind your current suffering? If you discover your suffering is through your own sin, you need to repent. If your suffering is caused by others, because of your ministry, through the circumstances of life, or by direct Satanic attack, what might be the purposes God has for allowing this?

2. Review the positive benefits of "suffering according to the will of God" listed below. Identify the ones you feel God is working to accomplish in your life, then begin to cooperate with the process.
    -Your faith is tested.
    -You are equipped to comfort others.
    -You learn not to trust in self.
    -You develop positive spiritual qualities.
    -The works of God are manifested.
    -The power of God is perfected.
    -That which is unstable is removed.
    -Your focus is changed.
    -The old self-nature is changed.
    -You are prepared for ministry.
    -You are prepared to reign with Christ.
    -You receive spiritual blessings.
    -You learn obedience.
    -The Word of God is tested within you.
    -You are humbled.
    -You are enlarged spiritually.
    -You come to know God intimately.

3. In natural warfare, soldiers help one another in the battle. When one soldier is under attack, others come to help him. They fire their weapons at the enemy to provide cover for him so he can run to safety. Do you know of a wounded warrior, a casualty of war for whom you can provide such spiritual cover? Can you help someone in their battle with the enemy by praying for them and encouraging them?

4. Study more about suffering in I Peter. This book focuses on the subject of suffering.

5. Study the following references about suffering:

Hardness: II Timothy 2:3

Tribulation: Acts 14:20; Romans 5:3; 12:12; I Thessalonians 3:4, II Thessalonians 1:4

Persecution: Matthew 5:10-12, 44; 13:21; Mark 4:17; Luke 11:49; 21:12; John 15:20; I Corinthians 4:12; II Corinthians 4:9; Acts 8:1; 11:19; 13:50; II Timothy 3:12; Romans 8:35; Galatians 6:12

Suffering: I Peter 5:10; Philippians 1:29; 3:8; 4:12; II Corinthians 1:6; II Timothy 2:12; 3:12; Galatians 5:11; 6:12; Acts 9:16; I Thessalonians 3:4; II Thessalonians 1:5

Affliction: Psalms 34:19; 119:67, 71, 75; Matthew 24:9; Acts 20:23; II Corinthians 2:4; 4:17; 6:4; I Thessalonians 3:3; II Timothy 1:8; 3:11, 4:5; II Corinthians 1:6; James 5:10; Hebrews 10:32-33.

CHAPTER TWENTY-THREE
HOW TO LOSE A BATTLE AND WIN THE WAR

OBJECTIVES:

Upon completion of this chapter you will be able to:

- Write the Key Verse from memory.
- Identify four Biblical examples of men who lost a battle but won the war.
- List four steps for winning the war despite losing a battle.
- Give a Biblical reference which proves you can recover from spiritual failure.
- Give a Biblical reference to use when Satan condemns you for failure.
- Explain how you can learn from spiritual failure.

KEY VERSE FROM THE ARTICLES OF WAR:

I have fought a good fight, I have finished my course, I have kept the faith. (II Timothy 4:7)

INTRODUCTION

In this course you have studied many strategies for spiritual warfare. As you apply this knowledge you will advance in your ability to fight in the strength and power of the Lord Jesus Christ. But despite your knowledge of these strategies, from time to time you may face failure. Do not be discouraged...some of the greatest men of God faced similar situations.

In this chapter you will study about four great men who lost battles but went on to win the war. You will learn steps for recovering from defeat and going on to victory despite failure. You will also learn how to deal with the condemnation of the enemy. Failure can teach important spiritual lessons... and remember... it is possible to lose a battle and still win the war.

LOSING A BATTLE

There are several examples in Scripture of men of God who lost battles with the enemy:

JOSHUA:

Joshua was a great military commander who assumed leadership of the nation of Israel after the death of Moses. One of the challenges God gave Joshua was to lead Israel across the Jordan River to claim their promised land. One of the warriors of Israel sinned by taking spoil (property) from the enemy, something God had forbidden. Because there was "sin in the camp," Israel lost the battle at Ai (Joshua 7).

KING DAVID:

King David lost an important battle when the evil Amalekites invaded the southern portion of his kingdom and burned the city of Ziklag. They took the women captive, including David's wives. David's friends and soldiers were so upset with him that they threatened to stone him to death. David was greatly distressed and discouraged (I Samuel 30:1-6).

King David also lost a great battle in the spiritual world at one point in his life. He committed adultery with a woman named Bathsheba who was another man's wife. When this resulted in Bathsheba becoming pregnant, he had her husband killed to try to cover his sin (II Samuel 11 and 12).

THE PROPHET ELIJAH:

A wicked queen named Jezebel sent a messenger to the prophet Elijah informing him she was planning to kill him. Elijah...

> **...went a day's journey into the wilderness and came and sat down under a juniper tree: and he requested for himself that he might die; and said, It is enough; now, O Lord, take away my life; for I am not better than my fathers. (I Kings 19:4)**

Here was the great man of God who had healed the sick, raised the dead, and commanded the elements of nature in the name of the Lord. Now he was hiding, fearful, despondent, and wanting to die.

THE APOSTLE PAUL:

The Apostle Paul also faced defeat. He wrote once that due to experiences in Asia he was "pressed out of measure" and "despaired even of life" (II Corinthians 1:8). He had times when he was troubled, perplexed, persecuted, fearful, and cast down (II Corinthians 4:8-11; 7:5-6).

WINNING THE WAR

Each of the great leaders mentioned lost battles with the enemy. As you engage in spiritual warfare, you too may experience a loss. But although you lose a battle with the enemy, it does not mean you have lost the war. A war is made up of many battles. Just because you lose one battle does not mean you have lost the war.

Each of these men lost a battle, but recovered to win the war. The spiritual strategies they used will help you when you have lost a battle. It is possible to recover from the snare of the enemy when you lose a battle:

> **And that they may recover themselves out of the snare of the devil, who are taken captive of him at his will. (II Timothy 2:26)**

The word "recover" means to awake or arouse yourself. A snare is a hidden trap. (See the "For Further Study" section of this chapter). "They may recover" indicates that YOU must take steps to recovery after losing a spiritual battle. Here are the steps to take to recover from the snare of the enemy:

STEP ONE: RECOGNIZE YOUR FAILURE:

-Joshua recognized and admitted the failure at Ai. He said:

> **O Lord, what shall I say, when Israel turneth their backs before their enemies. (Joshua 7:8)**

-It was not hard for David to admit failure in the incident at Ziklag. The loss was apparent to the natural eye. The city was burned and the women taken captive. But it was more difficult for David to admit failure in the incident with Bathsheba. No one knew of his sin except himself, Bathsheba, and the prophet of God. But David admitted, "I have sinned against the Lord" (II Samuel 12:13).

-Elijah admitted failure. He said:

> **...It is enough: now, O Lord, take away my life; for I am not better than my fathers. (I Kings 19:4)**

-Paul recognized his failures. He said he had been "troubled, perplexed, persecuted, cast down, and even despaired of life" (II Corinthians 4:8-9; II Corinthians 1:8).

Do not let pride prevent you from admitting you have lost a battle. In order to recover from the snare of the enemy, you must first acknowledge you are in his snare:

> **If we say that we have no sin, we deceive ourselves, and the truth is not in us. (I John 1:8)**

STEP TWO: REPENT:

It is not just enough to admit your failure. You must also ask God to forgive you:

> **If we confess our sins, He is faithful and just to forgive us our sins, and to cleanse us from all unrighteousness. (I John 1:9)**

-David repented of his sin with Bathsheba. Read his great prayer of repentance in Psalms 52. This is a good Psalm to use as a prayer when you have failed.

-Joshua searched until he found the cause of the failure at Ai. He discovered that a military leader among the people had disobeyed God and caused the army to lose the battle. He and the people repented before God (Joshua 7).

-Elijah repented. He admitted he was no better than his sinful ancestors (I Kings 19:4).

-Paul indicated that although he had a great battle with the flesh (Romans 7) he was able to gain victory through "repentance from dead works" (Romans 8; Hebrews 6:1).

STEP THREE: REBUILD YOUR SPIRITUAL STRENGTH:

In the natural world when an army has experienced a military loss, time is taken to rebuild combat forces before returning to the battlefield. Commanders analyze the problems, take corrective action, and strengthen and encourage the troops. This is an important principle in the spiritual world also. When you have experienced failure in spiritual warfare you must rebuild your spiritual strength.

-Joshua waited before the Lord in prayer to regain spiritual strength before returning to the battlefield. He prayed to discover the reason for failure and receive guidance for corrective actions (Joshua 7:6-15).

-David fasted and prayed after his failure with Bathsheba. Later he received physical food after the death of his child by Bathsheba. In the Ziklag incident David "encouraged himself in the Lord" and reorganized his forces before returning to the battlefield (I Samuel 30:6).

-Elijah rested, was ministered to by an angel, and waited on a mountain until receiving strength through a special manifestation of God's power (I Kings 19).

-Paul encouraged himself in the Lord. He reminded himself that nothing, not even his failure, could separate him from God:

> **Who shall separate us from the love of Christ? Shall tribulation, or distress, or persecution, or famine, or nakedness, or peril, or sword?...**
>
> **Nay, in all these things we are MORE THAN CONQUERORS through Him that loved us.**
>
> **For I am persuaded, that neither death, nor life, nor angels, nor principalities, nor powers, nor things present, nor things to come,**
>
> **Nor height, nor depth, nor any other creature shall be able to separate us from the love of God, which is in Christ Jesus our Lord.**
> **(Romans 8:35, 37-39)**

Here are some ways to rebuild your spiritual strength:

> -Study the greatest handbook on spiritual warfare ever written...The Word of God. Spend time in prayer and fasting. Incorporate the prayer and fasting principles you learned in this course, including binding the power of the enemy in your life.
> -Ask God to reveal causes for the failure you experienced and what to do to correct the situation.
> -Review the strategies of spiritual warfare in this course. Ask God to renew your strength and help you put these strategies into practice.
> -Rest physically. Man is body, soul, and spirit. When your physical body is exhausted, Satan can take advantage and affect your soul and spirit.

STEP FOUR: RETURN TO THE BATTLEFIELD:

One of the main strategies of the enemy is to tempt you to give up when you have lost a spiritual battle. While it is true that the Holy Spirit will sometimes convict you when you fail, there is a difference between the condemnation of the enemy and the conviction of the Holy Spirit. The Holy Spirit always singles out a specific sin while the condemnation of Satan is generalized.

Satan will speak generalized words of defeat to you:
"You might as well give up.
Everyone has lost confidence in you.
God does not care, or He would have helped you.
You are so weak and good for nothing.
You will never be able to make it as a Christian.
You are no good."

Do not listen to the condemnation of the enemy. Acknowledge your failure, repent before God, and recognize that...

There is therefore now no condemnation to them which are in Christ Jesus, who walk not after the flesh but after the Spirit. (Romans 8:1)

Use this verse to defeat the condemning strategies of Satan and then... return to the battlefield!

-Joshua continued military campaigns in the Promised Land with great success. He returned to Ai and conquered the same military forces which had caused his defeat. When you return to the spiritual battlefield after failure, you can not only recover all the enemy has taken from you, but you can also go on to win new victories.

-After the loss at Ziklag, David returned to the battlefield to great military victory. He recovered all the enemy had taken from him: And David recovered all that the Amalekites had carried away...

And there was nothing lacking to them, neither small nor great, neither sons nor daughters, neither spoil, nor any thing that they had taken to them: David recovered all. (I Samuel 30:18-19)

-Elijah recovered from his despondency, returned to spiritual battle, and performed some of the greatest miracles in the history of his ministry.

-And as for Paul...read the remaining portion of a passage we previously mentioned:

We are troubled on every side, yet not distressed; we are perplexed, but not in despair;

Persecuted, but not forsaken; cast down, but not destroyed. (II Corinthians 4:8-9)

Here is a spiritual warrior who overcame. He said he was:

> Troubled.....BUT NOT DISTRESSED.
> Perplexed....BUT NOT IN DESPAIR.
> Persecuted...BUT NOT FORSAKEN.
> Cast down....BUT NOT DESTROYED!
> Remember, "A just man falleth seven times, and riseth up again" (Proverbs 24:16).

LEARNING FROM FAILURE

Paul wrote to the Church at Corinth:

> **For we would not, brethren, have you ignorant of our trouble which came to us in Asia, that we were pressed out of measure, above strength, insomuch that we despaired even of life.**
>
> **But we had the sentence of death in ourselves, that we should not trust in ourselves, but in the God which raiseth the dead;**
>
> **Who delivered us from so great a death, and doth deliver, in whom we trust that He will yet deliver us. (II Corinthians 1:8-10)**

Paul explained that problems in Asia had taught him an important lesson. The lesson was that "we should not trust in ourselves, but in God." This is a great lesson to learn from failure. You cannot trust in yourself in spiritual warfare. Your power, your authority, your victory is assured only in Christ Jesus.

Paul looked beyond the natural world to see the spiritual benefits of problems, temptations, trials, and failures:

> **For which cause we faint not: but though our outward man perish, yet the inward man is renewed day by day.**
>
> **For our light affliction, which is but for a moment, worketh for us a far more exceeding and eternal weight of glory;**
>
> **While we look not at the things which are seen, but at the things, which are not seen:**
>
> **For the things which are seen are temporal; but the things which are not seen are eternal. (II Corinthians 4:16-18)**

Paul had learned that even though the outward man perished, the inward man was being renewed. The light afflictions of battle were resulting in spiritual growth. It was not what was visible that was important, it was what was happening in the spirit world.

Instead of giving up the battle, Paul learned from failure and went on to victory. In II Corinthians 1:10 he indicated that God...

- "Delivered" (In the past)
- "Doth deliver" (In the present)
- "Will yet deliver" (In the future)

ON TO VICTORY

Despite all the perplexities, persecution, trouble, and despair, Paul was able to say in the closing days of his life:

I have fought a good fight, I have finished my course, I have kept the faith.
(II Timothy 4:7)

If you learn how to win the war with the enemy despite temporary failure from a lost battle, you too will be able to echo... "I HAVE FOUGHT A GOOD FIGHT!"

INSPECTION

1. Write the Key Verse from the Articles Of War.

   _____

   _____

2. From the examples used in this lesson, name four men who lost a battle but won a war.

   _____ _____

   _____ _____

3. List four steps for going on to win the war despite losing a battle.

   _____ _____

   _____ _____

4. Give a Biblical reference to use when Satan condemns you for failure.

   _____

5. Give a Biblical reference which proves you can recover when you have lost a battle with Satan.

   _____

6. What lesson did Paul learn from his defeat in Asia?

   _____

   _____

(Answers to tests are provided at the conclusion of the final chapter in this manual.)

TACTICAL MANEUVERS

1. Have you been defeated in a battle with Satan? Follow the four steps given in this lesson to overcome this defeat:
    - Recognize your failure.
    - Repent.
    - Renew your spiritual strength.
    - Return to the battle field.

2. One of the main strategies Satan uses to defeat believers is deception. "To deceive" is to mislead or cause someone to believe something that is not true. Here are some things the Bible teaches about deception:

    - We are told that Satan is deceptive and deceives not only individuals but nations: Revelation 20:10
    - Satan works with "all deceivableness of unrighteousness": II Thessalonians 2:10
    - We are warned that deception will increase: II Timothy 3:13
    - Because deception will increase, we are instructed to be aware of the events indicating the return of Jesus: Matthew 24; Mark 13; II Thessalonians 2:3
    - We are warned of those used by Satan to deceive: II Corinthians 11:13; Titus 1:10; II Peter 2:13; II John 7
    - Every unsaved man is deceived by his own heart: Jeremiah 17:9
    - Every unsaved man is deceived by sin: II Corinthians 4:4; Hebrews 3:13
    - Do not accept deceptive "fair speeches" which do not agree with God's Word: Romans 16:18; II Corinthians 4:2

    You are deceived:

    - If you listen to vain philosophies: Colossians 2:8
    - If you trust in riches and permit the lusts of the flesh: Matthew 13:22; Mark 4:19; Ephesians 4:22
    - If you are a hearer and not a doer of the Word of God: James 1:22
    - If you say you have no sin: I John 1:8
    - If you listen to evil men: II Timothy 3:13
    - If you think you are important when actually you are nothing: Galatians 6:3
    - If you think you will not reap what you sow: Galatians 6:7
    - If you think the unrighteous will inherit the Kingdom of God: I Corinthians 6:9
    - When you think you are wise because you have the wisdom of this world: I Corinthians 3:18
    - By seeming to be spiritual when an unconquered tongue reveals your true condition: James 1:26
    - If you do not believe Jesus Christ came in the flesh: II John 7
    - If you think contact with sin will have no effect on you: I Corinthians 15:33

Having studied this list, do you see areas in which the enemy has deceived you? If so, acknowledge this deception, repent, and return to the battle field!

3. The Bible declares that God is your deliverer in spiritual warfare: II Samuel 22:2; I Chronicles 11:14; Psalms 18:2; 40:17; 70:5; 144:2; Daniel 6:16

   -He delivers your enemies into your hand: Judges 3:28
   -Jesus is called the Deliverer: Romans 11:26
   -Jesus came to preach deliverance: Luke 4:18
   -You are not delivered through the strength of man: Psalms 33:16
   -God delivers:
       The poor: Job 36:15
       Them that fear Him: Psalms 34:7
       The righteous: Proverbs 11:8,21
       Those who walk wisely: Proverbs 28:26
       The godly: II Peter 2:9
   -He delivers you from:
       Violent men: II Samuel 22:49
       The enemy: II Samuel 22:18; Psalms 18:48; 78:42
       Strivings of people: II Samuel 22:44; Psalms 18:43
       All fear: Psalms 34:4
       Fear of death: Hebrews 2:15
       Your troubles: Psalms 34:17; 54:7; 81:7
       Afflictions and persecutions: Psalms 34:19; Acts 7:10; II Timothy 3:11
       Evil rulers and evil people: Acts 12:11
       The law: Romans 7:6
       Corruption into glorious liberty: Romans 8:21
       The second death: II Corinthians 1:10
       The power of darkness: Colossians 1:13
       The wrath to come: I Thessalonians 1:10
       Unreasonable men: II Thessalonians 3:2
       Battle: Psalms 55:18
       Falling and your soul from death: Psalms 56:13; 116:8
       Those who hate you: Psalms 69:14
       Hell: Psalms 86:13
       Distress: Psalms 107:6
       Destruction: Psalms 107:20

FINAL BRIEFING...

...FOR THE LAST GREAT BATTLE OF SPIRITUAL WARFARE

There is a great and final conflict which will bring this spiritual war of the ages to a triumphant conclusion. Satan and his evil forces will be defeated and Jesus will reign forever as King of Kings.

CHAPTER TWENTY-FOUR

THE FINAL CONFLICT

OBJECTIVES:

Upon completion of this chapter you will be able to:

- Write the Key Verse from memory.
- Summarize the events leading to the final conflict.
- Describe the final conflict.
- Describe the final destiny of Satan and the spiritual forces of evil.

KEY VERSE FROM THE ARTICLES OF WAR:

> **And the Devil that deceived them was cast into the lake of fire and brimstone, where the beast and the false prophet are, and shall be tormented day and night for ever and ever. (Revelation 20:10)**

INTRODUCTION

As you learned in this course, final judgment upon Satan was already pronounced by the death and resurrection of Jesus Christ. But it is not until Jesus returns to earth that this judgment will be totally fulfilled.

This chapter focuses on the final conflict, that last great spiritual battle which will defeat all the forces of evil. This last great conflict will result in the crowning of Jesus as King of kings, the establishment of the Kingdom of God in its visible form, and final judgment of the spiritual forces of evil.

EVENTS PRECEDING THE FINAL CONFLICT

Here are the major events that will precede the final conflict:

THE RETURN OF JESUS:

The Bible teaches that the Lord will return to earth for believers. Jesus promised His followers:

> **...I go to prepare a place for you. And if I go and prepare a place for you, I will come again and receive you unto myself; that where I am, there ye may be also. (John 14:2-3)**

This return of Jesus for believers is also called the "rapture." Details about the return of Jesus for believers are given in I Thessalonians 4:13-18. These verses indicate:

-Jesus Himself will return (verse 16).
-There will be a resurrection from the grave of those who were believers when they died (verse 16).
-There will be a "rapture," which means "the act of taking a person from one place to another." Living believers will be taken from earth to meet Christ (verse 17).
-There will be a reunion between believers who have previously died, believers living at the time of Christ's return, and the Lord Jesus Christ (verse 17).

Some people believe the rapture will occur before the tribulation and that believers will not have to experience any of this terrible time on earth. Others believe the rapture will happen midway through this period. Still others believe the rapture will happen at the end of the tribulation. The most common belief is that the rapture of believers will happen before the tribulation period begins. The different views of the timing of the rapture result from various interpretations of the prophetic portions of Scripture. What is most important is to know you are a true believer and ready to go with Jesus in the rapture whenever it does occur.

No man can know the exact time of this great event:

> **But of that day and hour knoweth no man, no, not the angels of Heaven, but my Father only. (Matthew 24:36)**

Although no man knows the exact timing of the rapture, Jesus did identify some prophetic signs that will indicate when the time is near. You can read about these in Matthew 24.

THE TRIBULATION:

The Bible tells of a terrible time on earth which is called the tribulation during which the spiritual forces of evil will be more active than ever in the history of the world. Satan will set up his unholy Trinity, the beast and the false prophet (Revelation 13; 16:13-14). Through "spiritual wickedness in high places" they will do signs, wonders, and deceive many. They will seek worship and condemn men with a special mark of ownership.

The tribulation will last for 42 months or 1,260 days. (Daniel 9:24-27). It will be a very difficult time. There have been many difficult times in the world before, but three things will distinguish the tribulation from all other times of trouble:

1. **It will be worldwide, not just local:**

   > **...I also will keep thee from the hour of temptation, which shall come upon all the world...(Revelation 3:10)**

2. **People will realize the end of the world is near:**

   > **And said to the mountains and rocks, Fall on us, and hide us from the face of Him that sitteth on the throne, and from the wrath of the Lamb;**

> For the great day of His wrath is come; and who shall be able to stand? (Revelation 6:16-17)

3. The intensity of the trouble will be greater than ever before experienced:

There are a series of judgments from God which will come on the earth during the tribulation period. These judgments are described in Revelation chapters 6, 8-9, and 16 and in Matthew 24:4-14. The reason for these judgments is that the world must be punished for sin and rejection of God.

THE MILLENNIUM:

The Millennium is a period of 1,000 years after the tribulation during which Jesus will rule the earth in righteousness:

> And the Lord shall be King over all the earth: in that day shall there be one Lord, and His name one. (Zechariah 14:9)

The city of Jerusalem will be the center of government:

> And it shall come to pass in the last days, that the mountain of the Lord's house shall be established in the top of the mountains, and shall be exalted above the hills: and all nations shall flow unto it.
>
> ...for out of Zion shall go forth the law, and the word of the Lord from Jerusalem. (Isaiah 2:2-3)

Before the start of and during this Millennial period Satan and his evil forces will be bound. A great war will occur on earth and...

> ...the beast was taken, and with him the false prophet that wrought miracles before him, with which he deceived them that had received the mark of the beast and them that worshiped his image. These both were cast alive into a lake of fire burning with brimstone. (Revelation 19:20)
>
> And he laid hold on the dragon, that old serpent, which is the Devil, and Satan, and bound him a thousand years.
>
> And cast him into the bottomless pit, and shut him up, and set a seal upon him, that he should deceive the nations no more, till the thousand years should be fulfilled; and after that he must be loosed a little season. (Revelation 20:2-3)

THE FINAL CONFLICT

After the thousand years, the final conflict with Satan will occur:

> **And when the thousand years are expired, Satan shall be loosed out of his prison.**
>
> **And shall go out to deceive the nations which are in the four quarters of the earth...to gather them together to battle: the number of whom is as the sand of the sea.**
>
> **And they went up on the breadth of the earth, and compassed the camp of the saints about, and the beloved city (Jerusalem)...(Revelation 20:7-9)**

God will send fire from Heaven and end all opposition of the forces of evil:

> **...and fire came down from God out of heaven, and devoured them. (Revelation 20:9)**

The reason for this final battle is that Satan must at last be defeated and Jesus acknowledged as Lord of all. This completes God's plan of the ages:

> **Having made known unto us the mystery of His will, according to His good pleasure which He hath purposed in Himself;**
>
> **That in the dispensation of the fullness of times, He might gather together in one all things in Christ, both which are in Heaven, and which are on earth; even in Him. (Ephesians 1:9-10)**

This is the final battle in the spiritual warfare that has raged from the rebellion of Satan down through the history of the world.

SATAN'S FINAL DESTINY

The final destiny of the trinity of Satan is the lake of fire:

> **And the Devil that deceived them was cast into the lake of fire and brimstone, where the beast and the false prophet are and shall be tormented day and night for ever and ever. (Revelation 20:10)**

The demonic angels of Satan will also be cast into the lake of fire:

> **Then shall He say also unto them on the left hand, Depart from me, ye cursed, into everlasting fire, prepared for the Devil and his angels. (Matthew 25:41)**

Demons themselves recognize their own final destiny. In Matthew 8 when Jesus went into the country of the Gergesenes, he met two demon possessed men they cried out to Jesus saying...

> **...What have we to do with thee, Jesus, thou Son of God? art thou come hither to torment us before the time? (Matthew 8:29)**

JUDGMENT

All created beings will be judged by God. This is known as the time of eternal judgment. Those who died as unbelievers will be resurrected to face judgment. Because they did not repent from sin and accept Jesus as Savior they will be condemned to eternity in Hell:

> **And I saw the dead, small and great, stand before God; and the books were opened; and another book was opened, which is the book of life: and the dead were judged out of those things which were written in the books, according to their works.**
>
> **And the sea gave up the dead which were in it; and death and hell delivered up the dead which were in them: and they were judged every man according to their works.**
>
> **And death and hell were cast into the lake of fire. This is the second death. And whosoever was not found written in the book of life was cast into the lake of fire. (Revelation 20:12-15)**

True believers who repented from sin and accepted Jesus as Savior will spend eternity in Heaven in the presence of God (Revelation 21).

The great spiritual battle will be over!

> **And there was given Him (Jesus) dominion, and glory, and a Kingdom, that all people, nations, and languages, should serve Him; His dominion is an everlasting dominion, which shall not pass away, and His Kingdom that which shall not be destroyed. (Daniel 7:14)**

VICTORY IN THE SPIRIT WORLD

This chapter concludes this course on spiritual warfare. In reality, you will never stop studying and learning about this subject. Just as a soldier in the natural world, you will continue to develop your skills and strategies as you battle with the enemy.

As we close this study, we want to assure you that you can be victorious over all the power of the enemy and in every battle of life. Just remember...

- Your victory in warfare is assured, because it is not dependent upon YOU...It is dependent upon God:

  Who is this King of glory? The Lord strong and mighty, the Lord mighty in battle. (Psalms 24:8)

- You are protected by God as you battle:

  O God the Lord, the strength of my salvation, thou hast covered my head in the day of battle. (Psalms 140:7)

- When you are discouraged, you are comforted by God in battle:

  For when we were come into Macedonia, our flesh had no rest, but we were troubled on every side: without were fightings, within were fears. Nevertheless God, that comforteth those that are cast down, comforted us... (II Corinthians 7:5-6)

- God will encourage you in the midst of your warfare:

  Fear not, nor be afraid (in the coming violent upheavals); have I not told it to you from of old and declared it?...(Isaiah 44:8 The Amplified Version)

  For I the Lord thy God will hold thy right hand, saying unto thee, Fear not; I will help thee. (Isaiah 41:13)

  I, even I, am He that comforteth you; who art thou, that thou shouldest by afraid of a man that shall die, and the son of man which shall be made as grass. (Isaiah 51:12)

- No weapon formed against you will succeed:

  No weapon that is formed against thee shall prosper... (Isaiah 54:17)

- Victory can be attained over the world:

  For whatsoever is born of God overcometh the world: and this is the victory that overcometh the world, even our faith.

  Who is he that overcometh the world, but he that believeth that Jesus is the Son of God? (I John 5:4-5)

- Victory can be attained over the flesh:

  And they that are Christ's have crucified the flesh with the affections and lusts. (Galatians 5:24)

- Victory can be attained over the Devil:

    And the God of peace shall bruise Satan under your feet shortly... (Romans 16:20)

- Victory can be attained over death and the grave:

    I will ransom them from the power of the grave; I will redeem them from death... (Hosea 13:14)

    O death, where is thy sting? O grave, where is thy victory? (I Corinthians 15:26, 55)

    He will swallow up death in victory... (Isaiah 25:8)

- Victory can be attained over ALL that exalts itself against God:

    ...bringing into captivity every high thing that exalteth itself against the knowledge of God...(II Corinthians 10:5)

- Victory can be attained over ALL the powers of the enemy:

    Behold, I give unto you power...over all the power of the enemy... (Luke 10:19)

- Always remember to thank God for victory in battle through Jesus Christ:

    But thanks be to God which giveth us the victory through our Lord Jesus Christ. (I Corinthians 15:57)

- And when the battle is over, you will stand victorious:

    So use every piece of God's armor to resist the enemy whenever he attacks, and when it is all over, you will still be standing up. (Ephesians 6:13, Living Bible)

INSPECTION

1. Write the Key Verse from the Articles Of War.

2. Describe the events leading up to the final conflict.

3. Describe the final conflict. When will the conflict occur? What will happen to defeat the enemy forces?

4. What is the final destiny of Satan and the spiritual forces of evil?

(Answers to tests are provided at the conclusion of the final chapter in this manual.)

TACTICAL MANEUVERS

1. Satan sets spiritual "snares" for believers. A snare is like a trap set for animals. It is hidden, but springs open suddenly to take its victim into captivity. Examine your life to be certain you are not snared by...

    -The fowler: Psalms 91:3; 124:7
    -The wicked: Psalms 119:110
    -Your lips: Proverbs 18:7
    -Evil associates: Proverbs 22:24-25
    -Fear of man: Proverbs 29:25
    -The Devil: I Timothy 3:7; II Timothy 2:26
    -Riches: I Timothy 6:9
    -Sin: Proverbs 29:6
    -Scorn: Proverbs 29:8
    -False gods: Exodus 23:33; Judges 2:3
    -Sinful mate: I Samuel 18:21
    -Covenants with unbelievers: Exodus 34:12

2. Study the seven churches in Revelation chapters 2-3 in terms of spiritual warfare. In what areas of warfare were they failing? What instructions does the Spirit of God give to them to correct the situations?

3. You are now an overcomer! From this course you have learned...
    -That you can overcome the power of the wicked one: I John 2:13-14
    -Jesus overcame the world: John 16:33
    -Because He lives in you, you can overcome the world: I John 4:4
    -You overcome by the new birth experience and your faith: I John 5:4-5
    -You overcome by the blood of Jesus and your testimony: Revelation 12:11

Some beautiful promises are made to the overcomers. Those who overcome the spiritual forces of evil through waging effective spiritual warfare...

    -Will eat of the tree of life: Revelation 2:7
    -Shall eat of hidden manna: Revelation 2:17
    -Will be clothed in white raiment: Revelation 3:5
    -Will be pillars in the temple of God: Revelation 3:12
    -Will sit with Jesus in His throne: Revelation 3:21
    -Will have a new name: Revelation 2:17
    -Will have power over the nations: Revelation 2:26
    -Will have the name of God written upon them: Revelation 3:12
    -Will have a special relationship with God: Revelation 21:7
    -Will have the morning star (Jesus): Revelation 2:28
    -Will be confessed by Jesus before God the Father: Revelation 3:5
    -Will not be hurt by the second death: Revelation 2:11
    -Will not have their names blotted out of the book of life: Revelation 3:5
    -Will inherit all things: Revelation 21:7

4. This is your last lesson in this manual of spiritual warfare, but in reality you will never stop learning about this subject. You will continue to fight spiritual battles until you go to be with the Lord. As you fight each battle you will learn more about warfare from your successes and even from your failures. Start a "spiritual warfare journal" to record your battles and victories Always remember that "failure" is a temporary word as long as you return to the battlefield and continue to war. You may lose a battle now and then, but the final victory has been assured by our Lord of Hosts!

APPENDIX

DECISIVE BATTLES OF THE BIBLE

The Apostle Paul explained one important purpose for the Old Testament record. He said:

Now all these things happened unto them for ensamples: and they are written for our admonition, upon whom the ends of the world are come. (I Corinthians 10:11)

The Old Testament provides an "ensample" (examples) from which we are to learn. When you read the Old Testament, you will find many records of battles fought in the natural world. You may wonder why these records were included in the Bible. The importance of these battles extends beyond their immediate results. The strategies of Old Testament warfare in the natural world can be applied in the spiritual world to defeat our enemy.

This Appendix analyzes the historical record of Old Testament battles and applies these natural strategies to spiritual warfare. Just as a soldier in the natural world improves his skills by studying the historical record of previous battles, you can develop your spiritual warfare abilities by studying decisive battles of the Bible.

A DECISIVE BATTLE

A "decisive battle" is one that decides an issue by force of arms. It is a battle fought in a time of crisis. It results in advance or retreat, victory or defeat. It is the result of an offensive action (taking territory) or a defensive action (defending territory). In other words, it is an important conflict. This Appendix focuses on "decisive battles" of the Old Testament. Strategies used in these battles will help you fight "decisive battles" in the spiritual realm.

REASONS FOR OLD TESTAMENT BATTLES

The natural battles of the Old Testament were fought for three spiritual reasons:
1. For God's people to defeat evil forces which would enslave them.
2. For God's people to take from enemy forces territory He had given them.
3. To chastise God's people for evil when they turned from Him.

Our spiritual battles occur for the same reasons.

GENERAL PRINCIPLES

Before you study specific battles, it is important to understand general principles of Old Testament warfare because they are also applicable to spiritual warfare:

PRINCIPLE ONE:

In a properly conducted war authorized by God, He promised protection to the warriors (Deuteronomy 20:1-4).

PRINCIPLE TWO:

Israel's enemies were God's enemies. The people were to trust in Him for victory rather than their own strength (Judges 5:31, Exodus 17:16). When they did this, God fought with them.

PRINCIPLE THREE:

The ark of the covenant served as the symbol of God's presence with the Israelites during battle (Exodus 30:6; 25:21-22). The ark went before the armies of Israel to symbolize God's active presence with His people. It had no power in itself, but was only a symbol of God's presence with His people (I Samuel 4:1-11). In the New Testament, Jesus said the Holy Spirit was to dwell in believers and was God's actual, active presence within them (John 14:16-17).

PRINCIPLE FOUR:

If God was to fight for His people, they had to be holy (Deuteronomy 23:9-14). They were to separate themselves from anything sinful.

PRINCIPLE FIVE:

The fearful were exempted from war (Deuteronomy 20:8; Judges 7:1-6). Cowards will turn and run in the middle of the battle.

PRINCIPLE SIX:

People engaged in the affairs of life were exempted from war. Deuteronomy 20:5-8 records that a recently married man did not go to war for one year. This was because he was primarily concerned with his wife, setting up a household, getting established, etc. He was too busy with these affairs of life to be effective in warfare. This is why Paul warns Timothy "No man that warreth entangleth himself with the affairs of life" (II Timothy 2:4). Jesus also warned us about being overcome with the cares of the world. In the prophecy of Daniel, we learn that one of the main end time strategies of the antichrist is to "wear away the saints of God" by the affairs of this life.

PRINCIPLE SEVEN:

God's people were to fight until the enemy was completely destroyed (Numbers 31:10-11).

PRINCIPLE EIGHT:

The walls surrounding Israeli cities were important to their defense. These walls were approximately 10 feet in width and as high as 30 feet. Watchmen watched from the top of the walls for enemy activity. The New Testament compares the believer to a "city set on a hill". As you learned in this course, you have spiritual walls of defense against the enemy.

PRINCIPLE NINE:

A trumpet signal by the commander in chief opened each battle (Judges 7:18) and, when it was over, the trumpet called the soldiers away from the fight (II Samuel 2:28; 18:16). Jesus sounded

the trumpet in the spirit world when He commissioned us to go into all the world with the Gospel and gave us power over the enemy (Matthew 28:18-20). Someday in the future a trumpet will call us away from the fight (I Thessalonians 4:16-18).

ORGANIZATION OF THIS STUDY

Each battle discussed in this Appendix includes the:

- Scripture reference: Read the story of each battle in your Bible.
- Battleground: The geographic location of the battle.
- Opposing forces: Identity of the forces involved in the conflict.
- Reason for the battle: Why the battle occurred.
- Strategies: Strategies for victory or reasons for defeat. Some strategies appear repeatedly in the Biblical record. For example, the people are told repeatedly not to fear the enemy. Where duplications such as this occur, they are not repeated in this analysis after their first mention.

DECISIVE BATTLES OF THE BIBLE

- Scripture reference: Genesis 14
- Battleground: Dan, near the River Jordan.
- Opposing forces: Abraham and the four kings of the east.
- Reason for the battle: The kings had taken captive a relative of Abraham named Lot.
- Strategies:
    1. Anytime you go into enemy territory you can expect a battle.
    2. Abraham organized his forces into two easily controllable groups. His small forces conquered the armies of four kings. Victory is not dependent on size of the forces, but on organization, planning, readiness, and execution of the plan of God.

* * *

- Scripture reference: Exodus 14-15
- Battleground: The edge of the Red Sea located at the border of Egypt
- Opposing forces: Israel and Egypt
- Reason for the battle: Israel was escaping slavery in Egypt. They were fleeing the Egyptians when they were trapped by the Red Sea ahead and the enemy behind.
- Strategies:
    1. Do not look at the circumstances: Israel "lifted up their eyes" and saw the Egyptians pursuing them (Exodus 14:10-11). When they looked to the circumstances instead of God, this caused fear.
    2. Do not look back: The people began thinking of the good things of Egypt, which is a natural example of the spiritual bondage of sin (Exodus 14:12). When you are looking back you cannot advance spiritually.
    3. Fear not: The first message to Israel was "fear not" (Exodus 14:13). Fear paralyzes you in the face of the enemy. Faith energizes you to take action.
    4. Stand still: (Exodus 14:13). Until you receive specific direction from God, this should always be your response to the enemy. Do not flee in terror.
    5. Let the Lord fight for you: The battle is not yours. You do not have to do the fighting. God will fight for you (Exodus 14:14).
    6. Hold your peace: Do not let the threats of the enemy cause you to lose your peace (Exodus 14:14).
    7. Advance, do not retreat: God told Israel to step into the waters of the Red Sea. They were to advance into the flood, not retreat from it (Exodus 14:15-16, 21).
    8. Be assured that God will move for you supernaturally (Exodus 14:19-31). When you follow Biblical principles in spiritual warfare, God will move supernaturally to defeat the enemy. Repeatedly in these battles, you will see God moving supernaturally on behalf of His people.

* * *

- Scripture reference: Exodus 17:8-16
- Battleground: Rephidim
- Opposing forces: Israel and Amalek, a tribe of fierce nomads
- Reason for the battle: See Deuteronomy 25:17-18. The Amalekites had attacked Israel from the rear, making a cowardly assault upon the "faint and weary" stragglers.
- Strategies:
    1. Conquer through prayer: Israel could not conquer by the sword alone. The action taken by Moses is considered an act of prayer (Exodus 17:9-11). It expressed an attitude of dependence upon God that affected the outcome of the battle (Exodus 17:11).
    2. Grip "the rod of God": Moses took firm hold of the rod of God, a symbol of divine authority (Exodus 17:9). When you go into battle you must have a firm hold on your divine authority. You must know who we are in God and the authority He has given you.
    3. Obey spiritual leadership: Joshua did as Moses instructed him (Exodus 17:9-10). God has placed among us those to whom He has given special abilities to lead. He enables these leaders to give direction so His purposes will be accomplished.

Confusion results when everyone tries to give direction.
4. Go out and fight: All fighting is not defensive from the place in which you find yourself. There are times when offensive strategies are needed and you are to be aggressive in attacking your enemy (Exodus 17:9).
5. Seek assistance: God raises up men to assist you in meeting spiritual challenges. God called Joshua to assume military leadership while Moses gave spiritual leadership. Aaron and Hur assisted by holding up Moses's hands when he grew weary.
6. Recall past victories: Remembering past conquests through the power of God gives renewed vigor to face present opposition. God told Moses to write the story of this battle in a book for a memorial and rehearse it in the ears of Joshua (Exodus 17:14). Joshua, destined to be Moses' successor, would later lead Israel in the conquest of the Promised Land.

* * *

- Scripture reference: Numbers 14
- Battleground: Hill country in the vicinity of Hormah
- Opposing forces: Israelites against the Amalekites and Canaanites
- Reason for the battle: The Israelites went up to drive out the Amalekites and Canaanites to possess the land.
- Strategies:

1. Do not grumble: The Israelites complained about their situation (verses 2,3). To grumble and complain is displeasing to God (verse 11).
2. Do not rebel against the Lord: Rebellion is sin. You must totally renounce it (verse 9).
3. Beware of slanderous reports: Satan leads astray through evil reports and persuades by a multitude in agreement with these reports. The majority is seldom right (Numbers 14:36-38).
4. Obey the voice of God: God had made it plain that Israel must return to the wilderness but they proceeded in the opposite direction (verse 25).
5. Do not be overconfident: The Israelites moved in presumption and overconfidence (verses 42-44). They proceeded into battle without the blessing of God. God's presence is necessary for victory.
6. Make decisions in faith, not fear: Decisions based on fear result in defeat.

* * *

- Scripture reference: Numbers 21:1-3
- Battleground: Hormah
- Opposing forces: Israel and Arad the Canaanite, a tribal chief
- Reason for the battle: Israel was forced into this battle. It was not their plan to enter the land from the south.
- Strategies:
    1. Recognize that failure is a temporary word: This battle against King Arad and the Canaanites was fought in the same area as the aborted attempt to enter the

Promised Land 38 years earlier (Numbers 14:45). Though Israel failed then, this time they succeeded. Failure should never be considered permanent defeat. You will never fail until you stop trying.
2. Learn from past failures: God can use failure to teach spiritual truths. Israel learned they must have God with them in battle (verses 2-3). Ask God what He wants you to learn through your failures.

* * *

- Scripture reference: Numbers 21:21-32
- Battleground: Jahaz
- Opposing forces: Israel and the Amorites

- Reason for the battle: Moses wanted to gain access to the land west of Jordan which had been promised by God. He asked for peaceful passage (verses 21,22), but Sihon, king of the Amorites, refused (verse 23).
- Strategies:
    1. Understand that conflict is unavoidable: If you are to possess the promises of God, spiritual conflict is unavoidable. The enemy will not permit peaceful passage to claim God's promises.

* * *

- Scripture reference: Numbers 31
- Battleground: Plains of Moab
- Opposing forces: Israelites and Midianites
- Reason for battle: The Lord commanded the destruction of the Midianites because they were evil people involved in Baal worship (Numbers 25).
- Strategies:
    1. Purify yourselves: God instituted a purifying process that Israel was to follow before going into battle. He established the process, but they had to act upon it. If God is to fight with you in battle, you must be spiritually purified. He has established the way through Jesus Christ, but you must act upon it.
    2. Subordinate private interests: (verses 25-54). In battle, private interests must be subordinated (laid aside) for the cause of corporate victory.

* * *

- Scripture reference: Deuteronomy 2:24-37
- Battleground: Jahaz
- Opposing forces: Israel and Sihon the Amorite, king of Heshbon.
- Reason for the battle: Sihon refused to let the Israelites peacefully cross over the Jordan River into the land God gave them.
- Strategies:
    1. Claim what God has given: God had already given the Israelites the Promised Land of Canaan which is a type of the Spirit-filled life (verse 24). He has also given you an inheritance. It is already yours, waiting for you to claim it. (See also

the battle at Endrei in Numbers 21:33-35. This same strategy of taking possession of what God has already given is reflected in this battle.)
2. Let God fight for you: Sihon made a hostile attack on Israel and suffered defeat because the Lord fought for His people (verses 31,33).
3. Recognize nothing is too hard for the Lord: There was not one city too strong for Israel to defeat (verse 36). There is no stronghold of Satan in your life which cannot be overcome.

* * *

- Scripture reference: Deuteronomy 3:1-11

- Battleground: Edrei
- Opposing forces: Israel and Og the Amorite, king of Bashan
- Reason for the battle: Og, a giant such as had scared the spies when they first explored the land (Numbers 13:33), came with his men in battle against the Israelites.
- Strategies:
  1. Be assured that God will deliver the enemy into your hand: God's command to Israel to advance against Og was accompanied by His promise to deliver the enemy into their hands (verse 3).
  2. Overcome all obstacles: The height of the enemy's fortified cities and the size of their king did not defeat the army of the Lord. Nothing is too difficult for those empowered by Him.
  3. Claim the fruits of victory: Deuteronomy 3:8-11 summarizes the fruits of Israel's victory at Edrei. Each battle in which we engage presents an opportunity to claim new "fruits of victory" in your spiritual life.

* * *

- Scripture reference: Joshua 6
- Battleground: Jericho
- Opposing forces: Israelites and the king of Jericho and its mighty men
- Reason for the battle: God told Joshua to lead the Israelites to conquer the city of Jericho.
- Strategies:
  1. Recognize that God's ways are not your ways: No matter how foolish a situation appears, you must trust God. His thoughts and ways are not as yours (Isaiah 55:8). What the world calls weak, God uses to put the strong to shame (I Corinthians 1:27). God sometimes intervenes in ways that seem foolish to the natural mind. Israel was doing battle God's way, no matter how foolish it appeared. See I Corinthians 1:25.
  2. Seek assurance of God's presence: The ark of the Lord, mentioned nine times in verses 6-13, symbolized to Israel that God was with them. Before entering battle, seek assurance of God's presence.
  3. Use the strategy of silence: Israel was told to march in silence (with the exception of the sounding trumpets) until they heard the command to shout (v. 10). The strategy of silence should be used in warfare until you receive directions from God of when and what to speak.

* * *

- Scripture reference: Joshua 7
- Battleground: City of Ai
- Opposing forces: Israelites and the Amorites
- Reason for the battle: Joshua was leading the Israelites in battle to possess the land God had promised them.
- Strategies:
  1. Do not violate God's instructions: Achan's sin caused God's favor to be withdrawn which resulted in disaster for Israel (verses 1-5). Sin lurks in the shadow of victory.
  2. Do not underestimate the enemy: The spies underestimated the population of Ai (verses 2-4). Do not underestimate the power of the enemy to kill, steal, and destroy. At the same time, do not let the rational assessment of his powers bring fear. You have power over all the power of the enemy.
  3. Discover and deal with the cause of defeat: When there is defeat, there is a cause. Israel dealt with the guilty as instructed (verses 13,25,26). This discipline resulted in restored approval by God. To maintain the presence of God, you must deal with sin by confession and repentance.
  4. Abstain from fleshly lusts: Achan's sin was a progression...he saw, he coveted, he took (verse 21). In I Peter 2:11 we are told to "abstain from fleshly lusts, which war against the soul". The lust of the eyes is not of the Father, but is of the world (I John 2:16). From the very first attack of the enemy on man, fleshly lusts have been instrumental in defeat (Genesis 3).

* * *

- Scripture reference: Joshua 8
- Battleground: Ai
- Opposing forces: Israel and men of the city of Ai
- Reason for the battle: God told Israel to take the city of Ai and that this time they would be victorious.
- Strategies:
  1. Support one another: Working as a team, Israel defeated the enemy by setting an ambush. Ecclesiastes 4:9-12 indicates we have added strength against the enemy when we stand in support of one another.
  2. Be ready: Joshua told the men of war to be ready (verse 4). You are engaged in spiritual warfare. You must be ready to advance and be on guard against the enemy at all times.
  3. Use the sword: Joshua's sword was the signaling weapon to the men hidden in ambush (verse 18,19). Believers have a spiritual sword which is the Word of God (Ephesians 6:17). You are to use it to warn others of the approach of the enemy.
  4. Turn and face the enemy: The Israelites who fled into the wilderness turned back upon their pursuers and slew them (verse 21). Turn and face your enemy in the strength of the Lord. "Submit yourselves therefore to God, resist the Devil, and he

will flee from you" (James 4:7).
5. Focus on the Victor rather than the victories: Joshua led the people in worship after the victory was won (verses 29-31). Sometimes we make the mistake of emphasizing a spiritual victory and our part in attaining it. We are warned, "let him that thinketh he standeth take heed lest he fall" (I Corinthians 10:12).

* * *

- Scripture reference: Joshua 10:1-27
- Battleground: Gibeon
- Opposing forces: Israel and the five Amorite kings of Jerusalem, Hebron, Jarmuth, Lachish, and Eglon with their forces
- Reason for the battle: Joshua was called to aid the Gibeonites because the king of Jerusalem organized troops to punish them for making a treaty with Israel. These five kings wanted to prevent the Israelites from occupying this strategic location.
- Strategies:
    1. Put the enemy under your feet: Putting the feet upon the necks, the ancient symbol of subjugation, is acted out here by Joshua's field commanders (verses 24-25). Jesus said He is the head of His body, the Church. He has put all the power of the enemy under His feet. If we are His body, then this means our feet are upon the neck of the enemy.
    2. Be strong and of good courage: This is God's Word to you in the face of battle. Your strength comes in knowing God is on your side. This assurance causes you to be strong and of good courage as you face opposition (verse 25).

* * *

- Scripture reference: Joshua 10:28-43
- Battleground: Southern Palestine
- Opposing forces: Israel and the cities of Southern Palestine
- Reason for the battle: Joshua launched a battle to take Southern Palestine.
- Strategies:
    1. Attack key strongholds: Joshua's battle strategy was a series of lightning-like raids against key Canaanite cities with the purpose of destroying the fighting ability of the inhabitants (verses 28-43). By attacking key strongholds of the enemy in your life (for example, the flesh) you weaken the ability of the enemy to attack you.

* * *

- Scripture reference: Joshua 11
- Battleground: At the waters of Merom
- Opposing forces: Israel and the Canaanite kings of the north under the leadership of Jabin, king of Hazor
- Reason for the battle: Following God's instructions, Joshua led the Israelites to possess another portion of the Promised Land.
- Strategies:

1. Persevere: Joshua waged war with the kings of the land for around six years (verse 18). Perseverance (remaining faithful in battle) is essential in capturing strongholds, driving out the inhabitants (old sin nature) and possessing all God has promised.
2. Do not fear the size of enemy forces (verse 4).

* * *

- Scripture reference: Judges 6:1-8:35
- Battleground: Valley of Jezreel
- Opposing forces: Gideon and 300 men against the Midianites and Amalekites
- Reason for the battle: Because Israel sinned, God delivered them into bondage to the nation of Midian for seven years. When Israel repented and cried to the Lord, He sent Gideon to deliver them.
- Strategies:
    1. Heed the warning...Sin results in bondage: Israel's sin left her powerless before her foes (6:1-5). Sin brings you into the spiritual bondage of Satan.
    2. Restoration comes from God: The Midianite oppression brought Israel to the place where they finally sought God for deliverance (6:6-8). When you have been taken captive by the enemy through your own sin, God is your only hope of restoration.
    3. Get alone with God: Gideon was by himself when he was commissioned to deliver Israel (6:11-14). Valiant leaders of spiritual warfare must spend time alone with God. If you are to help others through a deliverance ministry, this strategy is vital.
    4. Pull down the altars of idolatry: Gideon pulled down and destroyed the altars of Baal (6:25-31). You are to pull down the strongholds of the enemy and destroy every idolatrous thing that stands in the way of total commitment to God.
    5. Be endued by the Spirit of God: God's Spirit came upon Gideon to empower him to accomplish the divine purpose (6:34). The endument of power by the Holy Spirit must come upon you for the same reason. See Acts 1:8.
    6. Seek deeper levels of faith: Gideon needed a fleece as a sign to be willing to trust God (6:36-40). Some Christians cannot believe unless they have certain favorable signs in the natural world. You need to seek a deeper level of faith that takes God at His Word even when natural circumstances are contrary. See Acts 27:20-25.
    7. Do not be self-reliant: God prevented self-reliance by reducing the army to a small number. God works in your life to eliminate self-reliance so you will recognize the victory comes from Him.
    8. Do not hesitate: In spite of God's confirmations, Gideon hesitated to face the enemy. He had never led an army before and his men were untrained and inexperienced (7:9,10). There are times when you may hesitate to move in a new direction God has told you to go. You may feel inexperienced and inadequate. Do not hesitate...God equips those He calls.
    9. Target the fear of the enemy: God allowed Gideon to hear the fears of the Midianites. In identifying fears, weaknesses are discovered. James 2:19 says that the devils believe in God and tremble in fear. Target the fear of the enemy with the power of God.

***

- Scripture reference: Judges 15
- Battleground: Lehi
- Opposing forces: Samson and the Philistines
- Reason for the battle: Samson attacked the Philistines over a family matter. The Philistines blamed the attack on his wife and her family and retaliated by destroying them with fire. The retaliation continued back and forth between Samson and the Philistines.
- Strategies:
    1. Know that God turns defeat to victory: While Samson's enemies were shouting in triumph, the Spirit of the Lord came upon Samson and he broke the cords binding him (verse 14). He took a jawbone of an ass, attacked his enemies, and killed a thousand men. What appeared as defeat was turned into victory for the Israelite champion (verse 15). There is no binding defeat of the enemy that cannot be turned to victory by God.
    2. Acknowledge God as your provision: After the exertion of killing 1,000 Philistines, Samson was thirsty. His weakened condition would leave him prey for other Philistines seeking to avenge the death of their countrymen. In his distress he called on the Lord (verse 18). God is not only our strength in battle, He is your provision.
    3. Be refreshed at the spring of the Lord: In answer to his call, God caused water to spring forth. Samson drank, and he was revived (verse 19). Jesus said, "If any man thirst, let him come unto me, and drink" (John 7:37). Just as soldiers in the natural world need times of rest and refreshment, we need refreshing spiritually. Many seek this refreshment through recreation, hobbies, and entertainment. True spiritual refreshment comes at "the spring of the Lord."

***

- Scripture reference: Judges 20
- Battleground: Gibeah
- Opposing forces: Benjaminites against all the other Israelites.
- Reason for the battle: A Levite's concubine was raped and killed by a group of men of Gibeah. The Levite called for the elders of each tribe to hear charges and consider appropriate action. All but the Benjaminites agreed to punish the men of Gibeah. They defended them.
- Strategies:
    1. Ask counsel of God: Israel went before God repeatedly seeking counsel concerning battle strategies (verses 18, 23, 26, 28).
    2. Exercise corporate discipline: The other tribes of Israel asked the tribe of Benjamin to turn over the offenders for punishment. Israel wanted to remove evil from their corporate life by punishing the offenders (verse 13). As believers we must cooperate with God in removal of evil from our lives by offering these areas to Him.
    3. Do not quit fighting: In the first two battles the Israelites were defeated by the forces of Benjamin. The Israelites wept, fasted, and went before the Lord again

for counsel. He said they should resume the battle and promised them victory (verses 18-28).

* * *

- Scripture reference: I Samuel 4
- Battleground: Between Aphek and Ebenezer
- Opposing forces: Israelites and Philistines
- Reason for the battle: Israel battled against the Philistines, God's enemies.
- Strategies:
  1. Do not trust in spiritual "forms": The ark of the Lord was the visible symbol of God's presence among His people (verse 4). But the people were not to trust in the form. They were to trust in the God it represented.

* * *

- Scripture reference: I Samuel 11
- Battleground: Bezek
- Opposing forces: Nahash the Ammonite and the men of Jabesh along with Saul and the Israelites
- Reason for the battle: The Ammonites attacked the Israelite town of Jabesh-gilead. Saul organized an army and defeated them (verse 11).

- Strategies:
  1. Prepare for battle in the morning watch: Saul attacked the Ammonites in the early morning hours (verse 11). Come before the Lord in the early morning hours and "put on the whole armor of God" (Ephesians 6:11-17).

* * *

- Scripture reference: I Samuel 13-14
- Battleground: Michmash
- Opposing forces: Israelites and Philistines
- Reason for the battle: Jonathan killed a Philistine military officer at Geba.
- Strategies:
  1. Be patient in the hour of crisis: Saul's impatience cost him his position of king (verse 13). He became fearful as he saw his army fleeing before the Philistines. He disobeyed the instructions of God to wait. In the hour of conflict do not let fear force you to act foolishly.
  2. Stress dedication, not numbers: Israel won battles not with superior numbers, but with dedicated men of valor (14:6).

* * *

- Scripture reference: I Samuel 17
- Battleground: Valley of Elah
- Opposing forces: Israelites (David) and Philistines (Goliath)
- Reason for the battle: The Philistine army had assembled to attack Israel. The Israeli army had set up a defensive position on the opposite side of the valley. A Philistine giant, Goliath, suggested that the battle be settled in a fight between him and an Israelite warrior.
- Strategies:
    1. Draw strength from previous victories: David had experienced victories in saving his flocks from wild beasts. He assured Saul he could protect the flock of God from this Philistine (verses 24-36). Faith strengthened in past difficulties yields faith for new crises.
    2. View obstacles as God's opportunity: Every difficulty is actually an opportunity for God to reveal His power through you. David saw the giant as an opportunity rather than a challenge (verses 32,45-47).
    3. Use proven armor: David refused Saul's worldly armor because he had not used (proved) it in battle (verses 38,39). Spiritual battles cannot be fought with worldly strategies. They must be fought with tried and proven spiritual armor.
    4. Face the enemy in the name of the Lord: Goliath came with a sword, spear and javelin but David faced the giant in the name of the Lord (verses 45-47).
    5. Remember that the battle is the Lord's: The enemy may appear to have the advantage, but when the battle is the Lord's the victory is certain. David confirmed that the Lord, not man's power, determines the outcome of battle. "...Not by might, nor by power, but by my spirit, saith the Lord of hosts." (Zechariah 4:6)
    6. Do not be limited by your own abilities: The giant looked on David in the natural as a youth with no experience in battle (verse 33). God does not see us as we are, limited by our own inabilities. He sees us as what we can become if we permit His power to flow through us.
    7. Confess the victory: David confessed past victories in God and spoke words of faith in confessing future victories.
    8. Recognize the purpose of spiritual warfare: David stated it in verse 46..."That all the earth may know that there is a God..."

* * *

- Scripture reference: I Samuel 30
- Battleground: Near Ziglag
- Opposing forces: Israelites and Amalekites
- Reason for the battle: While David and his forces were away from Ziglag, the Amalekites made a raid and took captive their families and burned the city.
- Strategies:
    1. Do not give in to despair: David's men were so grieved that they spoke of stoning him (verse 6), but David encouraged himself in the Lord. In times of discouragement when you are standing alone, encourage yourself in the Lord. Do not give in to despair.
    2. Claim restoration of all the enemy has taken: The enemy comes to kill, steal, and

destroy (verse 1). God told David to pursue the enemy and take back all that had been stolen. God wants to restore to you all the enemy has taken (verses 8,18).
3. Realize that a victory for one is for all: Verse 24 gives a key principle in spiritual warfare. Those on the front lines and those who "stay with the stuff" share equally in the victory.

* * *

- Scripture reference: II Samuel 5:1-16
- Battleground: Jerusalem
- Opposing forces: Israelites and Jebusites
- Reason for the battle: The Jebusites inhabited Jerusalem and considered their stronghold so great that it could not be captured. David captured the city and it became the center of Israel's national life.
- Strategies:
    1. Do not be intimidated by the ridicule of the enemy: The Jebusites ridiculed David saying their stronghold was so great that it could be defended by "the blind and the lame" (verse 6). David did not allow this ridicule to hinder him (verse 7). When the enemy makes you feel inadequate by ridicule, claim John 8:44.

* * *

- Scripture reference: II Samuel 5:17-25
- Battleground: Valley of Rephaim
- Opposing forces: Israelites and Philistines
- Reason for the battle: When the Philistines heard David had been anointed king over Israel, they organized an attack against him.
- Strategies:
    1. Fight offensively: David did not wait for the attack of the enemy. He went out against them. Do not wait for the enemy to come and get you!

* * *

- Scripture reference: II Samuel 10
- Battleground: Area of Helam
- Opposing forces: Israelites against Ammonites and Syrians
- Reason for the battle: The king of the Ammonites died. David sent servants to console his son and affirm his loyalty. But the new king listened to false accusations and insulted the Israelites instead of accepting David's goodwill gesture. He shaved off half of their beards, cut off their clothing, and sent them away in disgrace (verses 1-5).
- Strategies:
    1. Cooperate in battle: When David's general realized he was faced with a battle on two fronts, he divided his forces putting his brother in charge of half of the troops. Although divided, these forces fought together to defeat the enemy. Although divided geographically, culturally, or denominationally from other believers, we should cooperate in battle against the enemy, not fight each other.

* * *

- Scripture reference: II Samuel 21:15-22
- Battleground: Gob and Gath
- Opposing forces: Israelites and Philistines.
- Reason for the battle: The Philistines continued to war against the Israelites. This is another brief account of the ongoing conflict.
- Strategies:
    1. Conquer the giants in the land: A number of Philistine giants were killed in these battles. These giants had plagued Israel over the years. Is there some "giant" of your old flesh that continues to plague you? Continue the battle until the giants are conquered.
    2. Recognize that God uses different methods: Once David had faced Goliath and defeated him in the power of the Lord with a simple sling and stone. This time God used a different method to defeat the giant (verses 16-17). Do not limit God on the basis of how you have seen Him move in times past.
    3. Strengthen the leadership: Even great leaders can become weak in battle (verses 15-17). This is not the time to criticize, but the time to support them.

* * *

- Scripture reference: I Kings 20
- Battleground: Samaria and later at Aphek
- Opposing forces: Ahab king of the Israelites and Benhadad king of the Syrians
- Reason for the battle: Benhdad, king of Syria, gathered his army and 32 kings with him to war against Samaria.
- Strategies:
    1. Recognize that the enemy will return: The prophet told the king of Israel to strengthen himself because the king of Syria would return against him (verse 22). However great a victory has been, it is not the end of the fight. The enemy will renew his effort to defeat God's people.
    2. Do not be deceived by flattery: Flattered by the Syrian king's submission, Ahab consented to let Benhadad depart in peace. The motive behind flattery is self-interest. It leads to pride, a selfish emotion which acts apart from God. See Proverbs 16:8.
    3. Set proper priorities: Ahab was concerned about getting back his lost territories. The statement "and as thy servant was busy here and there, he was gone" (verse 40) reveals he did not set proper priorities. The will of God requires first place.
    4. Do not compromise with the enemy: It was within the power of Ahab to end the struggle between Syria and Israel. But with Benhadad free, the struggle would continue with disastrous results (verse 42).

* * *

- Scripture reference: II Kings 3
- Battleground: Moab
- Opposing forces: Israel and her allies, Judah and Edom, against the Moabites
- Reason for the battle: Moab rebelled and refused to pay taxes to Israel. Jehoram asked the king of Judah to help him fight Moab. When they started to battle they were joined by the king of Edom.
- Strategies:
  1. Praise God for revelation: Elisha had music played to make him receptive to the Word of the Lord. As the minstrel played, the power of the Lord came upon Elisha and he received the revelation of God (verses 11-15). Praise is a key strategy of warfare. It brings your spirit into a proper attitude to receive revelation from God.
  2. Prepare for victory: Sometimes you cannot receive victory because you have not prepared for it. There was a drought and the armies of Israel and Judah were in danger of death from lack of water. Elisha prayed for a miracle. God said, "Make this valley full of ditches." God caused the ditches to be filled with water (verses 16-17). You must be properly prepared if you are to be channels for the life giving flow of God. Sometimes this involves digging some "dirt" out of your spiritual life!

* * *

- Scripture reference: II Kings 6:8-23
- Battleground: Dothan and Samaria
- Opposing forces: Israel and Syria
- Reason for the battle: When Syria was fighting Israel, Elisha revealed to the king of Israel the location of the Syrian army. When the King of Syria learned what Elisha had done, he sent armies to capture him.
- Strategies:
  1. Pray: As you have probably noted, prayer to God was made repeatedly in Old Testament battles. In this account, Elisha prayed for the Syrians to be struck blind (verse 18). Prayer is one of the most powerful weapons of spiritual warfare.
  2. Develop spiritual insight: Elisha's servant saw nothing but the natural circumstances. Elisha had spiritual insight and could say: "Fear not, for those who are with us are more than those who are with them (Syria)" (verse 16).
  3. Allow God's power to be demonstrated: When the Syrians were struck with blindness, Elisha led them to the king of Israel. He asked the king not to destroy them, but to send them home as a demonstration of God's power (verses 18-23).

* * *

- Scripture reference: II Kings 6:24-7:20
- Battleground: Samaria
- Opposing forces: Syria and Israel
- Reason for the battle: Benhadad and his army surrounded Samaria and a terrible famine resulted in the city. Food was so expensive and scarce that people were eating garbage and even their own children.

- Strategies:
    1. Move toward the impossible: As the four lepers pondered their situation, they knew the worst the Syrians could do was kill them. They would die anyway if they did nothing. They decided to move toward the impossible situation. God made the Syrians hear sounds of an approaching army which caused them to flee, leaving behind their belongings (7:3-7). When you move towards the impossible, God acts in your behalf.
    2. Share with other believers: The lepers shared the good news of the defeat of the enemy (7:8-10). You have a responsibility to share with others what God has done for you in impossible situations. Through this, other believers are strengthened.
    3. Do not be skeptical of God's supernatural power: One leader did not receive the blessings of God because of skepticism of God's power (7:2, 17-20).

* * *

- Scripture reference: II Kings 17
- Battleground: Samaria
- Opposing forces: Israel and Assyria
- Reason for the battle: Hoshea, king of Israel, was to pay tribute annually to the King of Assyria. Israel stopped paying tribute, so Assyria attacked them.
- Strategies:
    1. Worship is a key to effective warfare: Israel ceased to worship God and He delivered them into the hand of Assyria. Worship is the highest form of spiritual warfare (see Job 1 and 2). If you fail in worship, you will soon be captive of the enemy.

* * *

- Scripture reference: II Kings 19
- Battleground: Jerusalem
- Opposing forces: Assyria and Israel
- Reason for the battle: Israel's king, Hezekiah, trusted in God and tried to destroy idolatry. To assure safety for his kingdom he paid tribute to the Assyrian king. Then he received a threatening letter.
- Strategies:
    1. Do not fear the threats of the enemy: Hezekiah took the threats of the enemy to the Lord. God told Him there was no need to fear, for the enemy would be removed from the land. Just as God defeated the Assyrians, He has defeated Satan. You need not fear his threats.

* * *

- Scripture reference: II Kings 24:1-25:30
- Battleground: Jerusalem
- Opposing forces: Judah and Babylon
- Reason for the battle: Judah did evil repeatedly in the sight of the Lord. Finally God permitted the people to be taken captive by the Babylonians who were the dominant world power. Jerusalem was burned and the walls were torn down.
- Strategies:
    1. Understand that sin results in captivity: God's people were taken captive by the enemy because they permitted repeated, unconfessed sin in their lives. Instead of being used by God to defeat the enemy, they were taken captive by their foes.

* * *

- Scripture reference: I Chronicles 14:8-17
- Battleground: Valley of Rephaim and Baal-perazim
- Opposing forces: Israelites and Philistines
- Reason for the battle: When David became king of a united Israel, he was a threat the Philistines could not ignore. They immediately launched an attack against him.
- Strategies:
    1. Hold out for decisive victories: David and his forces won the first battle, but it was not decisive because they did not completely possess the land (verses 9-13). In the second battle, God gave Israel a decisive victory. They forced the Philistines out of Israelite territory (verses 13-17).
    2. Wait for proper timing: Timing is a key to effective warfare. David waited until he knew God had gone before him as promised (verses 14-16). Many battles have been lost and won on the basis of this one principle of proper timing.

* * *

- Scripture reference: II Chronicles 12
- Battleground: Jerusalem
- Opposing forces: Egypt and her allies against Rehoboam, king of Judah
- Reason for the battle: Rehoboam was unfaithful to God and turned to sinful practices of the Canaanites. The invasion by Shishak, king of Egypt, was permitted as judgment from God.
- Strategies:
    1. Prepare spiritually; Spiritual preparation is necessary for victory: Rehoboam did evil because " he prepared not his heart to seek the Lord" (verse 14). Prepare your heart to seek the Lord before entering the battlefield.
    2. Humble yourself: When Rehoboam humbled himself, God granted him "some deliverance". He did not allow him to be totally destroyed (verses 5-7).
    3. Submit to God's service: Although God forgives, there are consequences for disobedience (verse 8). Compared to the service demanded by the world, how much better it is to submit to God. See Matthew 11:28-30.

* * *

- Scripture reference: II Chronicles 18
- Battleground: Ramoth-gilead
- Opposing forces: Syrians against Ahab king of Israel and Johoshaphat king of Judah
- Reason for the battle: Johoshaphat made an alliance with Ahab and together they battled the Syrians.
- Strategies:
    1. Do not make unholy alliances: After 65 years of hostility between Israel and Judah, Jehoshaphat made an alliance with Ahab. This included the marriage of his son to Ahab's daughter. This unholy alliance proved disastrous for Jehoshaphat personally as well as for Judah because it brought in the evils of heathenism. Alliances with evil never produce positive spiritual results.
    2. Use discernment in choosing counsel: Before going to battle, Ahab called for his prophets to bring a word from God. But these professional prophets were more interested in saying what Ahab wanted to hear. Jehoshaphat insisted they call a prophet who was not dependent on Ahab for sustenance. Ahab sent for Micaiah whose prophecy was from the Lord (verses 1-16). Discernment must be used in seeking spiritual counsel. A majority in one accord is not always verification of God's will.

* * *

- Scripture reference: II Chronicles 20
- Battleground: Valley of Berachah
- Opposing forces: Men of Moab, Ammon, and Mt. Seir against Jehoshaphat, king of Judah
- Reason for the battle: Several nations joined in a conspiracy against Judah.
- Strategies:
    1. Use the strategy of fasting: Jehoshaphat proclaimed a fast in all Judah (verse 3). God deals with you on the basis of your relationship to Him. Fasting does not change God, it changes you. It alters your relationship to Him which affects His response to you. See Jonah chapter 3.
    2. Keep your eyes upon the Lord: Jehoshaphat prayed, "We do not know what to do, but our eyes are upon You" (verse 12).
    3. Remember that it is better to trust than try: God's answer came to Jehoshaphat, "The battle is not yours, but God's" (verse 15). When only God can do what is needed, it is better to trust than to try in self-effort.
    4. Rejoice in the midst of battle: Singers were appointed to sing as they went out before the army. God set an ambush against the enemy and they were defeated.

* * *

- Scripture reference: II Chronicles 25:5-16
- Battleground: Valley of Salt
- Opposing forces: Edomites and Amaziah, king of Judah
- Reason for the battle: Amaziah battled the heathen nation of Edom.
- Strategies:
    1. Follow Godly advice: In an attempt to strengthen his own forces, Amaziah hired

mercenaries from Israel. This was displeasing to God who spoke by a prophet to send Israel home or else be defeated. Amaziah followed this Godly advice and victory was his.
2. Destroy all idols: Amaziah began to worship the Edomite idols (verse 14). Effective spiritual warfare will destroy all idols in your life, whether they be of stone or wood or materialistic possessions.

* * *

- Scripture reference: II Chronicles 25:17-24
- Battleground: Bethshemesh of Judah
- Opposing forces: Jehoash, king of Israel, against Amaziah, king of Judah
- Reason for the battle: Pride over success in defeating Edom led Amaziah to challenge Israel to battle.
- Strategies:
  1. Pride results in defeat: Amaziah was filled with pride over a former victory. This led him to challenge Israel (verses 17-19). See Proverbs 16:5.

* * *

- Scripture reference: II Chronicles 28
- Battleground: Jerusalem
- Opposing forces: Judah against invading forces of Syria, Israel, Edom, Philistia, and Assyria
- Reason for the battle: Judah was invaded by Syria, Israel, Edom, Philistia, and Assyria.
- Strategies:
  1. Worldly corruption brings spiritual ruin: Ahaz worshiped foreign gods thinking they would strengthen him. Instead, they were his ruin (verse 23). Corrupting influences of the world will result in spiritual ruin.
  2. Even valiant men fall when they forsake God: See verse 6.

* * *

- Scripture reference: II Chronicles 32:1-23 & II Kings 19
- Battleground: Jerusalem
- Opposing forces: Sennacherib, king of Assyria and Hezekiah, king of Judah
- Reason for the battle: The king of Assyria invaded Judah and surrounded the fortified cities.
- Strategies:
  1. Cut the supply line of the enemy: Hezekiah's strategies were to cut off the water supply for Assyria and build up the walls of the city (verses 3,5). Division in the Body of Christ is one of the main supply lines of the enemy. We equip Satan when we supply him with ammunition against other believers through wrong use of the tongue. Instead of criticizing and gossiping about fellow believers, we should build walls of protection around them.

* * *

- Scripture reference: II Chronicles 35:20-24
- Battleground: Valley of Megiddo
- Opposing forces: Necho, king of Egypt, and Josiah, king of Judah
- Reason for the battle: Egypt wanted to pass through Palestine to fight Nebuchadnezzar, king of Babylon. Josiah would not permit them to pass.
- Strategies:
    1. Reject deception: Josiah disguised himself when he went out to battle, hoping for protection from the fate spoken by the "words of Necho from the mouth of God" (verse 22). Deception is not effective in spiritual warfare, as Satan is the master deceiver.
    2. Listen when God speaks: Josiah had previously been in right relationship with God. The acts of his goodness are noted in verse 26. He knew the voice of God, but in this case did not listen when God spoke.

* * *

Now it is your turn...

Begin to keep your own historical record about spiritual battles you fight. Record what the battle concerns, the reason for the battle, strategies Satan used to attack, and counter strategies you used for victory.

ANSWERS TO INSPECTIONS

CHAPTER ONE:

1. For we wrestle not against flesh and blood, but against principalities, against powers, against the rulers of the darkness of this world, against spiritual wickedness in high places. (Ephesians 6:12)
2. The major division of all things into either that which is natural or that which is spiritual. See I Corinthians 15:44-49.
3. The Kingdom of Satan and the Kingdom of God.
4. Satan, demons, the world, the flesh.
5. God the Father, Jesus Christ, the Holy Spirit, and angels.
6. The word "king" means the sovereign ruler of a territory or people.
7. A kingdom is the territory and people over which a king rules.
8. Spiritual warfare is the analysis of and an active participation in the invisible spiritual war. It includes study of the opposing forces of good and evil, the strategies of Satan, and spiritual strategies for overcoming the enemy. Spiritual warfare moves beyond mere analysis into active participation by application of these strategies in life and ministry.
9. The reason behind this great spiritual conflict is that Satan still wants to be the supreme ruler. He is waging an intense battle for the heart, mind, soul, and spirit of man. His strategies are directed at God, His plan, and His people.
10. We must recognize that all battles of life, whether physical, spiritual emotional, mental, financial, or with human personalities are only outward manifestations of a spiritual cause. Although in the natural world they may seem to occur through circumstances of life, the basis of these natural battles is in the spirit world.

CHAPTER TWO:

1. I came not to call the righteous, but sinners to repentance. (Luke 5:32)
2. Repentance is "an inward decision or change of mind resulting in the outward action of turning from sin to God and righteousness."
3. Review the discussion on this subject in Chapter Two.
4. When you ask for forgiveness of sins you experience "conversion." Conversion means "to turn." When it is used in connection with Biblical repentance, it means to "turn from the wrong way to the right way." You leave the Kingdom of Satan and join the Kingdom of God.
5. Review the discussion on this subject in Chapter Two.
6. When you repent from sin and make the decision to turn from your sinful ways this establishes a right relationship with God. This right relationship or right standing before God is called "justification."
7. When you are justified by repentance and conversion, you are "saved" from a life of sin as well as from the penalties of sin. This is what it means to be "saved" and what the Bible is speaking of when the term "salvation" is used.

8. When the young man realized his sinful condition he made a decision to go to his father and repent of his sin. This is an example of repentance, an inward decision which results in outward action. He then arose and left the old life and went to his father to start a new life. This is conversion.

CHAPTER THREE:

1. Hear, O Israel: The Lord our God is one Lord. (Deuteronomy 6:4)
2. God the Father, Jesus Christ, the Holy Spirit, and angels.
3. God the Father; God the Son, Jesus Christ; God the Holy Spirit.
4. God the Father is the commander of the spiritual forces of good which combat the spiritual forces of evil. This is His special function in the realm of spiritual warfare.
5. The functions of Jesus Christ in relation to spiritual warfare are as follows: Redeeming mankind from sin: It is through the death of Jesus Christ that we are freed from the bondage of sin in which the enemy has ensnared us. Authority over the forces of evil: The death of Jesus not only freed mankind from sin, it resulted in triumph over the forces of evil. Because of this, you have authority over the enemy. Destroying the works of the Devil: This was one of the main purposes of His coming to earth in human form. Intercession for believers: In Heaven Jesus is at the right hand of God the Father interceding for believers who are engaged in spiritual warfare.
6. The Holy Spirit guides the warfare of the believer. He reveals spiritual things that cannot be known naturally. The Holy Spirit speaks the will and words of God to us. He also intercedes for the believer engaged in spiritual battles. He gives the believer spiritual power through the baptism of the Holy Spirit and equips him with spiritual gifts and fruit.
7. 1. h 7. c
   2. d 8. a
   3. b 9. f
   4. g 10. e
   5. l 11. j
   6. I 12. k
8. The Lord of Hosts.

CHAPTER FOUR:

1. The angel of the Lord encampeth round about them that fear Him, and delivereth them. (Psalms 34:7)
2. Heaven and earth.
3. They were created by God.
4. Study the various ministries of angels discussed in this chapter.
5. Study the attributes of angels listed in this chapter.
6. Hebrews 1:14.
7. True. See Colossians 2:18 and Revelation 22:8-9
8. False. See Galatians 1:8

9. Elect angels
   Messengers
   Cherubim
   Living creatures
   Seraphim
10. Good and evil.
11. Colossians 1:16

CHAPTER FIVE:

1. Be sober, be vigilant, because your adversary the devil, as a roaring lion, walketh about, seeking whom he may devour. (I Peter 5:8)
2. Satan was originally created as an angel by God.
3. In his former position, Satan was an angel named Lucifer, an anointed cherub.
4. Satan fell from his position because of pride and rebellion which was expressed in terms of five statements of "I Will."
5. See the results listed in Chapter Five.
6. Satan's sphere of activity is both Heaven and earth.
7. The general activities of Satan are always directed against God, His plan, and His people; their worship, the Word, their work, and walk.
8. Study the list given in Chapter Five.

CHAPTER SIX :

1. Now the Spirit speaketh expressly, that in the latter times some shall depart from the faith, giving heed to seducing spirits and doctrines of devils. (I Timothy 4:1)
2. God created them.
3. Their sphere of activity is on earth.
4. Like Satan, their activities are directed against God, His plan, and His people.
5. See the list of attributes listed in Chapter Six.
6. See the discussion in Chapter Six.
7. They were originally angels in Heaven.
8. They participated in the rebellion of Satan and as a result were cast out of Heaven. They no longer were good spiritual beings (angels) but became evil (demons).
9. See the discussion on this subject in Chapter Six.

CHAPTER SEVEN:

1. Love not the world, neither the things that are in the world. If any man love the world, the love of the Father is not in him. For all that is in the world, the lust of the flesh, and the lust of the eyes, and the pride of life, is not of the Father, but is of the world. (I John 2:15-16)
2. The word "flesh" as used in this lesson refers to the sinful nature that is in all men which is in opposition and rebellion to God.
3. The word "world" as used in this lesson refers to the present condition of the world system which is in opposition to God.
4. Satan.

5. Compare your summary to the discussion in Chapter Seven.
6. Sin.
7. The world hates believers.
8. Lust is strong desire, soulish emotions, the natural tendency of man towards evil. Lusting after evil things which will please our fleshly nature is "lust of the flesh."
9. Satan uses the environment of the world to appeal to the senses and cause evil desire or lust of the flesh.
10. Lust results in temptation, temptation leads to sin, and sin leads to death.
11. Galatians 5:19-21

CHAPTER EIGHT:

1. Be sober, be vigilant; because your adversary the Devil, as a roaring lion, walketh about, seeking whom he may devour; Whom resist steadfast in the faith, knowing that the same afflictions are accomplished in your brethren that are in the world. (I Peter 5:8-9)
2. Read the discussion on this subject in Chapter Eight.
3. Read the discussion on this subject in Chapter Eight.
4. Read the discussion on this subject in Chapter Eight.
5. Read the discussion on this subject in Chapter Eight.

CHAPTER NINE:

1. He that committeth sin is of the Devil; for the Devil sinneth from the beginning. For this purpose the Son of God was manifested, that He might destroy the works of the Devil. (I John 3:8)
2. See the discussion on this subject in Chapter Nine.
3. To destroy the works of the Devil.
4. The Word of God, power and authority, prayer, fasting, keys to the kingdom, and the name of Jesus.

CHAPTER TEN:

1. Neither give place to the Devil. (Ephesians 4:27)
2. Defensive warfare is battle waged to defend territory. It is a warfare that waits for the enemy to strike, then pulls its forces together in defensive response. This type of warfare does not advance into enemy territory. It defends territory already claimed.
3. Offensive warfare is aggressive warfare. It is not a warfare of waiting and responding like the defensive military strategy. It is warfare which takes the initiative of attack. The enemy is identified his strategy recognized, and offensive advances against him are made in the spirit world.
4. In both offensive and defensive warfare, personal action must be taken by the believer.
5. See the discussion on this subject in Chapter Ten.
6. See the discussion on this subject in Chapter Ten.

CHAPTER ELEVEN:

1. Put on the whole Armor of God, that ye may be able to stand against the wiles of the Devil. (Ephesians 6:11)

2. See the discussion on this subject in Chapter Ten.
3. Ephesians 6:13-17.
4. See the discussion on spiritual armor in Chapter Eleven.

CHAPTER TWELVE:

1. The Lord hath opened his armory, and hath brought forth the weapons of his indignation: for this is the work of the Lord God of hosts... (Jeremiah 50:25a)
2. Compare your summary to the discussion on this subject in Chapter Twelve.

CHAPTER THIRTEEN:

1. This charge I commit unto thee, son Timothy, according to the prophecies which went before on thee, that thou by them mightest war a good warfare. (I Timothy 1:18)
2. Natural principles are used to explain what is happening in the spirit world. We can understand what we see in the natural world. When parallels are drawn between something in the natural world and the spiritual world, we understand the spiritual because of the natural. God used the natural example of warfare because there are many natural principles of warfare applicable to the spiritual world.
3. Compare your summary with the discussion on Chapter Thirteen.

CHAPTER FOURTEEN:

1. Knowing this, that our old man is crucified with Him that the body of sin might be destroyed, that henceforth we should not serve sin. For he that is dead is freed from sin. (Romans 6:6-7)
2. Strategies are the science of forming and carrying out military operations. They are the method or plan which leads to victory.
3. The word "counter" means to act in opposition to, to hinder, defeat, or frustrate. A counter strategy is an organized plan and method in opposition to Satan. It is designed to hinder, defeat, and frustrate him in his attacks in the spiritual world.
4. Compare your summary to the discussion in Chapter Fourteen.
5. Compare your summary to the discussion in Chapter Fourteen.

CHAPTER FIFTEEN:

1. For though we walk in the flesh, we do not war after the flesh: For the weapons of our warfare are not carnal, but mighty through God to the pulling down of strong holds; Casting down imaginations, and every high thing that exalteth itself against the knowledge of God, and bringing into captivity every thought to the obedience of Christ. (II Corinthians 10:3-5)
2. In the mind.
3. They are the fiery darts of the wicked. The enemy continuously hurls "fiery darts" at us in the spirit world. Most of these "darts" are aimed at the mind.
4. Compare your answer to the discussion in Chapter Fifteen.
5. Compare your answer to the discussion in Chapter Fifteen.

CHAPTER SIXTEEN:

1. But the tongue can no man tame; it is an unruly evil, full of deadly poison. (James 3:8)
2. The tongue.
3. Compare your summary to the discussion on this subject in Chapter Sixteen.
4. Compare your summary to the discussion on this subject in Chapter Sixteen.

CHAPTER SEVENTEEN:

1. Then answered I them, and said unto them, The God of Heaven, He will prosper us; therefore we His servants will arise and build: but ye have no portion, nor right, nor memorial, in Jerusalem. (Nehemiah 2:20)
2. Compare your answer to the list provided in Chapter Seventeen.
   Your spiritual walls Satan targets to destroy include:
   - Walls of salvation, gates of praise
   - Work of the cross in our lives
   - Christian witness
   - The old nature changed to the new nature
   - Proper attitude in suffering and testing
   - Elimination of works of the flesh
   - Work of the Holy Spirit
   - The Word of God
   - Spiritual warfare
   - The hope of the return of Jesus
   - Self-examination
3. Sin.
4. Compare your list to that given in Chapter Seventeen.
5. Compare your lists to strategies listed in Chapter Seventeen.

CHAPTER EIGHTEEN:

1. The thief cometh not, but for to steal, and to kill, and to destroy: I am come that they might have life, and that they might have it more abundantly. (John 10:10)
2. Compare your summary to the discussion of Satan's strategies against the physical body in Chapter Eighteen.
3. Compare your summary to the discussion of spiritual counter-strategies for victory in the physical body in Chapter Eighteen.
4. Compare your summary to the discussion of Satan's strategies of using human personalities in Chapter Eighteen.
5. Compare your summary to the discussion of spiritual counter strategies for victory over human personalities in Chapter Eighteen.
6. Compare your summary to the discussion of Satan's strategies against the family in Chapter Eighteen.
7. Compare your summary to the discussion of the spiritual counter-strategies for victory in the family in Chapter Eighteen.
8. Compare your summary to the discussion of Satan's strategies in the financial and material realm in Chapter Eighteen.

9. Compare your summary to the discussion of spiritual counter strategies for victory in the financial and material in Chapter Eighteen.

CHAPTER NINETEEN:

1. And I will come down and talk with thee there: and I will take of the spirit which is upon thee, and will put it upon them; and they shall bear the burden of the people with thee, that thou bear it not thyself alone. (Numbers 11:17)
2. To transfer means to convey from one person to another. The word "spirit" as used in this lesson refers to the character, attitude, or motive behind an action. A person can be under the influence of evil or good and transfer his spirit to others on a personal or group basis.
3. The story of Moses and the seventy elders in Numbers 11:16-17.
4. The story of the ten spies in Numbers 13.
5.
   Control your own spirit.
   Guard your tongue.
   Guard your affections.

   Carefully select your associates.
   Guard your physical senses.
   Use caution in "the laying on of hands."

CHAPTER TWENTY:

1. And no marvel; for Satan himself is transformed into an angel of light.
   Therefore it is no great thing if his ministers also be transformed as the ministers of righteousness: whose end shall be according to their works. (II Corinthians 11:14-15)
2. They were used for worship.
3. When Paul speaks of "spiritual wickedness in high places," he is referring to wicked spirits who have infiltrated the religious systems of the world. They have even crept into the congregations of the righteous.
4. Compare your summary with the discussion given in Chapter Twenty.
5. Compare your answer to the discussion in Chapter Twenty.

CHAPTER TWENTY-ONE:

1. How God anointed Jesus of Nazareth with the Holy Ghost and with power: who went about doing good, and healing all that were oppressed of the Devil: for God was with Him. Acts 10:38
2. Seducing spirits, spirits of infirmity, unclean spirits.
3. The gift of discerning of spirits enables a believer to discern the spirits operating in others and to immediately discern whether or not a person has an evil spirit operating through or against him. It prevents deception by seducing or lying spirits. One with this gift can recognize the tactics and evil motives of demonic powers.
4. Demon possession is a condition in which one or more evil spirits (demons) inhabit the body of a human being and take complete control of their victim at will.
5. Compare your list to the list given in Chapter Twenty-One.

6. To be demon obsessed means to be consumed by an interest in demons, Satan, and the occult.
7. Compare your list to the list in Chapter Twenty-One.
8. To be demon oppressed means demonic powers bear down, come against, or bind from the outside.
9. Compare your list to the list given in Chapter Twenty-One.
10. Compare your summary to the discussion in Chapter Twenty-One.

CHAPTER TWENTY-TWO:

1. Thou therefore endure hardness as a good soldier of Jesus Christ. (II Timothy 2:3)
2. Sin and Satan.
3. Review the five ways suffering enters the life a believer discussed in Chapter Twenty-Two.
4. Review the positive benefits of suffering discussed in Chapter Twenty-Two.
5. Review the proper attitudes towards suffering discussed in Chapter Twenty-Two.
6. a. False b. False c. False d. True

CHAPTER TWENTY-THREE:

1. I have fought a good fight, I have finished my course, I have kept the faith. (II Timothy 4:7)
2. David, Joshua, Elijah, Paul.
3. -Recognize your failure.
   -Repent.
   -Rebuild your spiritual strength.
   -Return to the battlefield.
4. Romans 8:1
5. II Timothy 2:26.
6. That we cannot trust in ourselves in spiritual warfare. Our confidence must be in God.

CHAPTER TWENTY-FOUR:

1. And the Devil that deceived them was cast into the lake of fire and brimstone, where the beast and the false prophet are, and shall be tormented day and night forever and ever. (Revelation 20:10)
2. Compare your summary to the discussion in Chapter Twenty-Four.
3. The final conflict will be after the Millennium when Satan is loosed for a period of time. Fire from God will come down to destroy the forces of evil. Satan and his evil forces will go to their final destiny.
4. They will be cast into the lake that burns with fire and brimstone to be tormented for eternity.